Breakout

BREAKOUT

Leo Kessler

CENTURY

LONDON SYDNEY AUCKLAND JOHANNESBURG

First published in Great Britain in 1988 by
Century Hutchinson Ltd
Brookmount House, 62–65 Chandos Place
London WC2N 4NW

Century Hutchinson South Africa (Pty) Ltd
PO Box 337, Bergvlei, 2012 South Africa

Century Hutchinson Australia Pty Ltd
89–91 Albion Street, Surry Hills,
New South Wales 2012, Australia

Century Hutchinson New Zealand Ltd
PO Box 40–086, Glenfield, Auckland 10
New Zealand

ISBN 0 7126 2220 9
Printed in Great Britain by
WBC Print Ltd, Bristol

Escape from Camp Death, Feb-Mar 1944

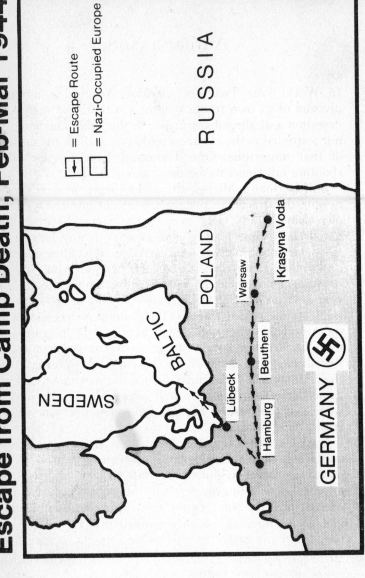

= Escape Route

= Nazi-Occupied Europe

RUSSIA

POLAND

Warsaw

Krasyna Voda

BALTIC

Beuthen

SWEDEN

Lübeck

Hamburg

GERMANY

Author's Note

In World War Two, the German Army shot a whole division of its own troops – some ten thousand men – for desertion and alleged cowardice in the field. This fate was not restricted to the common soldiery: by 1943, the masters of that monstrous 'One Thousand Year Empire' were shooting full Generals for those same 'crimes'.*

Still German soldiers continued to desert in their droves despite the draconian penalties, and not just to save their own skins. Many went over to the enemy because they hated the régime and refused to serve it any longer. By 1944, German soldiers were serving and fighting in the ranks of the Red Army, the Yugoslavian partisans, and the resistance movement of France, Italy and Greece. One year later, in early 1945, a whole company of ex-*Wehrmacht* soldiers were risking their lives back in the Reich, spying for the American Office of Strategic Services, the forerunner of the CIA. In that same year, it was German Generals, in British pay, who made an abortive attempt to bring about their Homeland's surrender before the inevitable collapse came. Deserters they may well have been, but these men were also the unsung heroes of the new post-war democratic West Germany

Karl Carstens, Ludwik Zimanski – known as 'Polack' and Adolf Steven Doepfgen – nicknamed 'Ami' – of the fourth Grenadier Regiment had no such high-falutin' aspirations. These young men, all in their early twenties, had been against the Nazi régime right from the start but they had no intention of working against their Homeland. All they wanted in early 1944, when they finally escaped from

*In comparison, the five million strong wartime US Army shot only *one* soldier – Private Eddie Slovik – for desertion.

Camp Death was to break loose from the tyranny of the hated Third Reich, which had destroyed their families and nearly destroyed them.

So the Three Rebels, as these ordinary young working-class men rather grandly styled themselves, set off on an epic journey into the unknown, crossing the length of Europe, braving 'chaindogs'*, partisans, homosexual priests and finally the most cunning enemy of all – Oberkriminalrat Hans Meissner. In those terrible, bloody years of late World War Two, there were many escapes by young men of various nationalities. But never one like this, when the Führer himself personally took a hand in the hunt for the fugitives. For this was a BREAKOUT – FROM HELL . . .

*Military policeman, so named because of their metal plate of office, suspended from a chain and worn around their necks.

BOOK ONE

Camp Death

CHAPTER 1

'SLOP OUT . . . DO YOU HEAR ME, YOU HOUNDS OF HELL . . . SLOP OUT!'

The great angry bellow echoed down the line of tiny cells. A moment later there was the vicious whack of a pick-handle being slammed against the iron door.

Grenadier Karl Carstens woke with a start. He sat bolt upright on his lice-ridden straw mattress on the concrete floor, blinking and for a moment unable to comprehend where he was. Then, with a sinking feeling it all came back to him as outside, the steel-shod jackboots stamped down the path. The narrow Russian cell, with the evil-smelling bucket in the corner, its dirty walls scrawled with the filth and crude sexual drawings of those who had gone before him – and that hated voice outside, yelling its morning call like a muezzin summoning the faithful. '*Slop out, you piss pansies . . . Los, los, los . . .* SLOP OUT!'

Stiffly, Karl put on his tattered uniform jacket, now devoid of all badges of rank and decorations. They had been the first thing the guards at the gate had ripped off him and his two comrades Polack and Ami – the 'Three Rebels', as they liked to call themselves. The guards had taken a real delight in it, crying out, as their breath fogged the icy air, 'Well, soldier boy, you won't be needing that shitting tin in here! This is where the real shitting war is being fought, *comrade*!' With that a tremendous kick in the seat of his pants had propelled Karl into Wehrmacht Punishment Camp Zero One – known throughout the Army in Russia as Camp Death.

There was a rattle of keys. Karl tensed. He assumed the correct position of attention, thumbs stretched down the side of his threadbare grey pants. The turnkey, 'Tinplate

3

Head', was totally unpredictable. Some of the jailbirds cursed that the shell which had failed to take his 'whole frigging turnip' off had turned him into a madman; and Karl did not want a run-in with the giant noncom this particular dawn. He felt cold and shivery, and his guts were rumbling like a drunken brass band. He had not eaten since four the previous afternoon.

The key turned rustily in the lock. The door swung open. Karl caught a quick glimpse of the Camp – several acres of hard-packed earth, which turned into ankle-deep mud when the rains came, shaped in the form of a hexagon by high, triple-wire fences. At regular intervals around the perimeter were the stork-legged wooden watchtowers manned by elderly reservists and mutilated veterans of the Russian War. But both groups were alert and positioned behind Spandau machine guns capable of firing a thousand rounds per minute. Between the lines of wire fierce, half-starved Dobermans padded back and forth restlessly. They were trained to go for a man's throat – or his testicles! Karl shuddered at the thought and took his eyes off the beasts.

Tinplate Head stamped in, his brutal face set in its usual black scowl, the silver plate which gave him his nickname glistening at the side of his shaven skull, as if it had just been polished. He towered above the handsome, open-faced young prisoner, pick-axe handle held ready in a hand like a small steam shovel, piglike eyes red and scummed as if he had been on the firewater all night again. 'Where's yer frigging chocolate pot, *prisoner?*' he demanded harshly.

Karl kept his gaze fixed rigidly on the horizon. 'Didn't use it, *Oberfeld!*' he barked, while all around him he heard the muffled groans and curses of the other inmates, the air heavy with the stench of their unwashed bodies and body waste, the reek of captivity and shame.

'No excuse, *prisoner!*' Tinplate snapped, his breath reeking of stale vodka. 'Don't I frighten the frigging shite outa ya, eh? Now look lively. Get that chocolate pot out

4

here – at the double! Or by the Great Whore of Buxtehude, I'll scare so much shit out o' them holler guts of yourn, that yer'll fill it right up to the frigging brim!' He laughed evilly at his own supposed joke and passed on to where the other miserable prisoners stood in line, obediently holding their piss buckets, or chocolate pots as Tinplate called them, in their left hands. Right hands were reserved for eating food – in Camp Death, the only tool prisoners were given was a spoon.

Karl waited, shivering in the cold. The icy wind seemed to be coming straight across the naked barren steppe, all the way from Siberia. God, was it cold! In two years in Russia he had never been as cold as during this last terrible week in Camp Death.

Suddenly, Karl forgot the bone-chilling cold as Tinplate roared, 'And what kind of chocolate pot do you call that, you dumb Polack barn-shitter? Answer me that!'

The words cut into Karl's skinny body like a knife. He risked a look to his right. Tinplate was poised in front of the second Rebel, Polack, hands on hips, looking dangerous. Inwardly Karl groaned. What had his old comrade gone and done now?

Ludwik Zimanski, known as Polack, flushed red. He put his free hand on his caved-in stomach and said in his accented German, 'It's the fodder, *Herr Oberfeld* . . . the fodder in here. It gives me the thin shits – all them peas. Real old fart-fodder. I get the thin shits all the time.'

Tinplate puffed out his cheeks in one of those artificial rages of his which they had all come to fear. 'God in Heaven,' he roared, 'what's wrong with yer filthy Polack fart-cannon, man! Don't it follow what yer brain – if yer've got one – tells it to do like any normal person? Why can't yer hit the inside of the chocolate pot like the rest of us do – or perhaps in Polackland, you didn't have a pot to piss in, eh?' He laughed at his own humour and one or two of the prisoners, attempting to curry favour, laughed with him.

Tinplate swung round. He fixed them with an evil stare. The laughter froze on their thin undernourished faces. He turned back to an embarrassed Polack. 'Right, you filthy man! You'll clean that chocolate pot out – *by hand*! I want to see my face in it when you've finished.' He lowered his ugly face close to Polack's. 'Otherwise, you know what I'm gonna do with you?'

Polack swallowed hard and said in a thin voice, 'No, *Herr Oberfeld*.'

'Well, I'll tell yer – fer free. I'm gonna sew up yer asshole with catgut, so that yer'll *fart through yer earholes from then onwards*!'

Satisfied with the impact of that terrifying threat, Tinplate stepped back a couple of paces and raising his voice, addressed the whole line of wretched, shivering prisoners. 'Now then, you bunch o' piss pansies, write this behind yer ears so yer don't forget it. After yer've slopped out in a minute, you'll march over to the hash slingers to take on yer half a litre o' fart soup,' – he meant the usual watery pea soup, which together with a hunk of stale black army bread, with bits of straw sticking out of it, made up their breakfast. 'Then there'll be an hour of physical training just to warm yer up.' He smirked evilly at them. 'Learn you lot o' shitheels not to play with the one-handed widow at night. Then,' he raised his voice even more, 'at zero ten hundred hours *precisely* – mark the time – it'll be the CO's parade and I can tell yer here and now that *frigging* Hauptmann *frigging* Howling Mad *frigging* Mueller ain't in one of his best moods this morning.' Tinplate flashed a quick look at the Camp Commandant's hut to ensure he was not being observed. 'That Popov gash of his must have had her monthlies or something last night. All right, you know the drill. Move it now . . . SLOP OUT!'

As one, the prisoners of Tract D jostled forward, with their evil-smelling buckets, leaving a trail of urine and faeces behind them, for they had been locked up for over sixteen hours. They were heading for the great concrete

6

trough which ran right through the Camp. There, Piotr the tame *Hiwi**, grinning all over his broad slavic face, waited for them, hosepipe in hand. In theory, it was his job just to flush their waste down the trough. But the Russian ex-prisoner was a kindly man. He would blast his first jet of ice-cold water along the line of piss buckets, cleaning them out the best he could before concentrating on the trough itself. The lucky ones in the first line were thus spared from trying to cleanse the nauseating receptacles with their bare hands and earth. So every morning the prisoners elbowed and shoved each other to be there in the first line at the trough.

However, this morning Tinplate, whose terrible head wound had left him in a state of near madness, was not going to allow the squat little Russian to 'spoil the barnshitters', as he would have put it. 'Listen, you Popov prick,' he cried, as Piotr turned on the tap, 'get that frigging hose right into the trough. This place is one big shitheap as it is. Let them clean out their chocolate pots with their pinkies.' He glared at Piotr, whose good-humoured face suddenly turned pale with fear. 'What do you think this frigging place is, anyhow? *A frigging finishing school for frigging gracious frauleins . . .*'

Camp Death was anything but a finishing school. Here, the scum of the German Army in Russia – deserters, cowards, black marketeers and the rest – were systematically terrorised, brutalised and eventually broken down until they pleaded on bended knees to be returned to the front. There were even some who volunteered to serve with a punishment battalion, from which virtually no one ever returned. A quick death at the front was preferable to a slow death in the Camp.

*Literally 'volunteer auxiliary'. A man given to ex-Russian POWs who had volunteered to serve with the German Army.

At Camp Death a prisoner entered at the double, laden down under his kit. Once he had been signed for by the Guard Commander, his punishment commenced. He was stripped naked there and then, no matter what the weather. Officially, this was to check the newcomer for contraband. In fact, it was to publicly humiliate him. Bent over, hands on knees, while some sadistic Sergeant, his forefinger clad in a finger-stool, poked it into his anus, he was the subject of coarse, sexual banter from the guards. '*Oh, sarge, put a bit more vaseline on it and give him a real thrill . . . Do yer think the rabbi docked too much off'n his dick. It ain't half small . . . D'yer know, I think I'm falling in love with that delightful arse. Oh, catch me somebody before I faint . . .*' and the like.

That was a new prisoner's introduction to Camp Death. Thereafter, each day brought fresh humiliations and hard, unrelenting physical labour, which had some of them breaking down in tears, sobbing unashamedly before the others like silly little schoolgirls. Even the 'hard men' in Camp Death cracked in the end. As the Camp Commandant *Hauptmann* Mueller informed each new intake, a sneer on his mad face, 'By the time we are finished with you here, prisoners, you will be begging me on bended knee to be allowed to go to the front. Here, the motto is "march or croak". And I, personally, don't give a twopenny damn either way. March or croak – it's all the same with me.'

Day after day, the prisoners exercised, starved and laboured, threatened and chivvied as they did so by sadistic NCOs who, like the CO himself were military criminals themselves saved from the punishment battalions only because they were experienced combat veterans who could serve some purpose in this remote penal camp. Brutal by nature, the NCOs' brutality was fed by the unlimited power they enjoyed in Camp Death, for here the officers of the Inspector General's branch never penetrated. '*Dead Men*, that's what you shower is,' as Tinplate often snarled. 'Real old carrion fodder!'

It was true, too, Karl realised after the first day of hell

at Camp Zero had finally ended and he had sunk exhausted, every limb trembling with fatigue and hunger, on to his lice-ridden straw pallet. They were little better than food for the giant hawks and buzzards which seemed to be the only wild life to inhabit the lonely steppe that surrounded the remote camp. That first day he told himself there were only two ways that a prisoner was going to leave Camp Zero: either as more cannon-fodder for a punishment battalion or feet-first as fresh meat for the hawks.

But on this freezing February morning, Karl and the other two Rebels, Polack and his undersized running mate Ami, had no time to ponder the uncertain future. In the hour that was to pass before the CO *Hauptmann* Mueller addressed them, Tinplate ran the prisoners through their paces with sadistic fury. They crawled on their bellies in the freezing mud, helped on by the toe of his big 'dice-beaker'* if they were too slow; they doubled back and forth while he leisurely smoked a cigar, red-faced and dripping with sweat, their breath fogging the icy air a dark-grey. They stood rigidly to attention for minutes on end, eyes fixed on the miserable, featureless horizon, saluting some imaginary General. All was hectic movement, punctuated by the staccato bark of Tinplate's voice as he stood in the middle of the square under the blood-red flag of the New Germany as if he had been specially planted there. 'PT,' Ami gasped leathern-lunged to Karl as the hour finally came to an end and they prepared to meet the Commandant. 'That must stand for frigging Physical Torture, that's what I think.'

But Karl was too beat even to reply.

Hauptmann 'Howling Mad' Mueller, the Commandant, was a strange man given when drunk – which was often this winter – to firing his pistol at mirrors, or windows or

*Soldiers' nickname for jackboots.

9

anything which reflected his own image, as if he hated himself – howling like a crazy man. Hence his nickname among the prisoners. His face was bitter, pinched and threatening when sober and wise prisoners immediately scuttled for cover when they saw him approaching. He bore them a permanent grudge because they were the reason he was here, desk-bound and a 'rear echelon stallion' instead of achieving some new glory at the front, as his heart desired.

This morning, despite the fact that he walked stiffly with the aid of a silver-knobbed cane, there was something about him almost physically menacing, as if it would take very little for him to raise the cane and begin thrashing wildly at the emaciated scared young men who faced him now, shivering noticeably in the icy air.

Next to Karl, Ami went through his new litany of hate, one he had composed the day after he had arrived in Camp Death, muttering it out of the side of his mouth in the fashion of an old lag. *'I hate the fucker . . . I hate all the fuckers . . . I'll kill the slime shitters before I'm through . . . Joseph Maria an' Jesus, I swear I'll croak the lot of 'em . . .'*

For a moment Karl indulged himself too, something new for that detached and realistic young man. In one of his favourite day dreams, Tinplate would be slightly drunk in a bar-brothel the *Wehrmacht* had set up behind the front. 'Scuse me *Oberfeld*,' he would say with apparent good-natured casualness as he entered, 'Ain't you from the Camp?' The conversation would start up. Karl would be generous with the fire-water. By the end of the evening the two would be buddies, drinking, singing sentimental ditties, arms round each other's shoulders as the whores poured more and more of the free white lightning down Tinplate's greedy throat – that is, until Karl got him outside. Then the punishment would start. Karl licked his cracked lips at the thought . . . The systematic smashing of the hated noncom down to his knees, the blood pouring from his ears and nose, his pleas for mercy, and then

10

Tinplate sprawled helpless on the ground in a bloody mess of his own dirt and muck, being kicked in the head. Karl could almost feel that glorious sensation of smashing his steel-tipped dice-beaker into the big swine's ribs, cracking them one by one . . . He stopped himself drooling just in time. 'Knock it off!' he hissed to Ami from the side of his mouth. 'He's watching us!'

Hauptmann Mueller was. He stared intently at his prisoners, running his silver-knobbed cane back and forth through the hollow formed by his thumb and forefinger as if it gave him some kind of pleasure, his thick red lips wet and sensual.

Karl tensed. Instinctively he knew there was trouble – *big trouble* – ahead.

CHAPTER 2

It had all started innocently enough. Indeed, there had been an element of knock-about farce about the whole episode – at least, at the start there had.

Karl had been squatting on 'his' stool next to the wooden table which served as a bar in the downstairs room of *Wehrmacht Brothel No. 10: other ranks only* talking to Tanya, who was off-duty that particular evening. Meanwhile, from above came the faint rhythmic squeak of rusty bedsprings, as some stubble-hopper who hadn't had a woman for months danced a mattress polka. Otherwise the place was quiet. The front was active and the rear echelon stallions hadn't been paid for a month. There wasn't much business about.

It was about nine o'clock that evening, just as Karl was debating whether to return to the Fourth Grenadiers' lines or spend his last five marks on Tanya, who did have a remarkable pair of breasts (every time she moved they shivered beneath the art-silk blouse she wore, like a pair of monstrous jellies) when the door was flung open to a flurry of curses and the howl of the icy wind outside.

'Damn and shit,' Tanya cried indignantly, those tremendous breasts rippling appetisingly beneath her blouse. 'Close the frigging door, willyer?' After two years of servicing the German conqueror, Tanya had learned the language to perfection.

The big figure staggered to the makeshift bar, while Tanya gave him a withering look which would have daunted anyone else not drunk beyond the bounds of belief. 'Gimme a drink, my little mountain lioness,' the newcomer said, slurring the words, as next to him Karl moaned inwardly. His pleasant little conversation with Tanya was

12

about to end. For the newcomer was none other than his old enemy and boss, the master of the Fourth Grenadiers' kitchens, the self-proclaimed 'King Bull'. Karl tried to hide his face in his mug of weak Russian beer.

It was no use. The big noncom recognised him despite the heavy load of firewater he had taken aboard this cold winter's night. 'It's that in . . . insubordinate prick of goulash cannon hero, Carstens, ain't it?' he stuttered, eyes revolving as if he might fall down in a faint at any moment. 'Christ on a crutch, Grenadier Carstens, you've been a jammy bugger ever since you've been with old King Bull, ain't yer?'

'*Jawohl, Herr Oberfeld*,' Karl answered tamely, still keeping his nose in his beer. He wanted no trouble with King Bull. It was three months now since 'Creeping Jesus' the Adjutant, had ordered them back to the cookhouse, and he and the other two Rebels were grateful. They'd had a noseful of the front. Even eight hours a day pearl-diving* in hot scummy water in King Bull's kitchens was preferable to having your ballocks shot off in the line.

But Tanya was not inclined to be tame. She liked Karl and was offended by the sudden intrusion. She pointed a finger, the nail of which looked as if it had been dipped in blood, at the silver stars on King Bull's epaulettes. 'You're not shitting allowed in here,' she snorted, proud of her command of the language. 'This is a knocking shop for other ranks, not for frigging noncoms!'

King Bull looked at her happily, too drunk to realise his danger. 'You remember me, Tanya *Schatzi*. I've bin here before.'

'Never seen you in my shitting life before!' she replied indignantly, breasts trembling once more with sheer emotion.

King Bull grinned inanely. An idea dawned on his drunken face. He ripped open his flies and taking a limp

*Dish-washing.

object out of his trousers let it fall with a soft plop on the table right in front of Tanya. '*Na*. Yer might have forgot my handsome face, Tanya,' he chortled happily, 'but yer can't say yer've forgotten *that!*'

Tanya was not impressed. Without a word she swung round, grasped the fork with which she had been eating her supper of dried *kiska* (sausage) and neatly skewered King Bull's pride to the table.

King Bull screamed!

He continued to shriek the whole way back to the Fourth Grenadiers' line as Karl assisted him. He even went with King Bull to the 'Pill', the Fourth's half-blind sawbones, and waited dutifully while the latter fumbled short-sightedly with his needle and thread. But it was all in vain. King Bull's penis – and his pride – had been hurt. Two days later, Karl and the other two Rebels found themselves back up at the misery of the front and it was here that the real trouble had commenced.

A freezing wind raced across the snowbound no-man's land. In the little holes scraped out of the iron-hard earth and frozen snow, the Grenadiers crouched in a state of shivering, trembling wretchedness. The wind slashed their unshaven faces with razor-sharp snow crystals. Icicles hung from their nostrils. Their eyebrows glittered a brilliant white with hoar frost. To their front in that swirling howling fog of white lay the enemy: the Russians dug in, in similar miserable holes.

But the enemy was silent. He had been for days now. Of course, the flares still sailed effortlessly into the evening sky to sweep down seconds later like fallen angels. At regular intervals there was the chatter of Russian machine guns like an iron bar being run along a length of railings to be followed a moment later by the high-pitched hysterical *burr-burr* of one of their own spandaus; and all

14

the while there was the constant boom and hollow thud of the permanent barrage.

The Three Rebels, crouched together in one hole, puffing moodily at their 'lung torpedoes' inside cupped hands, had spent several hundred evenings like this in these last terrible four years of total war. But still, as Karl told himself, you never got used to it. Always in the background there was danger and sudden, violent death lurking.

Karl raised his head slowly. Someone was shuffling through the gloom towards them. He sniffed, but he couldn't smell food. Those rotten hash-slingers of King Bull had screwed up the supper once again. The slime-shitters were probably too shit-scared to come out this night.

A slow figure hove into view. It was their Section Commander, Corporal Hau, wrapped in an old army blanket, his ragged tunic padded out with newspapers. Around his boots he had tied thick pieces of Russian sacking and to complete his *ensemble*, he had a woman's fur tippet, sent from Germany by the Winter Relief Organisation, strung about his ears. He looked like some cheap tart who was seven months pregnant and suffering from gout. If he hadn't been so depressed, Karl would have laughed out loud.

'Don't you friggers even challenge?' Hau wheezed, as he knelt down beside them. 'I could have been a whole army of frigging Popovs!'

'They can have this frigging hole any day,' Ami commented sourly. 'What's up, Corps? You shouldn't be out in this cold at your age.'

Corporal Hau held up his middle finger which peeped through his ragged mitten. 'Sit on it, you arse-with-ears,' he said gruffly. 'Cheeky young bugger!'

''Fraid I can't sit on it, Corp,' Ami replied unabashed. 'Got a bus up there already.'

Karl ignored the banter. 'Problems, Corp?' he snapped.

'Not for me, comrade,' the older man replied. 'Maybe

15

for you. 'Cos his nibs is due in thirty minutes. HQ called me up on the radio to let me know. They didn't want you lot of *eager*,' he emphasised the word, 'young spunk-sprayers to go and shoot or something without challenging him. You know how frigging keen you are.'

'His nibs?'

'Yer.' The Corporal scratched his pelvic area. The lice were running around his body hair again. It was always the same whenever his body started to warm up. Idly he wondered when he had last been free of lice. He concluded he had been lice-ridden ever since they had first marched into Russia. 'Creeping Jesus, he's coming up the line.'

'Major von Schorr,' they cried in unison. '*HIM!*'

'Yer, his nibs. Wonders never cease, do they, comrades?'

'But what's he coming up the line for?' Karl objected. 'Everybody knows he creams his satin drawers even if you mention the frigging word "Popov" to him.'

The old Corporal tapped his forefinger on the side of his big nose and said sagely, 'Wooden eye be careful. When a first-class prick like that who's been a devout coward all his military service comes up to where the shit flies, you can bet that something ain't all kosher. *Es kommt mir ganz schön spanisch vor, Kumpel.*'*

Karl absorbed the information in silence until Corporal Hau broke the heavy brooding atmosphere with, 'So you've been warned. Don't shoot the cunt. 'Cos there's better things to do with cunt than shoot it.' And with that piece of immortal wisdom, he turned and began to creak back the way he had come . . .

Exactly thirty minutes later, Major von Schorr, known throughout the Fourth Grenadiers contemptuously as Creeping Jesus from his habit of sneaking up on his troops in silence in the hope that he might catch them out, made his appearance. This time he made sufficient noise to alert them to his coming. He well knew how most of the frontline

*Literally, 'It's very Spanish to me, mates.' ie 'It sounds fishy'.

'stubble hoppers' would dearly love to pop him off if they could find a reliable excuse.

As he approached very gradually and with exceeding caution through the gloom, Karl could see he was armed like an American gangster, with grenades stuck down both sides of his boots, an extra pistol tucked in his belt and a machine-pistol slung over his back. In all his years with the Fourth Grenadiers, Karl had never seen the Adjutant armed like this. He wondered what was going on as he challenged and received the day's password in return.

A moment later Creeping Jesus slithered into their hole and announced in a whisper, as though the whole of the Red Army was just behind him, 'You're detailed for a fighting patrol.'

'Fighting patrol!' they exclaimed as one. Whatever would Creeping Jesus, who treasured his precious skin even above promotion, be doing going out on a fighting patrol?

'Yes, you heard me, Grenadiers. You are old hares, the lot of you, the most experienced men in the whole Regiment, even though you've spent most of this war skulking in the kitchens. You know the ropes better than those greenbeaks.' He waved vaguely in the direction of the other holes.

'What kind of fighting patrol?' Karl asked, deliberately omitting the 'sir'. Up front he knew the officer depended upon them one hundred per cent. Here they could get away with such heinous 'crimes'. 'What are we supposed to do?'

'Take a prisoner. We want to know who's opposing us –'

'– Popovs,' Ami muttered.

Creeping Jesus ignored him. 'The order has come down from the Corps Commander himself. There's something in the wind.'

'Yer, like a wet fart o' fear,' Ami again interjected and again Creeping Jesus pretended not to hear.

'The Corps Commander wants an identification on our front as soon as possible. You see, there's going to be a big push within days now. Not only our Corps, but the whole Army is about to launch an attack. They say the Führer himself is master-minding the offensive. So it's vital for us to identify what is opposing us on our section of the front. One prisoner should do the trick.'

Karl's brain moved quickly. A prisoner of such importance would mean that Creeping Jesus would be justified in escorting him personally to Corps HQ, where the poor shit of a Popov would be interrogated by Intelligence. By the time their poor fool of a Regimental Colonel had levered the Adjutant free from Corps, the offensive would have started and the Adjutant would have missed most of the dangerous shit that usually flew at the start of a new offensive. Despite his affected manner and the silly window pane of a monocle he usually had screwed in his eye, Creeping Jesus was nobody's fool. He was going to come out of this smelling of Attar of Roses and with his craven hide intact.

'What's the drill?' he asked, reluctantly adding a 'sir' to the question. He knew it was up to him to save himself and the other two Rebels from any mess the Adjutant might get them into. For he had long ago sworn he wasn't going to sacrifice himself for Hitler. He and his comrades were going to survive this unjust war, come what may. He wouldn't die to further Hitler's savage, arrogant conquest of Europe.

Von Schorr was abruptly very professional. 'All of you,' he snapped, 'look at that grove of shattered trees at three o'clock.'

They turned and stared to their right, as another flare hissed into the dark sky, burst in a flash of harsh unreal red and threw everything into stark relief for a few moments. 'Well – you got it?'

They nodded.

'To the immediate left of those trees there is a slight rise. See it?'

Again they nodded, as the flare started to fall, trailing

18

its blood-red light behind it, leaving them blinking and momentarily blinded.

'Well, HQ thinks that's an Ivan forward observer's post. The bright sparks at Div's listening station have pinpointed radio signals coming from the spot. Our guess is that it could well be that of a forward artillery observer linked to the Ivan's artillery network by radio. Must be something important at all events, because as you know those sub-humans over there are just about capable of using flags to signal with.'

Ami was unimpressed with Creeping Jesus's expertise. 'So what do the nobs at Div HQ want us to do with the place – put in a request for Zarah Leander to sing for us on a Saturday night *Wunschkonzert?*'*

Creeping Jesus caught himself just in time. The little half-American bastard with his damned cheeky tongue needed his arse shortening a little and in due course, he promised himself at that moment, he would take great personal pleasure in doing exactly that. But for the time being the Major curbed his tongue. He needed the little swine and those other two pieces of jailbait. They were real old hares, with hair growing out of their arseholes, as frontline veterans called such types. 'We feel,' he lectured the Three Rebels, 'that a forward observation post, especially if it's an artillery one, will be manned by more highly qualified personnel, perhaps even Popov officers. A little squeeze on people like that –'

Karl frowned at the word 'squeeze'. He knew what that meant. *Torture!*

'– And we could come up with some really useful information.' Creeping Jesus paused and flashed a glance at the green-glowing dial of his wrist-watch. Above their heads another flare exploded with a slight crack, bathing their suddenly upturned faces a sickly crimson, as if they had

*Zarah Leander was a well-known singer of the time who often appeared on the 'Request Concert' (*Wunschkonzert*) which linked the people back home with their men at the front.

been abruptly covered with blood. 'So, in five minutes we go over the top. *Klar?*'

'*Klar,*' they echoed without enthusiasm.

'Then get ready,' Creeping Jesus hissed, 'to move out . . .' His words died, as if he had suddenly realised what he was saying for the very first time.

Next to him, Karl could suddenly smell the strange odour the officer was giving off. At the time he was unable to identify it. Later, he did. Major von Schorr, the Adjutant of the Fourth Grenadier Regiment, whose tradition went right back to the time of the Great Elector himself, had been absolutely and totally scared shitless . . .

CHAPTER 3

Hauptmann Mueller could tell it was going to be one of his bad days, from the moment he'd vomited back his frugal breakfast and had found himself on his poor beatup knees, his face pressed against the cold unfeeling wood of his personal thunderbox, trying to fight off the waves of nausea and pain.

Pain he knewwell. It had dogged him for years now like a sadistic, shadowy torturer. What else could make him howl like someone half-demented? But nausea was new. Was he dying at last?

He pulled himself together ruthlessly, imposed his willpower on his wrecked body. God, to think that he had once led a full armoured regiment across France, remorselessly smashing down everything that lay in his way. It had been the same in this accursed Russia until . . . Why, the Führer himself had taken both his hands in his, after decorating him with *the* medal for valour, and had called him 'comrade'. He must not give in! He had to discipline himself to endure, overcome, survive. Perhaps one day he might be given a real command again, instead of this remote punishment camp with its inmates, the scum of the German Army.

But it was hard. Every single breath he ever took seemed to stab him in the lung like a sharp knife. Sometimes he spat blood for no apparent reason. Even the tablets he took all the time, washed down constantly by this Russian rotgut vodka, never really seemed to ease the torment. Only by inflicting pain and suffering on others – these oafs and scoundrels he had been condemned to command in this arsehole of the world – could he make his own agony let up for a while.

Now, as he faced the grey line of offal which were the new intake, he again felt that if he didn't get a grip on himself, he could start howling at any moment like a mad dog at the moon. '*Prisoners*,' he barked, as Tinplate stood them at ease, 'you have been with us a week now. We know you . . . and by now you must know us.' He peered hard at them. Karl felt a cold chill trace its way down the small of his back. The man was really barking mad, dangerously so! He swallowed hard and tried to avoid that frightening, glittering gaze.

'*Gut*. So we know where we stand with each other, don't we? Well, this morning your orders came in.'

There was a faint stir among the prisoners at the word 'orders'. Who, they asked themselves, was concerned about their fate? What kind of orders could concern them?

'You have four weeks,' Howling Mad continued, '*four* weeks to carry out a transformation of character, attitude and morale. You have come here as disgraced men – *prisoners*! You will leave as *soldiers*!' He paused momentarily to let the words sink in.

'In one short month you will be given time to redeem yourselves for the honour of our Folk, Fatherland and Führer. Then you will leave for the front immediately,' he paused again for a moment, 'to be posted to Punishment Battalion 333.'

The men stifled their gasps of surprise and fear. All of them knew of the 333rd. It was the worst punishment battalion of them all, a real Ascension Day commando*. The 333rd men cleared mines without detectors. They advanced in front of assault infantry, unprotected by aerial or artillery bombardments. No one ever returned from the 333rd unless he was too seriously wounded to move. A posting to the 333rd was virtually a death sentence.

Howling Mad Mueller seemed to have read their dread thoughts or perhaps he had seen what they were thinking

*i.e. a one-way or suicidal mission.

by the looks on the prisoners' faces. For he smiled in that strange cracked way of his, as if his lips were worked by rusty springs, and said, 'You have a one in ten chance of surviving, soldiers. You might console yourselves with the thought that you may be *one* of the ten. Or again, you might well be prepared to die for the cause of our Holy Fatherland. Or you might think, fools that you are, born rogues the lot of you, that you could escape from here.' His smile vanished suddenly. to be replaced by a mask of grim determination, his gimlet eyes boring into them, frighteningly.

Again Karl shivered.

'Forget it. There is *no* escape from Punishment Battalion 333 just as there is *no* escape from here. Where would you go, even if you did manage to get through the wire and past the dogs?' He indicated the stark, limitless steppe, bare of any feature right to the very horizon; there was no sign of life whatsoever. 'There are no German troops out there to catch you if you did escape, of course. The Army has better things to do than to waste manpower on your kind of trash. But there *are* partisans enough and they tell me they have peculiar little habits with any Fritz who falls into their hands. They'll dock your tail for you closer than any Jewish rabbi!'

Tinplate smiled happily. The thought obviously gave him a great deal of pleasure.

'All right, so you get through to Krasyna Voda, the nearest railhead. Do you really think that – dressed as you are without papers – you could go up to the nearest official and ask for a third-class single to Berlin – and please book me for midday dinner?' He chuckled. It wasn't a pleasant sound. 'Heaven, arse and cloudburst, the chaindogs would be kicking the crap outa you before you'd finished the sentence!'

Tinplate nodded his wooden head in agreement.

'But, say luck was on your side perhaps and you did manage to get on that troop train, leaving every day at

23

fourteen hundred hours - yes, that is the actual time of departure – heading for Berlin and Mother, as the stubble-hoppers put it – what then?' He smiled at them mercilessly. 'Every man's hand would be against you. Even if you do have mothers, which I doubt, they would turn you in. They would have no alternative. Hiding you is a capital offence. They'd be sent to the camps, too – and there'd be no return for them.' He shrugged carelessly. 'So you see, there is no hope. You either die here in Camp Death – or you go to the front and die there!' He paused to let his words sink in and then cried, 'All right, *Oberfeld*, wheel the slime-shitters away. I can't bear the sight of them any more.' He turned as Tinplate clicked to attention and threw him a tremendous salute.

Suddenly, Mueller's body betrayed him. He had turned too quickly and his gammy leg failed to support him. He went down on one knee, his face contorted, livid, mad with fury, as he flailed the ground with his stick. Tinplate looked away hurriedly. No member of his staff ever helped Howling Mad Mueller. They knew better. He behaved as if the incident wasn't taking place. Instead of rushing forward to help the stricken officer, he bellowed out his orders swiftly, crying, 'At the double now . . . *march* . . . *march*!'

So they doubled away, eyes fixed on some distant horizon, while behind them Mueller kept striking the earth with his stick, his eyes blazing madly . . .

The Three Rebels sat moodily in the evil-smelling 'ten seat crapper'. It had been another gruelling morning, rounded off by a sparse meal of 'old Man', tinned foul meat reputedly made from old men who had died in Berlin's work-houses. Now at last the prisoners had thirty minutes to themselves, away from the bullying, bellowing noncoms, before the afternoon misery commenced.

As always, the three of them stared ahead, faces

24

expressionless, as if they were totally absorbed in the business at hand, while they talked out of the sides of their mouths. By now, they knew they were safe nowhere, not even here in this foul privy. There were stool-pigeons in Camp Death and guards who pulled socks over their dice-beakers so that they could sneak up on unsuspecting prisoners chatting to one another: something which was forbidden even in the thirty-minute dinner break. Talking was not allowed between prisoners, even in the crapper; and the kind of conversation the Third Rebels were engaged in at this very moment was most definitely taboo.

'Put it like this, comrades,' Karl was presently saying, his lips motionless like those of a ventriloquist, 'we're between the wet fart and the side of the thunderbox. They're going to get us either way. If we refuse to go to the 333rd, they'll grind us into the frigging ground here. If we do go, sooner or later we'll be watching the taties grow from beneath two metres o' dirt.'

'Agreed,' Ami said moodily, at the same time scratching his crotch. What he called his 'felt-lice' were acting up again in the slight warmth of the latrine. 'They've got us with our hooters well and truly in the shit, mates. The bastards!'

'But what can we do about it, Karl?' Polack asked. 'You heard what the Commandant said this morning on parade. There's no escape from this place.' Morosely he flicked an opaque dewdrop from the tip of his big Slavic nose.

Karl pursed his lips. 'That's what *he* said. But there's always a chance of escape, if you're determined enough.'

'Natch,' Ami agreed. 'I'd be out of this dump in a shot give me half a chance, Karl. But the Commandant did mention the Popov partisans and we know that he was telling the truth there. Them Popov bastards'd slit yer throat as soon as look at yer.'

'We've dodged the partisans before, comrades,' Karl said, but there was little conviction in his voice. 'Besides, if the partisans are such a problem as the Commandant makes out, how come they haven't attacked this place before? It's pretty remote and that bunch of cripples and old farts who guard the Camp wouldn't be much good against a well-armed determined partisan band.' He flashed a glance at the door of the latrine, as if he half-expected to see Tinplate with his bull pizzle standing there, face contorted with fury. But there was nothing. Just the rustle of the icy wind making the piece of sacking which served as a door tremble.

Karl licked his wind-cracked lips and raised his voice slightly. 'We ought to tackle this thing step by step –'

'– You mean you really want us to have a go, Karl?' Polack interrupted, suddenly eager, a new light of hope dawning in his blue eyes.

'Yes, why not? But we ought to go at it bit by bit. First, we get out. Then, we worry about the Popov partisans. After that, we can start worrying about getting through Poland, though Polack here should be able to help us there.'

Polack nodded his cropped head hurriedly. '*Ja, ja, pan,*' he said in Polish.

'All right, all right.' Ami held up his hand patiently in that Rhenish manner of his which never seemed quite German to Karl, who came from Hamburg. But then, as he often reminded himself, Ami was not altogether German. His father had been an American soldier in the US Army of Occupation in the Rhineland after World War One. Hence his nickname of 'Ami'.* 'So we sort all that out, Karl. But what do we do when we get back to the Homeland? We can't take a dive there for ever, you know. What do we live off? Where do we hide? Where do we get papers, ration cards . . . hell, a heap of things. There we'd stand out like a sore thumb. What are three able-bodied young men wandering around in civvies for when they should be at the front? Any half-blind old cop would have

*German slang for American.

us inside the local lock-up, looking at Swedish curtains* in zero comma nix seconds!'

Karl listened to Ami's litany of woe calmly, a faintly superior smile on his lips. Finally, when the other man was finished, he said softly, 'But when we get that far, Ami, we're not going to stay in Germany, are we?'

'*What?*' the other two exploded together, forgetting in their surprise to talk out of the sides of their mouths.

'You heard me. Listen,' Karl said bitterly, 'ever since we first joined the frigging Fourth Grenadiers, we've talked about getting out of the Army. Why should we suffer under Hitler – serve the Austrian bastard? Up to now, we've talked a lot and done precious little. So this time we must make an end to it, once and for all.'

'But how, Karl?' Ami snapped almost angrily. 'The only place left in Europe not occupied by the Reich is Switzerland, and you can just imagine how the frontiers of the Homeland with Switzerland are guarded to prevent fellers like us from getting over there to them nice fat rich Swiss fleshpots.' He spat contemptuously into the frozen dust at his feet. 'Come off it, Karl, talk sense. You know as well as I do that Switzerland is frigging out!'

'But there is another country,' Karl said simply.

Polack opened his mouth to ask a question, but the tremendous voice roaring from the door beat him to it. 'What in three devils' name are you *frigging* load of jailbait doing there on yer *frigging* asses chattering away like *frigging* old women at a *frigging* tea party? Don't yer know I could slap the lot of yer on bread and water for three days for that?' Tinplate filled the whole doorway, as he thwacked his monstrous bull's pizzle against the support post. 'Hit the deck, do you hear! *Hit the frigging deck!*'

Hurriedly they 'hit the frigging deck'. Moments later, still pulling up their trousers, they were doubling for the square as if the devil himself were behind them.

*German slang for prison bars.

Tinplate waited till they were out of sight, a smirk of pleasure on his face. It pleased him to see that, like the rest of the scum who had come in with the new intake of prisoners, they too were shit-scared of him. Then his smirk vanished and he rapped the post urgently with the bull's pizzle three times, as if giving a signal.

A runtish soldier, with a cunning wizened face and a wall-eye, the armband of a trusty on his sleeve, emerged from behind the latrine, as if he had been waiting for the signal all the time.

'Well, Silvereye*?' the huge hulking noncom demanded. 'What did you hear?'

'Not much, *Oberfeld*,' the runtish man answered, rubbing his hands together the whole while, as if they were dirty and he was washing them with an invisible bar of soap. 'They've learned fast. They talk out of the side of their mouths all the time like old lags.'

'They'll get a thick lip from me one o' these days for doing that,' Tinplate growled sourly. 'But they're up to something, ain't they?'

The little man nodded. 'Ay, that they are, *Oberfeld*. In the years I've bin in here I've seen it often enough, I have. They're up to something all right.'

Tinplate considered for a moment, slapping the bull's pizzle to and fro menacingly, while the trusty cowered against the wall, both hands extended to feel it, almost as if he were reassuring himself that his back was covered by it. For Silvereye knew he was in the company of desperate men. His life wouldn't be worth a song if the other prisoners discovered he was a stool-pigeon for Tinplate. Still, the risk he took was better than the front any day. And besides, every so often Tinplate rewarded him with extra lung torpedoes and a bottle of fire-water. Once the big noncom had even allowed him to feel up the skirt of one of the whores the NCOs brought into camp once a month for

Silberblick, the German expression for a wall-eye.

28

their payday orgy. It had been lovely. She hadn't worn drawers.

Tinplate made up his mind. 'All right, Silvereye, I'm making you responsible for them from now onwards. Every time they're off the parade ground till they are locked up for the night, I want you watching them. I don't want any trouble-makers in this camp. Christ, the CO is bad enough as it is. But if there was any trouble–' he slammed the bull's pizzle against the support so that the whole latrine seemed to rattle, as if it might collapse at any moment – '*he'd have the eggs off'n the whole NCO corps with a blunt razorblade!*'

CHAPTER 4

'*Los . . . los, vorwaerts!*' Creeping Jesus had hissed urgently. Reluctantly they had eased out of their hole, with Creeping Jesus keeping well behind, and commenced moving forward, half-crouched. Every one of their senses was suddenly acute, and the hands holding their weapons were slick with hot sweat despite the biting cold.

Now they wove through the typical steppe bog which made up no-man's land, the hot gases beneath keeping it moist, soggy and treacherous even in winter. Carefully they crossed the rough causeway of logs which someone had once placed there, bodies tensed as if they were already anticipating the first steel slugs striking their soft flesh. Beneath them, the logs bobbed and sank under their weight and the marsh gases gurgled and bubbled obscenely.

Ahead of them, the flares still kept soaring into the night sky. Here and there multicoloured tracer arched across the horizon almost playfully. Occasionally, too, there would be the muted crump of a shell exploding, followed a moment or two later by a burst of cherry-red flame. Tonight, it seemed, the front refused stubbornly to settle down.

Karl frowned, worried. He wasn't going to waste his own life or that of his two comrades on some foolish mission dreamed up by the Adjutant just so he could reap the reward of it. He determined that at the first sign of serious trouble, he'd urge the others to turn and run. Creeping Jesus would be too worried about saving his own hide to be able to do anything about it.

Time passed. They were almost across the bog now. Soon they would be entering the Russian positions. Next to Karl, Polack hesitated momentarily, raised his head to the sky and sniffed hard like a dog trying to scent some elusive rabbit. 'They're there, Karl,' he whispered after a few seconds. 'I can smell 'em.'

Karl nodded: he could too. It was that typical Popov smell, the stench of unwashed bodies and the black *Marhokka* tobacco they smoked wrapped in scraps of newspaper. He tightened the grip on his rifle even more. They kept going.

Five minutes later the causeway ended and they stepped on to solid ground. They were across and in the Russians' outpost line.

Creeping Jesus halted them a moment. Voice shaky and barely under control, he hissed, 'I'll take the lead now. Not a sound, not a word,' he added. 'Let's get a prisoner and go back. Follow me.'

'Follow the officer – he's got a hole in his arse,' Ami intoned the old formula.

Creeping Jesus muttered something angrily, but didn't turn on Ami. He was too concerned by what lay to their front.

Spread out three metres apart, each man wrapped in a cocoon of anxious thought, nerves tingling electrically, every sense working at heightened pitch waiting for that sudden frightening challenge, they moved on in a lunar landscape of craters, shattered trees and abandoned rusting vehicles. This ground had been fought over all winter now, with tremendous losses – so many, in fact, that the dead had been allowed to lie where they had fallen, the snow their only shroud. Now, here and there, the dead were reappearing as the winter's severity wore off: crumpled broken corpses that looked like bundles of abandoned rags. Karl wasn't a sensitive young man, but suddenly he had a feeling he was walking through a massive graveyard on the Day of Resurrection with the dead about to spring back to life, and he shuddered in spite of himself.

Another five minutes passed in tense expectation. All of them, including Creeping Jesus, could smell the Popovs quite distinctly now. They were all around as the four men headed for the grove of splintered trees and forward observer's bunker. It seemed impossible that they wouldn't be discovered – and soon. What they were doing went against all the rules of war.

Suddenly, Karl halted. Behind him the others stumbled to a stop, hearts racing like trip-hammers. 'What is it?' Creeping Jesus snapped in fear.

'Somebody's coming!'

'Where?' Creeping Jesus asked in a cracked voice.

'Behind us . . . can't you hear?' Karl whispered urgently.

They froze. Karl was right. There was no mistaking the soft shuffle of padded feet through the snow.

Karl pressed his mouth close to Polack's ear, as the latter moved closer. 'The fart's gonna hit the thunderbox, Polack, if we don't nobble him. We're right in the middle of 'em. We don't want him yelling out and alarming the rest.'

'Creeping Jesus's at the rear.'

'*Him!*' Karl whispered contemptuously. '*He*'s scared shitless. It's got to be you, Polack.'

'I don't think I could kill even a Popov in cold blood, Karl,' the big Slav hissed hesitantly. 'Honest–'

'Don't frig about, Polack,' Karl cut him off sharply. 'It's him or us . . . Here he comes!'

'And there's another, Karl,' Ami interjected hurriedly. 'Just behind him.'

Karl swore under his breath and tensed, as the others froze. For the two unsuspecting Russians were almost on top of them now. It could be only a matter of seconds before the enemy spotted them. Karl felt a nerve begin to tick like a metronome at the side of his cheek. His nerves were virtually out of control. In half a minute he'd scream out loud with suppressed tension.

Suddenly, startlingly, the first Russian, weighed down by some kind of heavy pack, stopped. For what seemed an eternity, Polack stared at his victim and the Russian, frozen there with shock, did the same. '*Now!*' Karl hissed.

Polack lurched forward. His bayonet he held close to his

hip, like a dentist advancing on some frightened patient with his instruments concealed, so that the patient wouldn't be more terrified than was necessary.

The Russian opened his mouth. Polack lunged. The point of the razer-sharp blade grated against a buckle. There was a sudden gasp of shock, a sucking noise and the cruel blade sank deep inside the first Russian's guts. A soft keening started to come from the enemy's throat. 'Stop him, Polack,' Karl cried wildly, as he flung himself past a petrified Creeping Jesus at the second Russian, who was fumbling frantically with the sling of his tommy gun.

Blindly he lashed out with his own bayonet. *And missed*! The Russian, despite his bulky clothing, was not slow to take advantage. He stopped trying to get at his weapon. Instead, he encircled Karl's waist. Karl's nostrils were assailed by the stink of black tobacco, garlic and cheap perfume. But he had no time to ponder the smell of perfume. In a frenzy of fear, he brought up his knee sharply. But the Russian was as slippery as an eel. He turned the blow to his groin with his own knee. Next moment, the Russian had pressed his stomach into Karl's like a passionate lover. The Russian's body was supple and soft like that of a woman. But now Karl could no longer use his knees.

A few metres away, while Ami and Creeping Jesus watched in helpless horror, Polack writhed back and forth in the dirty wet snow on top of the other Russian, whose shattered body flung out great gobs of blood, as he stubbornly refused to die. '*Croak*,' Polack gasped fervently. 'For God's sake, please – *die!*'

In slow motion, panting hard as if with sexual ecstasy, Karl and the other Russian danced around the glade. The Russian thrust his fingers at Karl's eyes. Karl swung his head to one side at the very last moment. Hurriedly, with fingers that were wet with sweat, Karl changed his grip on the bayonet. Now it was ready for use as a dagger. Let the Russian bastard give him one chance . . .

Abruptly, the Russian slipped on the snow and went down on one knee. Karl didn't hesitate. Suddenly he was overcome by a great, red-roaring hatred of the Russian. Why had he made him do this? Almost as if he were hovering over the glade, watching detached this ritualised dance of death, he thrust home the blade.

The Russian let out a thin, eerie, almost female scream. Karl flung his free hand against the man's mouth to deaden the noise, and felt his palm flooded with warm thick liquid. Blood! Now the Russian's body was seized by a weird trembling. It was almost as though his opponent was suffering the throes of a violent epileptic seizure. He shook and quivered horribly.

Almost demented with fear, horror, hate and revulsion, Karl pulled out the bayonet with a dreadful squelching noise. Crazily, lathered in sweat, his every limb trembling totally out of control, he rammed the blade home once more. Over and over again now he hacked and sliced at the dying Russian, losing track of the time, obscene little animal cries and moans coming from his wet slack mouth until at last his crazed mind became aware of the fact that the Russian hung lifelessly in his blood-soaked arms and Ami was tugging at him urgently, hissing, 'Karl . . . Karl . . . he's dead, I say . . . *he's dead!*'

'I've killed a woman . . . Comrades, I've killed a . . . *woman!*' Polack croaked in horror, as he recoiled from that terrible apparition of long blonde hair matted with blood, that was now revealed by the fallen helmet. 'My God, *I've killed a woman!*'

Ami left Karl, who was hunched against the nearest shell-shattered tree vomiting helplessly and grabbed his old running mate. 'Polack . . . here, stop it, comrade.'

'But a woman.' Great tears were now coursing down the Polack's miserable, ashen face. 'A woman . . .'

Somewhere ahead of them, another flare sailed into the

sky, and Creeping Jesus peered down at the corpse of the man Karl had killed. 'This one is a woman, too,' he said disbelievingly, turning the corpse over with the toe of his boot gingerly. 'And by God,' he peered down harder, 'she's in the artillery – see those flashes.' He straightened up as the flare sank back to the earth and fizzled out. 'By Christ, the Russians are using female artillery observers.' He threw a quick glance in the direction of the small man-made hill which housed the Russians' forward observation post. 'This is going to make our task much easier. Women, we can deal with. They'll be no problem. We should have our prisoner and be back at the Regiment before midnight, I'll be bound.'

Polack turned and stared at the white blob of his Adjutant's face in the glowing gloom, and said, voice still heavy with shock, 'I'm going no further . . . I'm not going to kill no more women.' .

'What did you say, Grenadier?' Creeping Jesus hissed.

'You heard me,' Polack said with that typical Slavic stubbornness of his. 'I will not do it, *Herr Major*.'

Creeping Jesus gasped, as if someone had just struck him in the guts. 'But you . . . you,' he stuttered, 'you don't realise what you are saying!'

'I know,' Polack said dourly. Somewhere close by, an ancient Russian machine gun began to chatter like an angry woodpecker.

'I shall give you a direct order,' Creeping Jesus caught himself in time. 'If you refuse it, you will be court-martialled. Do you understand, Grenadier?'

Polack said nothing.

Karl wiped the vomit from his chin, trying to overcome the heaving feeling in his stomach. 'It's no good, sir,' he gasped thickly. 'Let's get back while there is still time . . .' His voice trailed away. Creeping Jesus wasn't even listening.

The Adjutant's visions of the coveted medal and the safe staff post were vanishing rapidly. If he didn't do something

35

decisive now, all would be lost. He had only volunteered for this damned dangerous mission to get out of the line before the next big push started. He had no desire to be killed by some hairy-arsed Popov in this God-forsaken country – and all for nothing. He wanted a safe base stallion's job. His hand fell to his pistol. 'Forget the court-martial,' he snapped, his mind made up. To his front tracer zipped through the darkness in a frightening lethal morse. 'I'm ordering you to move on. Otherwise–' the pistol appeared in his hand as if by magic, and even with the machine gun chattering, Karl could hear the click as the officer pushed off the safety catch.

'What are you going to do, sir?' Ami gasped fearfully.

Creeping Jesus didn't reply. Instead he barked, 'I'm going to count up to three. If you haven't moved by then, I'm going to shoot Grenadier Zimanski for disobeying an order in the face of the enemy. In my position as a Commanding Officer I am perfectly justified in doing so. Now – what is it to be? ONE!'

Polack stared back at him stubbornly in the gloom, fists clenched, but saying nothing.

Ami flashed a desperate look at Karl, who seemed frozen into immobility and then fumbled with his own safety catch. But Creeping Jesus beat him to it. 'I wouldn't do that,' he said, complete master of the situation now. 'Well, Zimanski? TWO!'

'Sir,' Ami cried. 'Please–'

'THR–' Creeping Jesus's finger, curled round the trigger, whitened as he took the final pressure. He felt a sense of power and contempt for the miserable Polack sub-human he was going to dispatch from this world.

The sudden burst of fire caught them all completely by surprise. Ami yelped as a slug clipped his shoulder with the sensation of a red-hot poker being thrust into his flesh, while Creeping Jesus slammed back against the nearest tree, the pistol clattering from his hand, a moment before he went down on one knee, crying out, 'I've been hit . . . Oh, Great God in Heaven, *I've been hit, men*!'

'*Stoi*!' The frightening challenge rang out in Russian. Then came, '*Nmentski*!'*

Karl knew only kitchen Russian, but that one word was sufficient. He roused himself from his stupor and cried, 'The Popovs have spotted us! *Duck*!' In that same instant, he pulled the stick grenade out of his pocket. With one and the same movement, he tugged out the little pin and hurled it violently in the direction from which the firing had come. There was a muffled thud, followed an instant later by a flash of ugly red light and someone screaming shrilly in absolute agony.

Next to him, Creeping Jesus sank to the ground, whimpering like a baby. 'My leg . . . my leg,' he moaned. 'Please help me, comrades. The bone is surely broken. Oh, comrades, please help me.'

Karl flashed a wild look in front of him. The Russians had disappeared. But only for a moment. They'd be back – and this time there would be more of them. 'Ready?' he gasped.

'Too fucking true!' Ami cried, weapon at the ready, peering into the darkness to their front. 'Let's move it, Karl.'

'But the officer,' Polack said simply. 'He's wounded. He can't move.'

Ami spat into the scuffed snow. 'Leave the candy-arsed bastard,' he said contemptuously. 'Leave him to the Popov women. They'll soon have his outside plumbing seen off.'

Creeping Jesus whimpered with fear. 'Please . . . *please*,' he quavered.

Karl considered. He guessed instinctively that Ami was right. Only a fool would trust anyone like Major von Schorr. All the same . . .

'Karl, let's go,' Ami interrupted and jerking up his rifle,

*Who goes there? Germans!'

aimed at the first of the shadowy figures looming up in front of them. 'Come on, stop farting about! The Popov pissers are coming!' He snapped off a swift burst and a voice screamed sharply.

'*Schnauze*!*' Karl cried, mind made up. 'Polack, sling us your rifle and grab a hold of the bastard!'

'Thank you, oh, thank you, Carstens,' Creeping Jesus breathed fervently with relief. 'Thank . . .'

Karl kicked him neatly in the ribs and in the same instant caught Polack's rifle.

With a grunt, the big Grenadier slung the officer over his shoulder, as from the Russian position a wild volley of angry fire exploded, the scarlet flame stabbing the darkness viciously. Next moment, they were running madly back to the bog, while Polack's spirits sank into his boots. Now they were in the shit, all right.

*'Shut your trap!'

CHAPTER 5

The whistle shrilled. The prisoners from Tract D surged forward. They came at the double, their breath fogging the morning air, their steel-shod boots stamping rhythmically on the concrete, arms crossing their chests like pistons. Tinplate barked an order. They halted as one, heaving for breath. Before them loomed the sewage channel into which they emptied their loathsome slops each dawn.

Tinplate took his time. He believed in allowing the prisoners' imaginations to run away with them when they were faced with something new and unknown. This, too, was part of the sadistic little games he liked to play with them. The scum deserved no better. For a few moments he ran his gimlet-like little eyes down the ranks, the men's gazes quailing before his. They knew they'd be on bread-and-water for three days in the 'dark cell' for the slightest infringement of the dress regulations. Finally he was satisfied he had let them wait long enough. He puffed out his chest and cried, 'Tract D . . . Tract D . . . stand at ease!'

As one the prisoners thrust out their right feet and threw their arms behind their backs as the regulations prescribed. Ami farted, but only very softly. Out of the corner of his eye he had seen Howling Mad Mueller gazing at the parade from the window of his quarters and Ami wanted no trouble with that unpredictable officer.

Tinplate opened his mouth again. 'So, you pissed off at Kiev, pissed off at Stalingrad, pissed off at half a dozen other frigging places in frigging Popovland and let your comrades take the flying shit. Well, you're not pissing off no more!' He glared at them, face flushed with one of his frightening artificial rages.

Karl waited. What was coming now?

'You heard the Commandant yesterday. Well, today we start real soldiering. Today you're gonna learn some real fighting soldiering agen.' He snapped up the whistle that dangled from his collar and blew three shrill blasts upon it.

As if it had all been rehearsed beforehand, a hand-cart appeared round the corner, pushed by two trusties and escorted by the little runt, known as Silvereye.

Despite the awesome discipline of Camp Death, the front line of the assembled prisoners gasped. The cart was piled high with the standard *Wehrmacht* '08 rifles, with sheathed bayonets attached. They were going to be given weapons, even though they were prisoners!

Tinplate saw the look in some of their eyes and smirked. 'Now don't go pissing in yer pants, you scum. They ain't loaded. Don't think I'd be cracked enough to trust one of you rats with my back turned and you with one up the spout. No, my lucky lads, you're gonna practise bayonet-fighting today with your old friend – me. When I've finished with yer, yer'll be ready to tackle the whole frigging Popov army single-handed.' He waited till the cart came level with him and then cried, 'Silvereye – the stick!'

Dutifully, the little man took the long bamboo contraption from on top of the pile of rifles and handed it to the noncom with a slight bow like a waiter presenting a dish to some favourite customer.

'Brown noser!' Ami hissed out of the side of his mouth to Karl, adding somewhat obscurely, 'Frigging good job he's got his army number stamped on the soles of his boots.'

Karl said nothing. He recognised the bamboo pole, a device he had not seen since his training days with the Fourth Grenadiers back in the summer of 1939. On one end of the three-metre long contraption there was a rope loop. In bayonet drill you were supposed to drive your blade through it as the training instuctor wielded the cumbersome thing. At the other end, there was a great padded leather bag. If you didn't manage to bayonet the loop, oftentimes the instructor would give you a tap with that end to encourage you to do better the next time. And sometimes the instructors weren't too gentle, either.

Tinplate waited with unusual patience for him as the trusties went down the line handing each prisoner a rifle with bayonet attached, though the blade of the latter was covered with its sheath. Karl shot the noncom a look. He didn't like what he saw. Tinplate had an unholy glint in his piglike eyes. He was up to something.

Finally they were ready. Handling the big bamboo rod like a kid's toy, Tinplate sprang across the drainage ditch which ran the length of the Camp and poised there holding the rod. 'Now then, get this, you bunch of arses with ears. I'm a Popov, yer see, defending this here front-line which is where you put yer chocolate pots in the morning. Gives off a real scent o' honeydew, don't it?' He smirked at his own humour and Silvereye standing to the side tittered obligingly.

'Arse-crawler,' Ami sneered.

'Now you lot are gonna come springing over this 'ere trench to attack me, just as you would if you was real soldiers, instead of a bunch o' piss-in-the-wind. And I'm gonna try to stop yer. So this is the drill. You'll attack individually – on command. Jump the ditch, give me the point and I'll try to parry.' He guffawed and hefted the big pole as if it were weightless. 'If I can. 'Cos I know how strong you lot are . . . All right, you're first.' He indicated a short bespectacled soldier from the Quartermaster's branch who had been sent to Camp Death for selling the men's rations on the Russian black market. 'Come on short-arse, don't frig around, like!'

The little ex-clerk hesitated. He swallowed hard and Karl could see his Adam's apple running up and down his skinny neck as if on an express lift.

'*Los*!' Tinplate commanded.

The ex-clerk took a deep breath and hurled himself

41

forward. Tinplate took up his stance, pole balanced across his body, held in those two great hams of his.

The attacker vaulted the ditch. He lunged. Tinplate lowered the rope loop a little. The attacker's point passed through it easily. Obligingly, Tinplate swung the pole to one side and the ex-clerk was stumbling on, without as much as a kick up the arse from the noncom to speed him on his way.

'See?' Tinplate proclaimed, as the ex-clerk stumbled to a surprised halt a few metres further on, obviously wondering just how he had managed it. 'It's as easy as falling off a frigging log.'

They waited for the next one. All of them knew Tinplate was playing with them. By letting the clerk through so easily, he thought he had lulled them into a false sense of security, but they knew otherwise. The sadistic swine was going to land some of them in the shit, that was for sure.

'All right,' Tinplate broke the heavy silence. 'You.' He pointed to Polack. 'Come on, yer big streak of pale piss. Move it . . . *Los*!'

Suddenly flushed with anger for some reason known only to himself, Polack tucked the rifle to his hip, cried something in Polish and sprang forward. He leapt the ditch and lunged. Tinplate parried easily. Next moment the great padded stick was swung round. The leather bag hit Polack a massive blow on the side. He yelped with pain and surprise. Then, arms flailing, rifle clattering to the ground, he was reeling backwards trying to save himself. But in vain. He shot into the nauseous drainage ditch, with a great bang.

Tinplate guffawed coarsely as a moment later Polack reappeared, soaked and furious, already smelling to high heaven, for Piotr had not done his job too well this morning after slopping out. 'God in Heaven,' the noncom chortled, 'don't you pong! And it ain't Attar o' Roses neither. Better watch your footwork next time around, soldier. All right,

42

don't just stand there like a wet fart. Pick up yer rifle and get back in the ranks.'

For a moment it looked almost as if Polack might disobey the big NCO. But suddenly his shoulders slumped and picking up his rifle, he returned to the others.

Highly pleased with himself, Tinplate now sought another victim. He looked along the front rank of prisoners and his gaze fell on Ami. 'Now then, you little short-arse,' he commenced, but before he could finish, Karl, red-faced and angry, had elbowed his running mate out of the way and had taken his place. '*Jawohl, Oberfeld, ich bin bereit,*' he snapped.

Before Tinplate could say anything more, Karl had clutched his bayonet lightly to his hip and was running forward to the attack.

Tinplate frowned. Even when a bayonet was covered by its scabbard a hard prod with it could hurt and the handsome blond young bastard charging toward him looked fit and tough – and very determined. He took up his stance, legs well spread, pole balanced across the upper part of his body and prepared for the attack.

Karl lunged. Automatically, Tinplate swung round, attempting to hit his attacker. Karl expected the tactic. He had not aimed at the ring, as Tinplate had anticipated, but straight at the big noncom's ample gut.

'*Ach du Scheisse!*' Tinplate gasped with pain as the sheath rammed his belly. For a moment he nearly dropped the pole as he bent double, face suddenly ashen. Then Karl was running on, a broad grin on his face, while on the other aide of the ditch, Ami hissed to a dripping stinking Polack, 'Now the big bastard has had a taste of his own frigging medicine.'

Little red eyes burning with rage, Tinplate straightened up and gripped his pole firmly once more. 'You,' he snorted, 'you fart-with-fans. Think you're frigging clever, don't yer?'

Karl said nothing. He could see just how dangerous

43

Tinplate had become. Again he realised with that old sinking feeling that Tinplate and all the rest of the sadistic bastards in charge of Camp Death could do exactly what they wanted with him. He was completely at their mercy.

'Right,' Tinplate ordered. 'Back across the ditch and try again. See if you get the point into me *this* time, soldier boy. There'll be an extra helping of fart-soup this dinnertime if you can. Now then – at the double. *Los!*'

Karl raced back the way he had come. As he came level with Ami, the latter gave him a worried look. Karl winked. But he knew now that Tinplate was out for blood. He had to be careful, very careful.

'All right!' Tinplate cried, after he had taken up his stance, bayonet at his hip. 'Let's be having yer, my lucky lad. *Charge!*'

Grimly, Karl doubled forward. He sprang over the ditch. Tinplate crouched. Watching, Ami and Polack held their breath. In theory, the instructor with the pole was supposed to wait until the trainee had made his lunge for the looped end. But Tinplate did not. As he saw the muscles of Karl's shoulders ripple, as the youth bent his head prior to lunging, he swung the big rod round with all his strength. The mighty blow caught Karl on his left side. He growled with sudden pain. Next moment he felt himself lifted from his feet, rifle tumbling from suddenly nerveless fingers, reeling backwards right into that disgusting trough.

'Ha, ha . . . now yer can really say that you're up to yer hooter in crap, mate!' Tinplate guffawed, hugely pleased with himself. 'You smart-arsed shiteheel!'

Karl for his part simply lay there, all wind knocked out of him, feeling himself sink a little lower into that disgusting mess and listening dully to Tinplate's booming laugh and the sycophantic mirth of the others, who wished to keep on the good side of the noncom. His face contorted with distaste as his nostrils were assailed by the obscene smell. Hell, how was he going to cleanse himself of the nauseating filth?

Suddenly, his rage and self-disgust vanished to be replaced by a sense of curiosity. He realised abruptly that he couldn't see anyone, not even their feet. He had disappeared from their view; it was natural. He was below ground level.

He frowned and stared the length of the stinking trench. There was a manhole at the far end, covered with an iron grating and partially coated with a noxious slime. Still, he could see the start of a shaft leading downwards at an angle. It was obvious why. If Piotr did his job properly at slopping-out time the muck and the water from his hosepipe would run off through the sloping shaft. There was one other thing, too. That shaft led right out of the Camp! Then Tinplate was bellowing his name urgently and he was scrambling hastily out of the stinking trench, his mind racing frantically.

Howling Mad Mueller watched the slime-covered soldier crawl out of the shit trench and turned from the window. He had seen enough. His noncoms were their usual sadistic selves. They were breaking the will of the prisoners. In a month he'd be able to send another bunch of cannonfodder to the front, for what they were worth. He sighed and limped across to the big table which dominated the room.

Once it had been a billiard table. But under his instructions a group of prisoners had transformed it into a rather superior sand table, covered now with papier-mâché trees and houses sweeping down to the broad wash of bright blue which represented the River Meuse.

Miniature tanks and half-tracks, opposed by miniature cannon and soldiers, clad in the uniform of the *Chasseurs Ardennais*, filled both sides of the river where he had won his first victory – the breakthrough at Dinant. He stared at the sand table suddenly happy and at the same time sad. What a great future he had once had – a full Colonel at the age of thirty when most of his contemporaries who had come with him from the regular *Reichswehr** into Hitler's Wehrmacht had still been Captains. Now they were Colonels themselves, a couple even Generals, and he was back to his old rank, running a camp for skivers and scum. He sighed. What a life!

Hauptmann Mueller limped to the sideboard next to the great green glowing Russian stove. It was still only zero ten hundred hours, but he needed a drink; otherwise he would start howling with the sheer absolute misery of it all.

Since that terrible wound in 1941, his whole life had been ruined. His wife had left him the day that Professor Sauerbruch in Berlin's La Charité Hospital had told her that her dashing, decorated husband would never be capable of frontline duty any more. There would be no more promotion and no more medals for valour from the Führer for the *Herr Oberst*. Divorce was easy in wartime. Now she was living with some fat swine of an SS Quartermaster-Colonel, who was getting ever richer in the black market in gold and diamonds probably looted from the Yids in the concentration camps.

Naturally he had tried other women, once he had been discharged from hospital. But they had not had the time for his little – er - *aberrations*, as Ilona had once had. Dashing Colonels of cavalry could afford to indulge themselves. Badly wounded Captains with no special employment could not. Thereafter it had been the whores and whatever kind of dumb Russian peasant bitch he could find. They were the best, however thick and ugly they were. They didn't object. They needed the food.

He drained his glass and poured himself another. Outside they were counting off the numbers in hoarse unison. The nagging pain in his leg was beginning to ease. He took another drink of the fiery spirits and felt a

*The name of the German Army before Hitler took it over and expanded it five-fold.

46

satisfying kick and burn at the back of his throat as he did so. He started to feel a lot better.

Suddenly he heard a noise from the next room. Instinctively his hand fell to the pistol at his hip. Next instant he relaxed. He knew who it was. It was Aniya, the 'laundry maid', who occasionally, when he felt in the mood, did more for him than just wash his shirts and underpants. He drained his glass and poured himself another.

Idly, glass in hand, he limped into the other room – his bedroom. For a few moments he watched the girl's shabby black dress ride up her thick farmer's leg, as she bent over the bedstead picking up his clothes. He licked his lips as her loose heavy breasts – for she had never heard of a brassière – swung free of restraint. God, wasn't she a real cow, but an utterly delightful one, too. He wondered whether she wore drawers. Most of the peasant women didn't. Why, he could just whip up her dress, as she leaned so provocatively over the bed and then –

He didn't think the thought to an end. Instead he finished the third drink and limped back into his study, calling, 'Aniya . . . *pashalasta!*'

She came humbly, hesitantly, wiping her hands on her black apron in the manner of the peasant. He sat in his chair, legs astraddle. She looked down at his loins. He had already ripped open the flies of his breeches. In one hand he had his cane, swinging it back and forth menacingly.

'*Gospodin, offisier?*' she queried, a little frightened. She knew him well by now – his moods, his brutality if he wasn't satisfied. 'You want?'

He said nothing, devouring her ample body with his greedy drunken gaze, the abundance of ripe warm flesh, just crying out for the pleasure he could never give her.

She repeated her query, half-hoping that he was already too drunk. Then he would whip up her skirt and slash her ample bottom a couple of times before sending her on her way with a couple of tins of meat the *Germanski* called 'old

47

man'. That she did not mind. Most Russian husbands beat their women when they were drunk. It was the other . . .

'Kneel!' His command cut harshly into her thoughts.

She hesitated.

He raised the cane.

Resigned she knelt, revulsion welling up inside her. What pigs these Fritzes were. Why couldn't they make love in the same honest way a Russian man did? He fumbled with his open flies. She waited until he was finished. Then closing her eyes, she commenced . . .

CHAPTER 6

It was snowing now – perhaps the last of the winter. The thick heavy wet flakes came down solidly as if God on high had decided He would blot out the miserable war-torn world down below for good. There would never be another spring.

In single file the prisoners, shrouded in snow, trudged around the circuit, hands behind their backs, as if they were tied. This was 'free time', the only period throughout the day when they were subjected to no pressures, save that of walking. In theory, they were not allowed to talk during free time, but in practice they did, safe in the knowledge, especially at this moment of bad weather, that their guards would be sheltering themselves, enjoying a quiet smoke out of the snow.

Karl walked in front. Behind him came Ami and Polack, their collars turned up against the snow while in the huts the lights were already burning; it was so grey. Their voices were muted by the snow and the Three Rebels felt safe from listening ears and prying eyes as Karl started on the subject which had been very much on his mind since the day he had fallen in the shit-trench.

'There is a way, comrades,' he said, while the other two broke the regulations as no one was looking and fell into step beside him, their feet muffled by the snow.

'Way to do what?' Ami asked.

'Get out of here.'

'You mean a tunnel?' Ami queried, always the quickest of the three in such matters.

'Of a kind,' Karl replied a little mysteriously.

'Karl,' Polack objected, his red nose swollen and dripping with the cold, 'we've got no tools to dig a tunnel.'

'Keep your hair on, Polack,' Karl soothed him, 'I know, I know. But it's a tunnel which has already been dug for us in a sort of way.'

'What kind of shit is that, Karl?' Ami demanded almost angrily.

Karl smiled softly. '*Shit* is the operative word, Ami,' he said. 'You remember the other day when that bastard Tinplate forced me into the shit-trench?' Hurriedly he explained what his thoughts had been that day when Tinplate had turfed him into the noxious pit.

The two of them nodded. Outside, between the layers of wire one of the sinister Dobermans was beginning to bay angrily. At what, they didn't know. All the same, Karl felt a cold finger of fear trace its way down his spine. He shuddered and said hurriedly, 'A louse must have run across my liver, comrades.'

'Piss or get off the pot, Karl,' Ami snapped, unimpressed. 'What's the drill?'

'This. I fell in the shit-trench as you both know and I realised . . .'

'You mean, Karl,' Polack said in that ponderous manner of his, his face red and wet with melting snowflakes, 'that you think that's the way out for us?'

'Yes,' Karl answered eagerly. 'It's a ready-made tunnel. Last night I checked it out the best I could from that hole in the plaster just over my cell door. As far as I can make out, the shit-trench itself is not covered by the searchlights. Once we're in the tunnel, we could crawl along it without being seen from up there.'

Ami tugged at the end of his nose. 'We've got to get out first, Karl.' He raised his hand hurriedly to prevent the others from interrupting. 'Let's forget about getting out of our cells – I suppose we're going to bugger off after dark so we'd be in our cells. What worries me is whether once we've got out of our cells and sneaked into the shit-tunnel, we can really get through to the other end?'

'You mean the manhole, Ami?' Karl said quickly.

'Yes.'

'I've been thinking about that, too. As I told you there's a manhole cover at the far end leading to the sewer which runs outside the camp. But natch, we don't know if it's bolted down or anything like that. Yes, we'd be in the shit, if we got that far and found out then it wouldn't damn well open . . .' He stopped short. Ami had ceased walking, a punishable offence in Camp Death. 'What is it?' he hissed urgently.

Ami licked his suddenly dry lips and looked around him in the swirling snow. The outer reaches of the Camp had already disappeared in the white moving fog of the snow-storm. Now he couldn't even see the towers. Somewhere to their right the column of prisoners were slouching past like silent grey ghosts, unaware that the Three Rebels were standing at the halt only a couple of metres away.

'Well?' Karl persisted irritably. 'What the frig's going on, Ami? Cough it up.'

'Well, there's no better time than now, is there? Ami replied brightly.

'Better time than what?'

'*Yo-yo*! To find out whether we can get into that shaft from the shit-tunnel, Karl!'

'But Ami – ' Karl commenced desperately, but already Ami was running lightly to the tunnel, calling softly over his shoulder, his words deadened by the falling snow, 'Keep your glassy orbits peeled.'

'Like a can of boiled tomatoes,' Polack answered without enthusiasm and then Ami was gone, eaten up by the white whirling fog . . .

Appalled by the stench, trying to breathe shallowly, Ami doubled down the trench-head below the surface, avoiding slipping and falling on the noxious slime time and time again. He knew he must make best use of every minute. If he were caught, it would be days in the 'dark cell' on bread-and-water – or worse. He couldn't afford to be nabbed.

Now the grating loomed up out of the snow. He gasped

51

with relief. Hurriedly he bent. His fingers were like ice, with hardly any feeling in them. He grunted and taking hold of the grating heaved with all his strength.

Nothing happened.

Ami cursed and tried again. Still nothing. The damn thing wouldn't budge a fraction.

For a moment he crouched there with the snow beating down, at a loss. Then he spotted the indentation at the side of the grating and realised its purpose immediately. You pressed there and the grating levered up. He bored his fingers through the slime and pressed. The grating came up at one end. Hastily he grabbed it and tugged. The whole thing was freed. He gulped and peered inside. The tunnel was definitely wide enough for them, even broad enough for Polack's bulk. It led downwards and then curved off towards the wire, but what lay beyond the curve it was impossible to see. He didn't have time to investigate.

Hurriedly, his heart beating excitedly, he slipped the grating into place and scurried back the way he had come like some human sewer rat. He poked his head above the trench. Nobody! He could hardly see the outline of his two comrades waiting tensely for him to reappear – it was that thick with flying snowflakes. He hesitated no longer. Hastily he heaved himself over the side of the trench and almost immediately the three of them resumed their progress around the yard.

'Well?' Karl demanded tensely.

Ami caught his breath. 'I couldn't see the whole way through, but I got the grating off without any trouble – as easy as falling off a log. And the shaft is big enough even for Polack here.'

'*Schnauze!*' Polack cut in suddenly with unusual vehemence for him.

'What's up?' Karl asked sharply.

Polack indicated with a nod of his head.

Karl followed the direction and just caught a glimpse of

a small, stoop-shouldered figure vanishing into the whirling white gloom.

'Silvereye,' he said slowly.

Polack nodded.

'And what's that bastard doing here? There's more shit on him than in that tunnel over yonder. He'd not be out here unless –'

Karl nodded grimly, face set and thoughtful. 'Unless he was spying on someone, Ami.'

'You mean us?'

Karl sucked his teeth and said, 'Yes.'

Polack, his face wet with melting snow, looked from one Rebel to the other in bewilderment. 'But what does it mean, comrades?'

'What does it mean, Polack?' Ami echoed scornfully. 'I'll tell yer what it frigging well means.' He drew his forefinger dramatically across his skinny throat. '*That!*'

Polack gulped, hard.

Now the days passed rapidly in unrelenting, brutal training during the day and equally hard labour at night as the Three Rebels prepared for their escape. Squatting in their freezing cells while the snow-laden wind howled outside, rattling the doors of the prison in one last fury before spring came at last, they prepared their imitation pistols – lengths of firewood stolen from the cookhouse – and blackened with boot polish which was in plentiful supply in the Camp. Holsters followed: pieces of shaped cardboard, marked to give them a leathery grain, before the long job of rubbing them with boot polish to give the right sheen.

Karl had decided that once they had crossed the steppe, they would board the leave train for the Reich – and to do that they would have to look like soldiers going on furlough. On the Eastern Front all men on leave travelled armed on account of the partisans. Their packs would be procured later by the simple expedient, he hoped, of stealing those left lying around in the train corridor by careless soldiers, busy already with getting drunk as most of them did on the day-long journey to Poland and from thence to the Reich. Badges of rank and medals were also currently in production – made from bits of silver cigarette paper thrown away by their guards and spoons filched again from the cookhouse.

'But what about our leave passes?' Ami had objected more than once, as their plans progressed. 'The frigging chaindogs will want to see leave passes once we change at Warsaw for Berlin. We might make it without them at that one-horse town on the other side of the steppe, but in Warsaw we haven't a chance.'

But each time, Karl, who didn't know the answer to that overwhelming question either, had soothed him with a calm, 'Ami, forget it, willyer? Let's worry about getting on the leave train first, eh?' And with that Ami had to be content.

Thus the three young men, over whose heads hung a virtual sentence of death whatever happened, laboured in the obscurity of their cells. Outside in the middle of the night while they worked and the rest of the inmates snored in heavy sleep, they could hear the half-wild guard dogs howling occasionally in that spine-tingling eerie manner of theirs. It was then that they would pause in their clandestine work and stare in sudden fear at the dirty walls of their cells. For those banshee-like, unreal howls were a reminder of the danger which lurked just outside the wire. Yes, they might just get safely through the shit-trench into the shaft. But what about the dogs? Were they allowed to roam *outside* the wire as well as between the various layers of inner wire?

More than once, the night-time howling had occasioned Karl to balance precariously on the three-legged *Wehrmacht* wooden stool, which was the little cell's only other furniture, and stare out through the crack above the door. But all was in the darkness, save for the usual finger of silver light sweeping across the compound. Nothing could be seen of what was taking place beyond the wire. Where the dogs were was a matter of conjecture.

But twice on such occasions, he had *smelled* not *seen* something unusual taking place outside Tract D. 'What do you mean – *smelled*?' Ami had snorted when he mentioned the matter to him.

Karl had hesitated. 'Well, Ami, it's hard to put your finger on.'

'As the soldier said to the female contortionist,' Ami had replied. 'Come on, Karl, get on with it, old house.'

'Well, it wasn't the smell of one of the guards. You know, decent soap, real meat, hair pomade – that sort of thing,' Karl had stuttered uncertainly.

'Well, what kind of smell was it?'

'Our kind of smell. You know – sweat and fart soup and all that.'

'Your arsehole must have been too near your own hooter,' Ami had snorted crudely. 'What in three devils' name would one of our lot be doing outside at night? No, Karl, you must be smelling your own pong.' Ami had shaken his head in mock sadness. 'You've got to take it easy, sunshine. This frigging place is getting yer down. Hope you're not gonna get like Howling Mad.'

But Karl had remained unconvinced. He was sure he had not been mistaken. 'I'm not shitting yer, Ami,' he declared fervently. 'There is somebody like us out there at night. Honest . . .'

But all that his old friend had been able to vouchsafe him as an answer was a sad shake of his blond head, tapping his temple as if poor Karl was already half-*meschugge*.

At the end of the first week of their preparations with three weeks to go before they were posted to the dreaded Punishment Battalion 333, Polack produced a bar of soap furtively, as they plodded round the circuit during their afternoon free time. 'Soap,' he announced somewhat stupidly.

'That's real nice of you, Polack, telling me what it is,' Ami snapped. 'Wouldn't have recognised it, if you hadn't told me.'

'Don't fuck around, Ami,' Karl hissed, noting that yet once again the little runt called Silvereye was dogging their footsteps as they trudged on. 'Is it from the guards?' he added urgently.

Polack nodded and held up his hand which had just pocketed the soap once more, for Karl to smell it. 'Get a whiff of that, mate.'

Karl did so and nodded his appreciation. 'Good work, Polack,' he whispered. 'Everything's working out just right.'

Ami looked angrily from one face to the other and snapped, 'Will one of you two queers let me know what's frigging well going on, eh?'

Karl did a quick look to left and right to check whether they were being overheard and said, 'It's for the dogs, Ami. We've got to smell like the guards – hence their soap. Maybe it'll stop them yapping when we come out of the tunnel. Anyway, it's the only thing I can think of.'

Ami was impressed for once. 'Smart damn thinking, old house,' he conceded. 'Very smart damn thinking.'

Karl nodded and decided to keep the fact that there might well be dogs running loose *outside* the compound to himself. Then all the frigging perfumed soap in the world wouldn't help them.

So, little by little, they prepared for their escape, that daring venture into the unknown – the like of which had never been undertaken before in the cruel history of Camp Death. Unknown to the Three Rebels, all previous attempts made by desperate men at the end of their tether had been nipped in the bud. The noncoms who ran the Camp valued their skins too highly to allow anyone to escape from the place for that would mean their being sent straight back to the front, crippled as most of them were. For self-protection, each of them employed stoolpigeons and spies among the prisoners to ensure that they were informed in time of any attempt to flee.

Tinplate, the most feared of all the noncoms, was no exception. He had taken the measure of most of the scum under his charge. They valued their own hides above everything. Comradeship and loyalty were foreign to them. They were all out for Number One pure and simple. Thus it was that he knew Silvereye was telling the truth - he was too shit-scared to tell a lie, even for profit – when he made his weekly report at the end of the second week of Tract D's training for the 333rd.

'There's no doubt about it, *Oberfeld*,' he reported in that hoarse, conspiratorial manner of his, his one straight eye fixed longingly on the bottle of firewater that Tinplate had promised him. 'The three of them are up to no good. Twice I've been out in the compound this week at night and heard them beavering away at something or other. They're organising' – he meant stealing – 'odds and ends from the hashslingers' cookhouse when they think they're not looking. Very definitely, they're up to something.' He licked his lips significantly.

Tinplate ignored the look. Let the frigging little sauce-hound suffer a while longer. 'But how're they gonna do it?' he demanded. 'The listening men report no tunnel. They ain't got a cat's chance in hell of getting over the wire – or under it either, for that matter. Them hounds'd soon see 'em off.' He grinned evilly. 'So how?'

'Don't know, *Oberfeld*,' the stoolpigeon admitted grudgingly. 'All I do know is that there's something going on. Feel it in my bones.'

'You'll feel my frigging dice-beaker up yer arse if you don't find out more soon,' Tinplate growled and reaching for the bottle of cheap vodka flung it at the little runt. 'All right, arse-with-ears, piss in the wind now. But don't come back next Saturday without exact details. Now be off with you.'

For a moment or two after his spy had departed, Tinplate sat there, thinking. Then from over at the Sergeants' Mess he heard the first clink of glasses and the high silly laughter of the whores they had brought in for the Saturday night orgy. He forgot the Three Rebels. There were better things to do on this particular night . . . Meanwhile, on the other side of Camp Death the desperate young men worked doggedly in the heavy silence of their cells. There were just two weeks to go . . .

CHAPTER 7

The Three Rebels had been tried by a Field Tribunal of the fourth Grenadier Regiment. It had consisted of the two senior Battalion Commanders and Colonel von Heinersdorff, the Regimental Commander, presiding. As usual the old cavalryman had seated himself on his saddle – that and his own personal thunderbox seat had followed him through four years of campaigning on three continents – swinging the broken sabre which he had carried in the Battle of Bzura back in Poland in 1939.

There had been no defence, only the prosecution, carried out by Creeping Jesus, still pale after his stay in hospital with his wound, but as vindictive as ever. Against the background of the lowering gunfire to the east and the coming and going of vehicles at the farmhouse regimental headquarters, the Adjutant had lammed into the three young men. 'Rank treachery . . . wilful disobedience . . . plain refusal of an order given by a superior officer in the field of battle . . . there is only one verdict this court can possibly give . . . *death!*' The words had poured from his twisted lips in an angry bitter stream.

While the two Battalion Commanders had leaned forward intently taking in every word, for both of them were seriously concerned about the morale of the men after the disastrous outcome of the recent offensive, von Heinersdorff seemed bored by the whole business, his mind apparently elsewhere. He slumped on his saddle, occasionally fiddling with his old-fashioned cavalryman's white moustache or swinging his sabre, as if he were mentally riding that great charge of Bzura.

Watching the tribunal, standing stiffly at attention, Karl had been overcome by a feeling of helplessness. The two

59

Battalion Commanders were against them, he could see that, even though they might not have been convinced by Creeping Jesus's angry rhetoric. Everyone in the Fourth Grenadiers knew just how much the Adjutant had fought to save his precious hide these last years. As for the Regiment Commander, whose vote carried the most weight of all, he wasn't even listening. The old fart was obviously just too senile to take in anything.

'So, *meine Herren*,' Creeping Jesus had summed up, flashing a glance of triumph at the pale young men standing beside a heavily armed guard in the middle of the big farm kitchen which served as a courtroom, 'there can be only one decision this tribunal can make. It has been clearly proved that the three accused refused a direct order while on active service. Not only that, but they prejudiced a major action, due to be carried out by the whole corps. They have blood on their hands. The sentence for that can be only – *death*!' He sat down without another word, but with a smirk on his face, as if he half-expected applause for his cleverness. Instead he was greeted by a heavy brooding silence, broken only by the urgent ringing of a telephone in the next room.

Slowly, very slowly, as if it required an effort of will, von Heinersdorff roused himself. He tugged at the end of his big bulbous nose, the usual semi-idiotic smile absent from his lean old soldier's face. 'Well, accused, you have heard the charges and you've heard the evidence against you, which is damning . . .'

At either side of him the tough Battalion Commanders nodded their heads in agreement as if they wanted to get the matter over with quickly and be off back to their hard-pressed troops.

'. . . And convincing. Not the sort of thing I expect from the Fourth Grenadiers, even if there were women involved – *Russian* women, of course.' He emphasised the word, as if it were of some importance . . . 'But in the past, all three of you have been good soldiers. You have shed your blood for the Fatherland. You have won decorations for valour in the field . . .'

Creeping Jesus shot the CO a warning look. What was the silly old fart up to now, it seemed to say. God, the CO was in his dotage. He should have been sacked years ago and he, von Schorr, appointed Commander in his place.

'Your conduct has been most deplorable, however, and we are fighting a battle here in the East for our very existence. If we fail, Germany, our beloved Fatherland, will go under.' He tugged again at his red nose, as if he was becoming aware of the full import of his own words for the first time. 'I am afraid that I must treat this case with the utmost severity.' He cleared his throat. 'Have you anything to say before I pass sentence upon you?'

Creeping Jesus's mood changed abruptly. He flashed a triumphant glance in the direction of the Three Rebels.

Karl shook his head numbly. Ami, for his part, glared defiantly at the Tribunal, angry and unbeaten to the very end. All his young life he had been taunted and maligned on account of his American father and his unmarried mother who brought him into a cruel provincial world as an American bastard. *Ami . . . Ami . . . Ami . . .* That name had accompanied him throughout his short life. Teachers, schoolmates, nuns, bosses, Nazis – the whole rotten lot of them had reviled and mocked him with it for as long as he could remember. How often had he cried himself to sleep as a kid? But he had become hard, too. If the New Order, this vaunted, racially pure 'One Thousand Year Reich', didn't want him, well then he didn't want it, either. Now they – the Nazis – were about to make their final reckoning with him. Let them!

'Well?' von Heinersdorff asked not unkindly. 'Not a word in your defence?'

'Sir!' It was Polack, face flushed, fists suddenly clenched.

'Yes, Prisoner.'

'I'd like to say something, sir.' Suddenly, the normally inarticulate Polack released a torrent of impassioned words, as if a dam had broken which had hemmed them in for years. 'Marching, marching . . . weeks on end . . . with nothing proper to eat . . . The Ivans behind us and in front of us . . . murdering bastards . . . dog eat dog . . . It's been going on for years . . .' The words came in a hectic desperate flow, straight from Polack's simple Slavic heart, the expression of the little man everywhere caught up in a global struggle far beyond the comprehension of his humble, small-town existence. A cry from the heart, which had nothing to do really with their 'crimes', but which had Colonel von Heinersdorff suddenly blinking hard and furtively rubbing the knuckles of his gnarled sabre-slashed hand in his old rheumy eyes.

'Sir, I don't want you to think we're cowards, because we're not. We didn't deliberately refuse Major von Schorr's order because we wanted to run away from the firing line. We did it, sir, because we thought what he asked us to do . . . wasn't proper . . . wasn't right . . .' Suddenly, the fire went from Polack's voice. He ended lamely, shoulders bent abruptly, as if in defeat, dropping his gaze like a humble little man who realised he had said too much.

Von Schorr fumed. He sprang to his feet to object. But the CO waved his broken sabre at him to desist and he sat down again, fists clenched with suppressed rage. Gently, the old Regimental Commander had nodded, as if he were agreeing with what Polack had just said, before stating in a voice that made his listeners strain to catch his words, 'There will be no death penalty. There has been enough killing, far too much as it is.' He had shaken his head regretfully. 'You will be sent to the Corps' Punishment Cage . . . Perhaps one day you might return . . .' He had not even finished the sentence. Swinging his booted leg over the well-worn saddle, he had ambled away, leaving the court and the prisoners staring at each other in complete bewilderment.

Now, as Karl worked at the door of his cell, the only noise the rasp of the sharpened spoon he was using as a tool on the stonework and the raucous drunken laughter coming from the Camp's Sergeants' Mess, he thought back to that scene – Polack's surprising outburst and the Colonel's seeming understanding of their motivation – and wondered yet again at the strangeness of life. One moment he had believed himself a dead man, with not a chance in hell of escaping from the cruel, all-powerful system. The next day they had been saved by a man who had always epitomised to him the old Imperial Prussian officers' corps. There had been no logic to it, no sense whatsoever. Yet there had to be some sense of purpose to their existence. They were here for something or other. *They had to be!* Why else life?

But as the cheap Russian mortar that had linked the two stones when it was slapped on hastily just before the war, started to crumble and he could begin to edge the first stone out, Karl forgot his philosophising. Now his pulse started to quicken. Things were falling into place! If he could find a means of getting out of his cell, it would be simplicity itself to rescue his two running-mates occu-pying the adjacent cells. For they were merely bolted from the outside . . . There was not even a padlock, for the rural prison had been designed to hold unruly members of the farming *kolhoz*, or collective farm, to which this prison complex had once belonged. Rough-and-ready herders and farmboys were imprisoned here for a few days for failing to meet their quota or for drinking more than their share of vodka on a Saturday night.

The beads of sweat trickling down his strained handsome young face, Karl worked even harder, removing now a second and then a third stone, feeling the icy wind of the steppe blowing against his head, the noise from the Sergeants' Mess getting ever louder.

By midnight, as the drunken voices of women singing the Russian soldiers' marching song *Katinka* in the Serge-ants' Mess grew in maudlin confusion, Karl paused in his labours, rested a moment and then rapped his tin cup on the wall of his cell. It was the signal to Ami next door to stand by. A moment later he heard the muted noise of Ami rapping on his cell-wall, signalling Polack to do the same. They were ready!

Hastily, Karl balanced himself on the three-legged stool once more. He had picked the spot above the door because he reasoned the guards always looked for anything suspicious at below eye-level or on the floor. They wouldn't conceive of anyone attempting to escape from a place above the door.

He took a deep breath and heaved himself upwards. Gingerly he placed his head inside the hole and started to wriggle through. The wind was blowing even stronger now, carrying the racket coming from the Sergeants' Mess with it. Karl was pleased. It would deaden any sound he might make. He didn't want one of the damned half-wild hounds at the wire beginning to howl its head off, alerting the guards on the stork-legged towers.

Again the searchlight swept across the courtyard, dragging its beam of bright silver light with it. He froze, as if shot. Nothing happened. The light swept on. God, he told himself with a fervent sigh of relief, if it had caught him half-in and half-out of the hole, he would have been a dead pigeon. The gunners on the towers would have shown no mercy. It would have been a welcome relief from the boredom of what they called the 'graveyard shift'.

He hesitated and then with one final heave he was through and dropping lightly to the ground. He was out. He was free, well free at least from the confines of his miserable, freezing cell. Crouched low, body pressed against the wall, hardly daring to breathe, he peered into the darkness. Nothing! There was no one in the yard. The guards were either in their towers or in the warmth and fug of the guardroom, knowing full well that both Howling Mad and the NCOs would be fully occupied this Saturday night with their whores and booze. He couldn't have picked a better time for the test run.

Karl hesitated no longer. He grasped the bolt to Ami's cell. It squeaked rustily. Karl started, heart pounding furiously. Nothing stirred. Next moment Ami sneaked out, hand extended. *'Himmel, Arsch und Wolkenbruch, Karl,'* he breathed excitedly, *'du hast es geschafft, Mensch!'*

'No time for congrats, Ami. Let Polack out – hurry!'

While Ami drew back the bolt of Polack's cell, Karl pulled out the socks he had deposited in his pocket and drew them on. Now all three of them had their clumsy heavy boots covered by their spare pair of socks so that as they doubled across the yard at a half-crouch they were almost noiseless, any little sound they might have made drowned by the racket from the Mess and the howl of the wind.

They paused at the trench, while Ami tied a rag around his nose and mouth against the stench. Then all three of them dropped hastily inside and ran its length, trying not to slip on the slime. Swiftly Ami, the smallest of the three, ripped up the grating and said in a muffled voice, 'Wish me luck, comrades.' Then without another word, while the other two crouched anxiously, he wiggled into the shaft. A moment later he was gone.

Karl's watch had been ripped off his wrist the day he had entered Camp Death. Now he timed Ami as he worked his way down the shaft and towards the wire with his fingers pressed to his pulse. Somewhere he had read that sewer gas could be poisonous and Polack, the fomer farm labourer on one of those vast Prussian estates in the east, had told of the dangers farmers sometimes faced from the gases engendered in closed-in silos. 'About three to five minutes at the most, comrades,' he had warned them gravely, 'then it gets to you and you keel over.' Now Karl prayed it would take Ami no more than two minutes to reach the outer wire and see if he could find the outside grating with more fresh air. That would mean a round trip of four minutes, one minute less than Polack had estimated before the danger point was reached. Hearing himself breathing harshly, feeling his pulse race, Karl ticked off the seconds, praying that nothing would go wrong – *now!*

Two minutes . . . two and a half . . . three minutes . . . three and a half . . . 'Shit on the shingle, Polack,' he cursed, beside himself with anxiety, 'where the frig is the little prick?' *Four minutes!*

Now it was Polack's turn to become worried. He bent his big head to the grating and whispered, his voice echoing hollowly down the shaft, 'Can you hear me, Ami?'

His only answer was an echoing silence. He swallowed hard. Dare he raise his voice more? My God, where was Ami?

Next to him, Karl, as worried and as anxious as he was, asked, 'Do you think I should go down after him, Polack? Didn't you say that –' He stopped short. There was a rustling, shuffling sound coming from the shaft. For an instant he wondered if it could be a sewer rat. But Ami's cheerful voice saying, 'All right, don't just wait there, give us a hand,' told him, with a sense of relief, that this particular creature hailed from the Rhineland not Central Russia and walked on two legs instead of four.

Hurriedly, Polack leaned down once more and extended his big hand. He heaved and Ami's head popped into view. A moment later he was out of the shaft, breathing heavily and gasping, 'It's easy, old house. There's another grating like this on the far end. Came off without any fuss.' He caught his breath and tried to calm his nerves, racing electrically with his discovery. 'And –'

'Go on!' they hissed together, nerves stretched to breaking point with tension.

'It lets out to the *other side of the wire!*' Ami prevented himself from shouting out his tremendous news just in time. 'Did you hear me, comrades? The shit-shaft leads right out of the Camp!'

'*Boshe moi!*' Polack exclaimed happily and gave Karl a nudge in the ribs which slammed him against the side of the tunnel. 'Did you hear that, Karl?'

'Well, in spite of the fact that you have just frigging well punctured a couple of my ribs and probably damaged my eardrum permanently with that bang against the concrete, I heard,' Karl hissed with mock sourness, as Ami clambered up into the trench and the three of them embraced.

Even as an old man Karl Carstens would recall every moment, every smell, every sound of that magic moment. The soft pad-pad of the guard dogs near the wire, the heavy resinous odour of the firs which fringed one of the towers, the drunken laughter coming from the Sergeants' Mess, the great bars of bright white light momentarily drenching the areas of darkness in cruel, artificial daylight; and far beyond the sombre stillness of the limitless steppe, the faint, mournful whistle of a train . . .

CHAPTER 8

Hurriedly, Silvereye pressed himself into the shadows as the searchlight swung across the yard yet once again, throwing everything into harsh relief. His heart pounded and his fingers trembled. Already he could taste the vodka to come – that pleasant burn, as it coursed its way down his gullet to slam into his shrunken stomach. Who could tell? Perhaps that big bastard Tinplate might let him have a feel of one of the whores. Of course, he was no longer capable – the years in prison had taken their toll. But a good feel underneath one of their skirts would do him; it would keep him content for many a long night in the loneliness of his little cell.

Last year, when he had betrayed that cocky young prick of a *Panzergrenadier*, always going on – the smartarsed handsome young bastard – about the hundreds of women he'd snaked and how no bit o' gash could withstand him, Tinplate had given him *two* bottles of sauce, and a ring of giddyup* sausage as well. For a whole day they had left the celebrated cocksman's corpse hanging on the wire as a warning to the others. Yes, that had been a grand day for him; he had savoured it for months afterwards.

Now he'd got an even bigger fish. Three of the bastards, obviously ready to try to escape. First they had broken out of their cells – and he had already spotted they'd been taking odds and ends from the cookhouse, despite the risks – now they were down in that shaft; and there was only one place that shaft led to – *the outside*!

Silvereye rubbed his crooked chin. How was he going to do it? He didn't like reporting to Tinplate during daylight

*Sausage made of horsemeat.

hours. The scum confined in Camp Death were nobody's fools. They were all crooks themselves; they had eyes in the backs of their heads. He didn't want to be spotted talking to one of the noncoms. Stoolpigeons didn't live long. But could he tackle Tinplate now?

He pondered. Obviously the big prick would have poured a lot of firewater down behind his wing-collar by now. Would he be in any fit state to take in the exciting information he had to pass on? Or would he already be upstairs in bed with one of the Popov whores, doing the two-backed, four-legged beast? Holy strawsack, it would be more than his life was worth to disturb Tinplate when he was going at it like a frigging fiddler's elbow!

Abruptly the mental picture of Tinplate dicking it to some piece of Popov gash, with her legs in the air, giggling and panting, her naked arse and everything showing, excited the little runt of a man hiding in the shadows. He licked suddenly parched lips. God, how he could go running his finger up and down a piece of lovely wet gash at this very moment! Christ on a crutch, he might even get a stiff 'un agen after all these years. He swallowed hard, his mind made up. He flashed one last look at the shit-trench. They were still in it. He could hear the slight movements they were making and in between lulls in the high wind blowing, he thought he could catch snatches of their whispered conversation. They were safe there for the time being, he told himself. Right, he'd better get on with it.

Carefully he detached himself from the shadows cast by the wall of the hut from which he had been observing the three would-be escapers. Across at the Sergeants' Mess, a sudden chink of light cut the darkness, followed a second later by the sharp hiss of running liquid. Someone was pissing out of the door. Silvereye gave one of his rare crooked smiles. The noncoms were having a real high old time this Saturday night. He felt his pulse racing again. He'd have a feel at that delightful female gash yet . . .

69

Cautiously, keeping his one good eye on the nearest stork-legged guard tower, he started to cross the yard towards the Sergeants' Mess, nerves tingling with suppressed excitement. The door slammed shut again. The noise was cut off. Up in the towers he knew the duty men would relax. They'd realise that the noncoms were too pissed or otherwise occupied to bother them tonight for sure.

Now he could easily hear the noise coming from the Sergeants' Mess. He could smell the typical odour of a Saturday night piss-up: a mixture of stale beer, cigar-smoke and cheap perfume, plus that delightful tang of female gash. He quickened his pace, heading for the back door. By now the Mess servants, all trusties like himself, would be back in their cells, he reasoned. The noncoms would be serving themselves, those still on their feet and capable of doing so. For he did not want to encounter any of his fellow trusties. In the dog eat dog world in which they all lived, he didn't trust a single one of them. They'd shop him, he knew, at the drop of a hat.

Hesitantly he tapped on the door. No answer. In a way Silvereye wasn't expecting one. He turned the knob and entered in his usual furtive shuffling manner.

The kitchen was a mess. A pan of green pea soup had overflowed on the stove and the already hardening lava of soup had run on to the floor, littered with broken bottles and scraps of sausage and bread. On the big table, awash with beer suds and debris, someone had doused a wet cigar in a pair of fried eggs so that it looked as if a yellow eye had been poked out. Silvereye licked his lips greedily. He would dearly love to scoop up the good egg and swallow it whole. But there were more important things to do. He turned the handle of the door which led into the Sergeants' Mess itself.

He peered inside. The place was a smoke-filled shambles! 'Beer corpses' lay everywhere, slumped in corners, lying full-length on benches, sprawled head-down on the tables, faces in their own vomit. Here and there drunken whores, some stripped down to their knickers were being fondled by bleary-eyed noncoms while in the centre of the floor a Sergeant, completely starkers save for his boots, stumbled through a foxtrot to the scratchy music of a gramophone, supported by a madly giggling whore, who for some reason unknown to Silvereye, was wearing a lampshade on her brashly peroxided curls.

Silvereye swallowed hard, his Adam's apple shuttling up and down his narrow throat nervously, at a loss for what to do. Tinplate was nowhere in sight, but there was the sound of bedsprings squeaking noisily upstairs. Was he already on the nest, he wondered. He licked his lips and tried to take his one eye off a whore who had raised her skirt and was now squatting over a flowerpot on the floor, giggling madly. She wasn't wearing any knickers. Christ, what was he going to do?

Suddenly the decision was made for him. A heavy hand fell on his skinny shoulder and he sank almost to his knees. 'Now then, jailbait,' a drunken bass voice demanded. 'Get them frigging glassy orbits o' yourn off'n that lady pissing in the jug over there. That's my fiancée, see. And tell me what a frigging one-eyed cripple like you is doing in here without permission!'

Silvereye looked up.

Above him towered Tinplate's assistant-*Unteroffizier* Hanno Hitler, known behind his broad back – naturally – as 'Adolf's Bastard'; and he was drunk, roaring drunk, swaying dramatically as he used Silvereye now to support himself.

'You know me, sir,' Silvereye quavered, face contorted with the weight he was supporting now.

'Yer,' chortled the big drunk. 'You're a pain in the pisser and you've been looking up my fiancée's knickers.' He wagged a finger like a small hairy sausage in front of Silvereye's nose. 'Naughty, naughty, frigging well *very* naughty!'

71

'But sir,' Silvereye pleaded urgently, sensing trouble with the drunken NCO. 'I've got important information for *Oberfeldwebel* Dietz.' He meant 'Tinplate'.

Adolf's Bastard chuckled throatily. 'For your information, arse-with-ears, *der Herr Oberfeldwebel* Dietz is presently dancing a mattress polka with Lubricated Luzie and don't want to be disturbed nohow. Got it?'

'Sir,' Silvereye protested. 'It's vitally important . . . I've got information about three prisoners preparing to escape . . .' His words ended with a sudden yelp as he felt himself seized by the scruff of the neck and propelled through the drunken scene inside the Mess, through the kitchen door into the sudden cold of the yard.

For a moment Adolf's Bastard held him aloft, snarling, 'I don't like treacherous little pricks like you . . . ever since they shot that *Panzergrenadier* on the wire. Didn't you know the poor shit came from my old Regiment . . . Besides, yer looked up my fiancée's frigging knickers. Now shit in the wind, you cockeyed bugger.' He grunted and suddenly Silvereye felt himself sailing through the air, propelled upwards and outwards by a tremendous kick from the drunken NCO's big dicebeaker. He couldn't help himself. He let out a loud yell of absolute pain. Next moment he crashed to the ground, all breath knocked from his skinny frame . . .

'*Did you hear that?*' Polack hissed.

'Yes, I heard it,' Karl answered grimly, as the three of them crouched there in the inky darkness, listening to Silvereye's soft moans as he lay in an awkward heap only metres away. 'And I heard something else.'

'Yer, so now we know who betrayed that poor shit of a *Panzergrenadier*, the one they told us about when we first came here.'

Karl, his mind racing furiously, nodded. 'Yes, the same swine who is now going to betray us, if he has half a chance.'

'What do you mean?' Ami asked quickly.

'Well, somebody's been watching us all along, I knew it. Now that *somebody's* over there.'

'Stoolpigeon?' Ami rapped.

'Yes.'

'But what can we do?' Polack protested unhappily. 'He's in prison and so are we.'

'*Nobble* him before he *nobbles* us. Come on!' Without waiting to see if they had understood, Karl darted forward in the direction from which he had heard the cry of pain.

Silvereye heard them coming. Instinctively he knew it was the prisoners he had been spying on. In absolute panic he scrambled to his feet, eyes wild with fear. What was he to do? Should he cry out? If he did, the guards on the nearest tower might open up. He'd be dead before he hit the deck. *The Sergeants' Mess*! That was it. He started to run, skinny little arms flailing like pistons across his narrow chest.

'There he is,' Polack hissed. 'Stop him, Karl!'

Karl changed direction. The stoolpigeon was perhaps some fifteen metres away from the back door of the Mess. Should he go after him? What if someone else opened the back door to take a piss on the steps and spotted them? It was a chance they had to take. He increased his pace. Now he could almost smell the fear coming from the running man. The bastard was running for his life. Karl flung in his last bit of strength. They were a metre apart . . . The door was within grasping distance. If he didn't nobble the little bastard now, it would all be over.

With a wild grunt Karl flung himself forward in a shallow dive. The little man yelped with pain as Karl's shoulder slammed into the small of his back. Next moment they had fallen together in a confused mass of flailing limbs while Karl's hand sought desperately for the other man's mouth to silence him before he woke up the whole Camp. The stoolpigeon had been well and truly nobbled. Now *what in hell's name were they going to do with him?*

*

73

Slowly, very slowly, Polack relaxed the grip of his brawny arm on Silvereye's skinny throat, saying softly, 'Now listen, arse-with-ears, one single peep out of you and I'll croak yer here and now. Understand?'

Gasping for breath, unable to speak, Silvereye nodded his head wildly. Polack let go and pushed the terrified spy against the wooden seat of the 'ten-seat crapper'.

For a moment there was no sound save that of the little man's hectic breathing and the soft keening of the wind outside the latrine. Even the Sergeants' Mess on the other side of the Camp was silent at last. Perhaps they were all safely tucked up in their bunks with their whores, Karl told himself before dismissing the matter.

'What we gonna do with the bastard?' Polack asked softly, towering over the terrified little man.

'I won't talk . . . honest I won't.'

Angrily Ami slapped him across the face snarling, 'Speak when you're spoken to, cunt! Of course he'll squeal the moment he gets a chance to, Karl,' he sneered.

Karl nodded agreement, his brain racing as he considered what to do. They couldn't let the man go, he knew that. But what could they do if they didn't release him? They were prisoners themselves. They couldn't hide him. In four hours it would be morning parade again and the usual count. He had to make up his mind and he had to make it up damned fast!

Silvereye seemed to read the way Karl's mind was moving for suddenly he folded his hands in the classic position of supplication, tears streaming down his wizened runtish face, voice choked with emotion. 'Please don't kill me,' he cried, 'I didn't mean to do it – with that *Panzergrenadier*. But you don't know what they're like – the noncoms . . . they force you to do things. After a while you don't even kn–'

Ami slapped him again and the sudden torrent of words came to a surprised halt. Silvereye slumped forward, skinny shoulders heaving as he sobbed like a heart-broken child.

74

Karl looked at Ami, then at the stoolpigeon and finally at the open seat of the nauseous crapper next to where Silvereye slumped. Slowly, very slowly, Ami began to nod, as if he were already in agreement with Karl's unspoken question.

Polack flashed a wild glance from one face to the other. He licked dry lips, opened his mouth as if he were going to protest, then thought better of it. He let his big brutal shoulders slump, as if in defeat. Now there was no sound save that of the sobbing stoolpigeon . . .

CHAPTER 9

'God in Heaven, Oberfeld!' cried Howling Mad, beside himself
with rage. 'It is impossible . . . You must still be drunk
from last night, man!' He grabbed the bottle of vodka from
the table and snatched a mighty slug from it. He caught
his breath and shuddered as the neat spirit flamed a searing
path down to his ruined stomach, not giving a twopenny
damn that he was drinking in the presence of an NCO at
eight o'clock in the morning.

Tinplate waited miserably, standing at attention, a
bandage soaked in vinegar hidden beneath his helmet in
an attempt to soothe his aching head, dark hollows under
his eyes. His mouth felt like the bottom of a parrot's cage.

Howling Mad Mueller wiped his hand across his lips
and barked, 'Are you sure you counted correctly, *Oberfeld*?
You might have missed someone. You know it's Sunday
morning and you swine were up to your usual piggery last
night. It is possible.'

Miserably Tinplate shook his raging head. 'Wish it was
true, sir. We counted 'em,' he indicated the shabby prisoners standing rigidly to attention outside in the freezing
wind, 'three times before I reported Silver – um, Prisoner
Schleim missing, sir.'

Howling Mad slammed his cane across the table in
sudden fury and made Tinplate jump. 'But I cannot
tolerate any prisoner escaping, *Oberfeld*! I will *not* tolerate
it. *Verdammte Scheisse*, the man must have been using you
all the time, pretending to supply you with information,
getting the run of the Camp at night, just so that he could
prepare his own escape.'

In spite of the pain he was in, *Oberfeldwebel* Dietz was
still prepared to argue. He knew he had been dropped

neatly into the shit by somebody or other but he wasn't prepared to take the blame. 'But *where* could he go?' Tinplate protested. 'And *why* would he go, sir? He was on a nice cushy number here, sir. He couldn't go home to the Reich. The only other alternative was the front and believe you me, sir, that was the last place that little heap of shit – excuse my French, sir – the prisoner Schleim would want to go.'

Howling Mad waved his hand in angry dismissal. 'All right, so one of your tame informers has disappeared. You don't think that he's left the Camp. That is something to be thankful for at least. I don't want to blot my record on escapes at Army HQ. So, if he's not *outsi*de, then he's somewhere *insi*de the Camp – yes?'

Tinplate nodded his agreement.

'So where and why is he hiding, if that is what he is doing? How do you explain that, *Oberfeld*, eh?' Howling Mad's demented eyes bored into Tinplate's menacingly.

'How do you mean?'

Howling Mad contained himself with difficulty. 'Man, what have you got between your ears – broad beans? Why should a stoolpigeon disappear, eh? *Think*! A man who is universally hated and feared – what happens if he's rumbled by the other prisoners?'

'You mean, sir,' Tinplate's mouth started to droop stupidly, as if he could not believe his own thoughts, as if *his* prisoners would never dare do that to *him*. 'You mean the other prisoners might . . .'

'Of course I damn well do, *Oberfeld*. If they've tumbled to your spy, they'll have done away with him!'

'But they wouldn't dare!'

'Now this is what you are going to do,' Howling Mad interrupted impatiently, no longer listening to the stupid oaf. 'Dismiss the men back to their cells at once. Take every off-duty guard – and the dogs too – and then you turn this place upside down, do you hear me? Turn it upside down till you find your missing man and then report to me immediately. At the double now – *move!*'

Tinplate 'moved', leaving Howling Mad Mueller, with his red-rimmed eyes gleaming crazily, staring out at the rigid ranks of the prisoners of Camp Death, murder in his heart . . .

Carefully, Karl rapped on the wall of his cell with his tin mug. Outside, all was noise and hustle as the guards doubled back and forth, running as if *they* were the prisoners, the hounds barking excitedly at their heels. Obviously they had cottoned on to Silvereye's disappearance and were turning the whole place apart. It wouldn't be long before they began on the cells, even though they would be the most unlikely places to hide someone. 'Listen,' he whispered, holding the inside of the mug to his mouth pressed close to the wall to function as a kind of primitive amplifier, 'stash the dummy pistol and any fodder you've got as soon as I sign off.'

Ami tapped twice to signal his understanding.

'We know we're safe for a bit yet. I don't think they'll find – well, you know what I mean.' Even now, ten hours after it had happened, he couldn't really bring himself to think of that horrific scene inside the latrine last night. 'But they will sooner or later. The shit'll put the hounds off for a bit, but once they really let them loose, they'll find . . .'

Again there came that double tap, indicating that Ami understood and didn't want to mention that subject openly, either.

'So, Ami, let's make a decision.' Karl hesitated, knowing that soon they would be committing themselves overwhelmingly; there would be no way back, once it was decided.

'What?'

'*Tonight.*'

78

'You mean we're going?' Even through the thickness of the wall, Karl felt he could hear the note of shock in his comrade's voice.

'Yes. We can't wait any longer than that. They've got us by the short and curlies. So pass it on to Polack . . . *Hurry*, there's somebody coming, Ami.'

Hastily, Karl flung his mug in the corner and squatted on the lice-ridden straw mattress on the concrete floor. An instant later the rusty bolt was ripped back and Tinplate, an evil black scowl on his face, stood framed there. Behind, one of the guards was holding a Doberman, straining at the leash, saliva dripping from its ugly yellow fangs. Karl sprang to his feet as regulations prescribed and stood to attention.

Sourly, Tinplate jerked a big thumb over his shoulder. '*Raus!*' he commanded.

Karl obediently moved outside, skirting the dog with care. It was the first time he had ever seen one of the brutes close to hand and he didn't like what he saw one little bit. The creatures were really savage. He shuddered slightly at the thought of what those terrible fangs might do to the human body.

Abruptly Karl forgot the dog, as the two guards began to turf out his cell. The mattress flew through the open door, followed an instant later by the piss-bucket which clattered after it. Fortunately, it was empty. Now while the two of them poked and prodded the walls, the black hound sniffed and smelled, running round the tiny place as if it were hot on the scent. Karl knew their imitation arms and medals were already hidden in the shit-shaft, but he was worried about the escape hole above the door. Earlier that morning, half-suspecting there might be a cell search when the disappearance of the little cockeyed traitor was discovered, he had taken extra care to fill in the cracks where the mortar was missing between the stones with bread from his meagre breakfast. He had chewed the hard black bread into a pulp, dragging the mixture across the dusty floor to give it the right look and had then wedged it into the joints. Now he prayed that neither of the two guards looked upwards. They didn't. But somehow the hound sensed something was wrong. It ferreted around the door jamb, cropped tail wagging furiously, sniffing all the while, as if it had scented something exciting. Once it almost escaped from its handler and attempted to spring upwards – exactly to the spot where the stonework was loose!

Just in time the guard caught the beast, jerking hard at the leash and crying angrily, 'Will you frigging well keep still, Lux!' while Karl's knees suddenly felt like soft india-rubber with relief.

A minute later and Karl found himself pushed into his cell, the bolt snapped behind him, staring at his jumbled bits and pieces and listening to the faint noise from next door where Ami was undergoing the same search. So far so good, he told himself and then suddenly sat down on the rumpled mattress, all strength gone. God, he realised, tonight – *this very night* – they were off into the unknown. They were going to do a bunk . . .

Hauptmann Mueller took another drink. Already the vodka bottle was nearly empty and it was not yet midday. Through the open door of the bedroom he could see the Popov woman bending down over the bed in her short dress, stripping the sheets he supposed. His red eyes took in the curve of Aniya's generous hips, and the soft dark creases revealed between her plump peasant cheeks. He swallowed hard. Why did she display so much overripe flesh so shamelessly? Why was she tempting him when she must have known the mood he was in?

He drained his glass and marched toward the window, trying to ignore her. He had more important things to do, he told himself. Outside, guards and dogs were doubling back and forth in a great hurry while self-important senior noncoms strode about shrilling their whistles and bellowing red-faced orders.

Mueller wasn't impressed. He had been in the Army since he was seventeen and knew the old adage – 'blind them with bullshit'. Carry a bucket around and walk smartish and the authorities would think you were doing something. For all their noise and fuss they obviously hadn't found the missing man yet. He cursed under his breath. Although he knew it didn't mean a damn that some wretch of a jailbird was missing, he was still professional soldier enough to want to keep a perfect record. In his monthly report to higher headquarters he didn't want to have to report a prisoner missing – though he was quite sure his reports were never read by anyone save the filing clerk who stowed them away in the cabinets.

'*Pashalasta?*' the Popov woman said softly.

He swung round. 'Yes?' he demanded.

She looked at him with her great brown bovine eyes, wordless.

Was the peasant bitch mocking him, he asked himself, flushing. By now she knew his problem only too well. What did she expect of him – to tumble her on to the newly-made bed, her legs splayed apart invitingly, her great milk tits thrust upwards in her hands, just asking to be sucked? Was she tormenting him, an officer who had once been personally received by the Führer before he had landed up in this arsehole of the world?

His hand tightened on his cane. Suddenly he was overcome by a desire to seize her, throw her face downwards on the bed, but not to copulate with the bitch, only to slash and beat, lash those proud plump buttocks until she writhed not with joy, but with pain and was screaming out for mercy.

The Russian woman must have seen the look in his eyes, for suddenly she turned, tucked the bundle of washing underneath her big muscular arm and walked out.

Mueller opened his mouth to say something, but stopped

short. Instead he sat down and poured himself the last of the vodka. There he slumped, brooding while outside the search   continued . . .

Aniya had recognised that look. The Fritz had been just about to beat her again. He had done it before. The Fritz was not only bad, he was mad. Face set and thoughtful, she stuffed the dirty linen into the sack she had brought for it. Before her lay a five kilometre tramp across the steppe to the handful of tumbledown *isbas** which made up the hamlet in which she lived. There were no men left there – they had long since vanished into the Red Army – and no work. The partisans had run off with most of their animals. All that she could do was to work – and do other things – for the Fritz so that she could get enough food, poor as it was, to feed the child and her old *babuska*. But God, how she hated him – and the rest of them!

Now this Sunday, for some unknown reason, the place was in total confusion, and so far the Fritz had made no offer to give her food. Should she wait and chance his rage and the usual humiliation he inflicted upon her in the end – God, why couldn't the Fritzes make love like a decent normal Russian man! Or should she go now while she was still safe from him? Her poor simple mind was in a turmoil. It was all so difficult. She was frightened, yet she needed that food, scraps though it would be, desperately. What was she to do?

A hundred metres away, on the other side of the Camp, midday brought with it not the usual hot soup, but a couple of slices of bread and a bowl of water. '*Jawohl*,' Tinplate had sneered at their objections, 'this is all you swine will get till we find Silvereye.' The Three Rebels were plagued like Aniya by doubts, worries, indecision.

For Ami, it was a question of the water. Tonight they

*Huts.

82

went, but would they be given anything to drink again before then? He slumped on his mattress, shivering a little in the cold, staring at the burnished tin bowl longingly. He had already eaten the bread, wolfing it down ravenously, stuffing it into his mouth so that it had vanished in a matter of seconds. Now still famished, his skinny litle stomach rumbling murderously, he looked at the bowl longingly, as if it contained delightful Bavarian suds instead of stale, chemically-treated water. Christ on a crutch, should he drink now or should he spin the water out over the after-noon? He licked his cracked parched lips, sensing the pressure of those damned prison walls, feeling them like a palpable band, squeezing at his guts. Despite the cold he started to sweat, choking a little, pulse racing. With a trembling hand, he reached out for the bowl.

Next door, Polack had closed his eyes to temptation. His bread and water remained untouched. For a while he had kept his mind off his lunchtime rations by thinking about what was to happen that night. But the prospect of the coming escape had palled, as his stomach had begun to rumble noisily.

With his eyes squeezed tightly shut like those of a child trying to blot out something unpleasant, he had fallen to thinking of those delightful Sunday dinners his mother had prepared before the war. How they had kissed their father's head as children before going into the 'best room', where it had been all laid out for them: great balls of cabbage filled with rice and chopped meat, long curly garlic saus-ages heaped on mountains of steaming red cabbage, rich dark puddings which they only ate on Sundays.

In his daydreaming, Polack licked his lips, nostrils atwitch as he recalled in loving detail the wondrous rich sights and smells of his childhood, savouring once again in memory the escaping steam, the warm strong odours, the delicious crackling sound of the fried pork. *Boshe moi*, it was better than having a woman! Of all the miserable, confined men in Tract Dat that moment, only the big young 'water-

83

Polack'* as they called him behind his burly back, was halfway content, for a moment at least, with no decisions to make.

In his cell, Karl had made the important decision. It was not only fear of the consequences once the guards discovered how Silvereye had disappeared; it was also the desire to escape from the horrific memory of what had happened last night in the ten-seat crapper.

Silvereye had panicked the moment they grabbed him. His eyes had been utterly wild with fear. With his foot Karl had kicked off the seat.'No!' the man had begun to scream, but Polack smothered that desperate cry with his big hand. Silvereye began to struggle. To no avail! Frantically the traitor freed one hand from Ami's grasp. He reached out, trying to hold on to something, to prevent this terrible thing from happening to him. But he had taken hold of the sacking. It had ripped and then he was going in, enveloped by that nauseous odour.

'No . . . no!' he managed to cry from beneath Polack's hand and then, his eyes wide with horror, he was in the pit, the dread yellow liquid spurting up on all sides. Hurriedly, the Three Rebels had started back, their own faces ashen with the appalling horror of it all.

For a moment, Silvereye had gone under. Then he was up again, spluttering and trying to scream, his teeth suddenly a brilliant white against the hateful yellow of the human ordure which dripped from his hair and his contorted, animal face. Feverishly he had started to claw his way out.

For a split-second they were rooted to the spot, stricken motionless by the horror of what they had just done. Suddenly Karl realised that this man had betrayed them and would do so again, if he survived. He seized the long-handled broom which Piotr used to clean out the latrine.

*Name given to Poles from the border region; they were regarded as German but were really 'watered-down' Poles ie. Walter-Polacks.

He raised it. Next instant, he had brought it crashing down.

There was a crack, and the ripple of splintering bone. The traitor's eyes rolled upwards. There was the terrifying sound of suction. Slowly, very slowly, the helpless runt began to disappear. His head tilted forward. The nauseous brew reached to his chin. Still he had not tried to help himself. Aghast at their own handiwork the Rebels watched. He was still conscious – his eyes were still open. But he did not attempt to close his mouth.

'*God . . . God*,' Polack had moaned, hugging himself in his utter despair. '*God . . .*'

Meaningless noises were now bubbling from Silvereye's mouth, as the liquid nearly reached it. Were they appeals for help? What was he saying in this last moment of his life? Suddenly they ceased. Bubbles began to explode obscenely on the surface. The top of his head vanished. For a moment a pale claw, the fingers extended outwards, surfaced. They jerked convulsively. Then it, too, disappeared. The surface of the pit was now without movement. Wordlessly they had begun to replace the lid, studiously avoiding looking each other in the eye.

Now in the stillness of his cell, a young man, brutalised by the war, as so many millions of other young men were all over Europe this Sunday in February 1944, remembered his lost innocence and began to weep. But young as the weeping man was, in the tight confines of his little prison, he knew that come what may, there would be no victors and vanquished in this terrible war – only losers. The coming night might well bring him and his two dear comrades freedom. But it would be freedom in name only. What they had done last night would place him in a mental prison till the day he died. In reality, *there was no escape.*

BOOK TWO

Stolen Journey

CHAPTER 1

Midnight!

All was silent in Camp Death. The search had been called off and those guards who were off-duty had long since tumbled exhausted into their bunks. Now all that disturbed the heavy silence which hung over the remote prison camp was the soft howl of the wind and the muted pad-pad of the watchdogs.

Gingerly, very gingerly, Karl edged the bolt free on Ami's cell and then moved on, on the tip of his toes to do the same at Polack's, hugging the deeper shadow of the wall as he did so. Somewhere, someone was snoring loudly. At any other time, the sound would have amused Karl, but not now. His nerves were too tense.

The other two emerged, their boots covered with a spare pair of socks, their little bundles tied securely to their backs. Karl nodded and jerked his thumb at the trough.

They nodded in their turn. In single file, crouched low, they started to cross the yard, ready to throw themselves flat at the least sign of the searchlight swinging their way. But they were in luck. The bright white eye of the search-light continued to play on the main gate.

One by one they dropped into the shit-tunnel, too tense now even to notice and remark upon the stench. Karl let them have five seconds, head cocked to one side alert to the slightest sound. But there was none. All was going to plan. '*Los*,' he whispered. 'You first, Ami.'

The little Rhinelander did not need to be told twice. He knew exactly what to do. He tossed Polack his bundle and then he was scurrying down the ditch like a sewer rat. Karl flashed a look at the nearest tower, but there was no sign of movement. Perhaps the guards up there were sleeping, too. He wouldn't put it past them. All of those who guarded Camp Death were skivers, feather-merchants, out for Number One. He nudged Polack. It was his turn now.

Polack moved with surprising stealth for such a big man, while Karl counted off the seconds. Polack's size might be a problem. If he got stuck in the shaft, they had agreed that Ami would pull from inside, while he, Karl, pushed from the outside.

Five! Now it was his turn. He darted down the trench, hardly making a sound. The night was cool and the disgusting goo at the bottom of the trench had solidified somewhat; that way he didn't make so much noise.

Polack was already disappearing, grunting a little with the effort, when Karl reached the entrance to the shaft. Karl paused and suddenly, all his doubts and worries vanished. He looked back. For the first time he felt he was seeing the Camp as a free man. He was going and they were remaining behind. It was a good feeling. But not one to dwell on. He wasn't out yet. He gave Polack another five seconds and then he was wriggling into the shaft himself. For a moment he fumbled awkwardly with the grating from inside in order to replace it and then he was writhing his way down the stinking tube, dripping with sweat with the effort in a matter of seconds.

Ahead of him he could hear Polack, and beyond him Ami, cursing softly to himself, for what reason he didn't know or care. They were almost free now. He burrowed on.

Two minutes later he was crouched next to Ami and Polack, kneeling in the wet grass and sucking in great breaths of fresh air like newborn babies filling their lungs for the first time, staring first to the rear, where the Camp showed up in stark relief *behind* the rows of high barbed wire, and then to their front: the limitless spread of the alien steppe.

Ami nudged Karl and pressed his mouth close to the latter's ear. 'We've screwed 'em,' he hissed triumphantly.

'Screwed the whole frigging lot of 'em – Howling Mad, Tinplate – ' He suddenly stopped short.

There was no mistaking that soft pad-pad, and that fetid stink. They froze.

Karl swallowed hard. Once again he had that nightmarish vision of one of those half-wild dogs which patrolled the perimeter of the Camp, with dripping open jaws revealing vicious yellow teeth. The short hairs at the nape of his neck stood erect and he shivered.

Ami nudged his friend. 'There,' he whispered urgently.

Karl strained his eyes in the gloom. A Doberman was trotting leisurely in their general direction.

The three of them dropped as one, hugging the earth like frantic lovers. *Would it spot them?*

The hound came closer. Its pace seemed casual, as if it were just carrying out a routine patrol. There was no sign of its handler, though now they could hear the rattle of a chain. The dog was tied by an iron chain to a bar running the length of the outer wire. Karl's mind raced. One bark from the dog and they were finished. The searchlight would flood the area with its cold merciless light and the shooting would commence. They'd be sitting ducks.

Suddenly the Doberman stopped. Karl's heart skipped a beat. It sniffed the air. Karl stared at the brute with its teeth that seemed too long for its vicious snout. *Had it spotted them?* Carefully, very carefully, his right hand reached down the length of his body searching for the sharpened end of the tablespoon which was his only weapon. Now his every nerve jingled electrically and he felt that the dog must hear the frantic, loud pounding of his heart at any moment.

The hound let out a low menacing growl. Karl held his breath. He could see, as the beast was silhouetted against the lighter gloom of the sky, how its ears were beginning to slope back against its skull. That was a sure sign of impending danger. The damn thing had scented something. Next to him, Ami stiffened and Karl felt he was going to spring to his feet. With his free hand he dug him in the ribs, indicating he should stay where he was. His other hand he raised slowly, holding the sharpened end of the spoon like a dagger.

The beast's muzzle dropped once more as it moved off, head weaving from side to side in the manner of a tracker-dog. It started to sniff the ground energetically. It was on to them! 'God help us . . . God help us . . .' Karl prayed fervently, as he had never prayed since being kicked out of the Confirmation class for looking up the pastor's wife's skirt all those years before. '*God help us . . .*'

Polack clenched his fist. 'Here it comes, Karl,' he hissed. 'Get ready!'

Instinctively Ami raised his hand to protect himself as the brute came level with him, but the Doberman reacted more quickly. Its paw lashed out. The claws caught Ami a raking blow on the side of his face. He yelped with pain and cowered backwards as his blood shot out from the lacerations in great gobs.

For a moment the beast hesitated. In front of him Ami trembled violently, one hand full of warm blood held to his wounded face. He wanted to scream out loud with sheer absolute fear, but no sound came from his lips; his throat was too constricted.

Very cautiously, his heart pounding furiously, Karl started to reach out one hand. The dog saw the movement. It went back on its haunches warily. Its wet upper lip curled back over those terrible long yellow fangs. A low menacing growl commenced somewhere deep inside its throat. Karl sweated, still he continued the advance of his hand, wondering in terror just when the beast would spring at him. At his side, Polack clubbed a fist like a small steam shovel and prepared to jump into action the instant his old friend needed him.

The growl grew in menace. The dog was completely on its haunches now, ready to spring. Karl could smell its nauseating fetid breath all over his face. He had perhaps only a second left now. Suddenly he lunged forward. In the very moment that the dog prepared to bark and spring, he wrapped his right hand brutally around the animal's snout.

The creature started violently, caught completely off-guard. But one of its heavy paws flailed out and Karl felt the claws rake his jaw. An electric hot pain shot through his body. But there was no time to think of that now. The fight had commenced and he must prevent the beast from breaking loose and beginning to bark. That would alert the whole damned Camp. *He must silence it!*

Blood splattering everywhere, the beast heaved and tugged, digging in its powerful hind-legs, dragging Karl with it. Desperately he hung on, as it swung its head from one side to the other, muffled growls coming from its throat, as it tried furiously to break that hold on its muzzle.

Polack did not hesitate. Country boy that he was, he knew the ways of animals, tame and otherwise. He grabbed for the beast's genitals and squeezed hard. The dog contorted with pain. In its throat it howled violently. Madly it tried to free itself from that murderous grip. For one horrifying moment it seemed it would break loose, dragging both of them forward over the wet ground.

Ami recovered from his fear. In the gloom, he saw the black beast twisting and turning wildly, exerting all of its crazy brutal strength to free itself. Any minute now it would break loose and then the clock would really be in the piss-bucket. He hesitated no longer.

Raising his spoon with the razor-sharp handle, he plunged it home. The narrow blade sank deep into its side. The beast's spine arched like a taut bow. With its last desperate energy, it dragged itself free from the grasp of the two Rebels. Its muzzle went up, as it slipped down to its hind legs, dying there and then. It was going to loose one last mad howl. Ami cursed. His blade flashed again. The sharp end sunk right into the dog, grating disgustingly off the rib-cage and plunging deep into the heart. His hand flushed hot with blood. An instant later the beast slumped to the red earth – dead at long last.

For what seemed an eternity, though in reality it was only a matter of seconds, the three of them lay there, unable to move, lungs gasping like those of men who have just run a great race. The fight with the dog seemed to have drained all their energy. Then Karl, the unspoken leader of the three Rebels, roused himself painfully. He knew they had to be on their way at once. The dog would have a handler. When the beast didn't report in at the other end of the circuit which it had patrolled attached to its chain, the handler was bound to raise the alarm, or at least come looking for the creature. They had a mere quarter of an hour or so at the most. It was time to be gone.

'Come on,' Karl hissed in a cracked voice, which was still not quite under control. In these past terrible years of war he had killed many men, but nothing had affected him as much as this slaughter of the guard dog. His hands were still trembling violently. When his friends didn't respond, he hissed once more, feeling his strength returning, as the new emergency pumped fresh adrenalin into his blood-stream. '*Los* . . . los . . . We've got to do a bunk while there's still time . . . Come on, you two.'

The urgent note in his voice did the trick. They staggered to their feet, avoiding looking at the dead beast which had occasioned them so much fear. Karl took a quick fix on the stars which were now beginning to appear, casting the lonely steppe in their silver spectral light, and then they were off, heading for the railhead of Krasyna Voda. There was a light-hearted, youthful spring in their step. They were free. They were on their way.

Five minutes later Camp Death had vanished into the pale gloom. They didn't look back . . .

In his quarters, Howling Mad Mueller reeled to the wash-basin, his throat full of hot bile, his stomach churning.

94

Below him the floor heaved and pitched as if he were aboard a ship tossing in a fully-fledged gale. Just in time he caught the edge of the basin with both hands and vomited, his shoulders jerking violently.

For what seemed an age he hung on there, face glazed with sweat, throat flooded with hot noxious bile, tears of effort in his bloodshot eyes. Then it was over and he turned on the taps, washing the stuff away, his head clearing rapidly. He cleaned his lips with his handkerchief and walking a little unsteadily, for he had consumed the best part of two bottles of vodka this Sunday, he slumped back in his chair. He sighed with relief. It was good to sit down and know the room was not dancing and swaying all around him like a backdrop in a theatre in high wind.

His gaze wandered and he saw his stick. It gleamed a dull red and he licked his rimed lips curiously, wondering why and what the stick was doing on the floor. Suddenly he moaned – he no longer had the strength to howl like a demented animal – as it all came back to him. A mixture of rage at the disappearance of the little stoolpigeon and frustration – sexual frustration, had made him do it. Just as the Popov whore had come in to ask if he had any scraps of food for her, flaunting that lush body of hers deliberately, his control had suddenly broken. He had started lashing her with the stick, mouthing impossible obscenities, cutting her breasts, her thighs and finally her sex with cruel blows as she lay huddled in the corner, hands protecting her face, sobbing heartbrokenly. In the end he had pulled himself together and she had fled into the night, spitting blood and empty-handed, sobbing and sobbing so that he felt he could still hear her cries long after she had departed from the Camp. Then he had seized the second bottle of rotgut and had drained it empty before falling into a drunken sleep.

Now he slumped in his chair, his head aching, throat parched and choked, listening to the silence of the night. But his mind was crystal clear. He had already forgotten the Popov whore. There were plenty more willing peasant girls where she came from. Instead, he concentrated on the main event of the previous day: the mysterious disappearance of Silvereye.

Of course, that big booby of an NCO, Sergeant Dietz, couldn't see further than the end of his red drunkard's nose. The noncom had made no attempt to reason the matter out logically. If the stoolpigeon really had not wanted to escape, as Dietz maintained, then he was still somewhere in the Camp. Either the other inmates had made him disappear *inside* the place simply because he was spying on them in general, or, the stoolpigeon had known something specific and *he had had to be silenced*.

Mueller's pulse quickened. What could Silvereye have possibly learned that made someone murder him? For the Captain was pretty sure that the little runt was dead by now. The answer was obvious. No inmate of Camp Death would even take such a risk unless he was sure he was no longer going to be there in the Camp when the corpse was discovered.

Mueller sat bolt upright. '*Natürlich!*' he cried and hammered his fist down on the table next to him so that the 'dead soldiers' rolled and rattled about. 'They're escaping!' It came to him with the clarity of a vision. The stoolpigeon had been silenced because he had known that someone was about to escape, or –!

Howling Mad Mueller did not think that dire possibility through to its conclusion. Instead, he rushed to the window, flinging it open, completely forgetting the Camp's strict blackout regulations, and cried into the night, '*Alarm alarm . . . stand to, the guard . . . ALARM!*'

Two kilometres away, bloody and weary, painfully edging her way across the silver steppe, Aniya heard the first dread wail of the Camp siren, and turned to shake her fist in that direction, her heart full of rage and bitterness. 'Do what you like,' she cried, face contorted with anger. 'You won't catch me . . . and by God, you'll pay – all of you Fritzes.' Her fist clenched in the salute of the partisans and she yelled their slogan defiantly at the night sky, '*Slava Krasyna Armya!*' Then she turned and hurried on as best she could. There was no time to be lost. The partisans must be told . . .

CHAPTER 2

They marched strung out in single file, with Karl in the lead. Their pace was that of heavy infantry, sixty steps to the minute for fifty minutes, with ten minutes at the end of each hour, judged the best they could, for none of them had watches. Despite the fact that they had been locked in prison for nearly three weeks now, they made good time. Tinplate's toughening up process was working. They felt little strain. Besides, they were all animated by a feeling of buoyant confidence. Hadn't they not only tackled and outwitted the Camp authorities, but also the whole of the *Wehrmacht*? The Top Brass had thought they had committed the three of them to a living hell from which there was no escape but death – yet these three ordinary stubble-hoppers of no education had made their getaway.

For the first hour, Karl kept them in the stunted trees which covered the higher ground of the steppe, but after the first fifty minutes, pushing their way through them and the frozen snow which lay there, he had given up. They had been lathered and dripping with sweat, gasping for breath like old men, despite their new fitness.

So after that first rest period, Karl had taken them down to the track leading roughly north, reasoning that they would be safe on it till dawn at least. Now they were covering, he calculated, some five kilometres an hour, which meant that they might make the area of Krasyna Voda within the next twenty-four hours. Vaguely he realised that they would have to spend one night hidden in that general area until they could catch the daily leave train, and that by then, the alarm would have been raised. But he determinedly thrust that thought to the back of his mind. Hadn't he told the others right at the beginning that

98

they'd take it step by step? And that's how they'd do it. First they'd concentrate on getting there. The rest would take care of itself in due course. '*Toi, toi, toi*,'* he whispered to himself hopefully.

Another hour passed. The moon had come out now. Before them, the steppe was silhouetted, stark black in its cold silver light. It was almost as clear as day and Karl knew that although they could be seen clearly themselves, they would be able to spot any potential danger in their path from some way off. It was a comforting feeling. The only danger he reckoned with at the moment was the partisans and he felt there was little risk of their being about in this lonely stretch of the endless grassland. They would be concentrating on their usual nocturnal work of sabotage on the *Wehrmacht*'s supply lines: the railway from the east and the two supply roads – 'the big Runway', as the troops called them – which ran parallel with the metal lines.

By three o'clock they had covered some fifteen kilometres and Karl guessed it was time for them to have a longer rest. He reasoned that soon they would become careless through sheer weariness and it was pointless to run unnecessary risks at this early stage of the game. Better to have a good half-hour break before continuing until first light. Then they would be able to make a decision about the way ahead. He suggested this to the other two and Ami said, 'Good idea, Karl. I've already worn my boots down to my frigging knees. Let's have a break.'

'But out of this wind,' Polack added. 'See them trees over there at two o'clock? Let's head for them. They're not far away and the trees'll act as a wind-break.'

Five minutes later they were just approaching the grove of firs, the frozen old snow sparkling crystalline here and there between them, when they spotted it – the dark shape

*The German equivalent of 'touch wood three times'.

of a cart, with what looked like a *panje*** pony between the shafts.

They stopped as one, hearts suddenly beating furiously, automatically going down, as if to take cover. 'Christ,' Ami whispered, 'what do you make of that, Karl?'

The latter tried the old soldier's trick of raising his head from the ground at an angle in order to get a better view of an object at night. 'Well, it's not moving,' he whispered a moment later. 'Neither the nag nor whoever is inside the cart.'

'Partisan?' Ami asked urgently.

Karl shrugged. 'Search me. But I can't see what they'd be doing in the middle of the steppe at this time of night. They'd be undercover long ago after getting up to their usual nasty tricks . . . What are we gonna do, comrades?' he added uneasily a moment later.

'There's only one thing we can do, Karl,' Ami answered grimly. 'Here, hang on.' He tiptoed to the nearest tree and swiftly cut himself a stout club with the sharpened end of the spoon. 'Come on. But at the first sign of danger, let's run for it like merry hell.'

The choice of phrase somehow perked Karl up. He grinned and said, 'You betcha, Ami!'

Gingerly they approached the lone cart, which remained completely motionless, automatically noting even from some distance away that the tarpaulin which covered its contents was *Wehrmacht*. Still they took their time, ready for flight at any moment. Then they were almost upon it and in the ghostly light of the sickle moon, they could see clearly that the nag between the traces was dead, held upright by the balance of whatever was beneath the tarpaulin.

They halted. They looked at each other in eloquent silence until Polack nodded his big head. Ami gripped his cudgel more firmly in his skinny little hand and they

---

*A sturdy little steppe horse.

100

continued again, hardly daring to breathe, all their nerves on the alert. But there was no need of the cudgel. For not only was the *panje* pony dead, but so was its driver. Sprawled out on the ground, his eyes were wide open, staring unseeingly at the silver heavens, his throat a jagged mess of jellied black blood, cut savagely from ear to ear!

'*Himmelherrje!*' Ami whispered.

Hastily Polack crossed himself.

For his part, Karl bit his bottom lip, then stepped forward to investigate, while the other two remained rooted to the spot. The back of the cart was piled high with dead German soldiers, all of them bandaged, some with bloody shell-dressings packed over their wounds, others with their arms in rough-and-ready slings, but all of them murdered in the same brutal manner.

Ami swallowed hard and advanced a few paces. 'What do you make of it, Karl?' he asked in a tight little voice, trying not to look at those pale, horribly-contorted faces set in the last savage grimaces of violent death.

'For what it's worth,' the other man answered, 'I think they must have been wounded first and then – well, you can see what happened to them then.'

'But the front's a good hundred kilometres or more over there,' Ami objected, indicating the east.

'I know, but they were obviously on some sort of anti-partisan operation, probably around the "Runway".' Karl indicated the fur-backed pack near one of the dead men. 'See that pack. If that poor devil had been wounded at the front, the sawbones would have taken his pack off him long ago.'

Ami nodded his understanding.

'But why are . . . they dead?' Polack stuttered, eyes round with horror. 'What happened after they were wounded? I mean, who did that to the poor swine?'

'Partisans,' Karl said glumly, and shivered suddenly. He cast a swift involuntary glance over his shoulder, as if half-expecting he knew not what exactly to be lurking there, grasping a knife dripping human gore. 'My guess is they were wounded in some anti-partisan op and were on their way back to Krasyna Voda to a collecting point when they were ambushed by the partisans and – ' He shrugged and left the rest of his sentence unsaid.

For a few moments the three young men relapsed into brooding silence, each one of them shrouded in his own thoughts. For his part, Karl wondered what fate had decided these men would be so cruelly slaughtered here in this nameless place? What had they done to offend the gods so that they had to be punished thus? Or was their slaughter just another example of the whole overwhelming purposelessness of life? Weren't they, in the end, mere insects to be crushed under the foot of the mighty, their lives serving no purpose whatsoever?

He shook himself violently and said, 'Louse ran over my liver,' as if that were explanation enough. 'All right, let's not stand here gawping like a bunch of shitting country yokels,' he snapped, almost angrily. 'Those stiffs are gonna come in handy.'

'*Karl!*' Polack said in mild outrage.

'What do you mean, Karl?' Ami asked.

'Food. That pack over there. There could be an iron ration in it. And they'll all have their paybooks on them – the partisans wouldn't have taken those. They were only interested in the poor devils' weapons. Now come on, stop looking as if you've just creamed yer skivvies, Polack, let's get on with it!' Karl's harsh voice and coarseness were calculated. He wanted them to move and move fast while there was still time, for already, like a lazy snake slowly uncoiling itself, a plan was beginning to form in his mind . . .

Elinka Shimsk, a big heavy woman who wore her hair cropped like a man and whose heavy White Russian face was graced with the vestiges of a moustache, whistled softly through her gleaming metal teeth, as she viewed the peasant woman's back.

Standing there in the middle of the *isba*,* full of blue cigarette smoke and lit by a guttering petroleum lantern, Aniya's shoulders showed red-raw from the beating she had received and both her back and heavy breasts were bruised blue and red with what were obviously bite marks. '*Boshe moi!*' the female partisan leader cursed to herself, her big hand reaching instinctively down to the pistol which hung from her hip. The Fritz who had done that to the peasant woman must have been crazy!

'All right. *Horoscho* – it's good. Dress yourself,' she commanded in her deep bass voice. 'I have seen enough.' The woman partisan leader had once been a well-respected doctor in Kiev until the fascist pigs had seized her hospital, raping the nurses and slaughtering the wounded where they lay in their beds. Soon after this, she had volunteered to the *Stavka*† to form her own female partisan unit behind the German lines. Now she waved a hand in the peasant's direction and took one of the long *papiroki* from her tunic pocket and lit it thoughtfully, while Aniya dressed.

The peasant woman's story was interesting. Most of the partisan effort these last few months, ever since the fascists had begun to retreat from West Russia, had been concentrated on that single vital railway line connecting the German front with the rear. But the Fritzes had thrown in massive troop reinforcements to protect it. It had become increasingly difficult to attack effectively the Runway, as the fascists called it. Might an attempt on that remote German Camp the peasant woman had described, draw off some of those troops and allow a full-scale partisan attack to be launched against Krasyna Voda itself? It was an interesting thought. She puffed thoughtfully at her long cigarette, held in fingers heavily stained with nicotine.

*Hut.
†Soviet High Command.

She waited till the peasant woman had replaced her blouse, wrapping the heavy tattered woollen shawl cross-wise across her ample bosom in the country fashion. 'Now then,' she said gruffly. 'Describe this Camp for me. Here on the floor. Knife!' she snapped.

Squatting on the shelf of the big green tiled oven which dominated the hut, her second-in-command Sonya neatly tossed the Commander her trench-knife. Elinka caught it just as neatly and handed it to the woman. 'Here, use this. Draw us a plan of the Camp in the dirt.' She indicated the centre of the floor.

Awkwardly, Aniya commenced doing so, knife held in the same manner a backward pupil might hold her pen in some rural school, tongue stuck out between her teeth with the effort. At any other time, the partisan leader might have grinned at the sight. But not now, for she was both angry at what had happened to the woman and excited at the prospect of a surprise attack against the Fritzes.

Slowly, just as the plan was beginning to unfurl in Karl's mind some ten kilometres away out in the steppe, one was forming in Elinka's mind, too, as she intently watched Aniya drawing a map in the smoke-filled fug of that peasant hut . . . But while Karl – and unbeknown to him the partisan leader – were making their separate plans, *Hauptmann* Mueller was demanding action - *immediate* action!

As the first ugly white of the false dawn began to flush the sky in the east, the Camp's trucks burst into angry life, their exhausts flooding the compound with the cloying stench of petrol. Hurriedly, the dog-handlers took their positions in the back, while their charges yelped and snapped nervously. From the towers the guards came huffing and panting, lugging their machine guns with them. Over at the armoury, angry red-faced NCOs, who had not had sufficient sleep, supervised the handing out of weapons

104

to the guards, now clad in the unaccustomed combat gear. In their cells the prisoners, alarmed by this sudden pre-dawn activity, rattled their tin mugs against the bars or knocked them against the walls, angry and yet anxious at the same time. *What was going on?*

It was the same question that a red-faced, sweating Tinplate was asking himself, as he shrilled his whistle urgently and bellowed orders to the confused throng hurrying to and fro, hauling cases of ammunition and toting their heavy weapons to the waiting trucks. What in three devils' name was that fart of a Commandant up to? So three of the prisoners had escaped from Camp Death, those fresh pricks from the Fourth Grenadiers. What did it matter? Why all the frigging fuss? They wouldn't get far, would they? If the chaindogs didn't get them, the Popov partisans would.

Tinplate shook his big cropped head in mock disbelief. The whole fucking world was *meschugge*, he told himself. The whole shitting lot of them had got a bloody bird in the head which went tweet-tweet. Crazy . . . *absolutely shitting crazy* . . .

And maybe for once in his short brutal life *Oberfeldwebel* Dietz, known behind his back, since Stalingrad 1942, as 'Tinplate Head', was right. This February dawn in that remote Russian backwater, which didn't even have a name, the world did seem 'absolutely shitting crazy'.

CHAPTER 3

A low, smoke-grey mist now covered the steppe to their front. It had come once the sun had risen. Now the sun was glimpsed through the rolling banks of fog like a copper coin glinting at the bottom of a green-scummed pool. But Karl, leading the little group, was pleased. The fog obscured their progress from prying eyes, though it did make navigation difficult.

Behind him the other two, both laden with packs taken from the massacred soldiers, marched in silence, conserving their strength. For all of them knew Krasyna Voda, the railhead, was half a day's march away still, and even when they reached the place they would need all their strength and alertness if they were to board the train without being spotted by the chaindogs. So they shuffled on almost soundlessly, with the mist swirling around their legs so that they might have appeared to some observer like grey ghosts condemned to wander this featureless grass plain for eternity.

While he led, Karl's mind was working furiously, as he hammered out his plan. By now, he guessed the Camp would have notified the local authorities at the railhead that there had been an escape. Surely Silvereye must have been found by now and with him, their escape. Even Tinplate's thick head could have worked out where they were heading. So, the chaindogs would be on the alert. They'd be *expecting* them to board that daily leave train, bound for Warsaw and the Reich. But was that the only train passing through Krasyna Voda?

Karl munched on a piece of Army black bread taken from one of the murdered men – 'first food, old house, then morals', he had told Polack when the latter had objected –

and considered the question. Surely the *Wehrmacht* wouldn't limit the traffic on the vital Runway to just one train a day. There must be others. Naturally there would be plenty of supply trains going the other way to the front. But what else would be bound for the Homeland?

The answer had been dawning on him ever since he had first spotted those poor devils heaped on the back of the *panje* wagon. Wounded! He knew the Top Brass. They didn't like the people back home knowing the extent of the casualties in Russia, so they fed the trains packed with wounded from the Eastern Front into the hospital towns back in the Reich *at the dead of night*. Was it possible that another train – a hospital train – halted at Krasyna Voda during the hours of darkness, tomorrow night for instance?

The possibility excited him. Of course, if there was one, there would be chaindogs about on the station, carrying out their usual patrols. But would they be expecting deserters or fugitives such as they were, to attempt to board the train.

'*Of course not!*' a hard little voice at the back of his mind snapped angrily. '*But grow up, man. You're jumping the gun, Karl . . . clutching at frigging straws. How the hell do you know there's a frigging hospital train in the first place? Oh, do let's try to keep our frigging feet on the ground!*'

'*Karl!*' Polack's voice cut into his reverie suddenly.

He swung round, a little startled. 'What is it, Polack?' he demanded.

The big man was standing quite still, head twisted to the wind, hand cocked to his ear. Country boy that he was, he had the most acute sense of hearing of all the Three Rebels.

Polack didn't answer and Ami said irritably, 'Come on, you silly wet fart – piss or get off the pot.'

Polack's hand fell slowly. His face took on a crestfallen look. 'I thought I heard something,' he said lamely. 'I thought –'

107

'You know what thought did, Polack,' Ami cut in crudely. '*He shat hissen*! Now don't go –'

Suddenly it was the red-faced little Rhinelander's turn to stop short. For to their rear he heard it, too, and there was no mistaking the sound now: that awesome hollow baying, muted a little by the wet mist, but very definitely there. He looked at Karl, his wizened little face aghast, eyes flushed with the wet sheen of fear. 'Did . . . did you . . . hear *that*, Karl?' he quavered.

Karl nodded, his plans forgotten in a flash. 'Yes, I heard it,' he said tonelessly. 'They've got those hounds after us. *Mueller's tumbled to it.*'

Not more than two kilometres away, the partisans moving into the attack on Camp Death heard the baying of those hounds, too, and Commander Shimsk immediately held up her hand. The long column of partisan wagons drawn by the *panje* ponies creaked to a halt one after another, the women springing from the carts at once, as they had been trained, forming a defensive perimeter, stubby little machine-pistols at the ready, peering into the grey gloom.

The big woman listened, head cocked to the faint wind. The baying was coming from their front and she guessed that those hounds belonged to the fascists from the Camp. Who else had hunting dogs like that but the Germans? The damned Tsarist aristocrats with their hounds had not hunted this part of the steppe since 1917.

She smiled slightly under her rakishly-tilted man's cap. Sonya, her second-in-command and lover for the last six months ever since they had discovered each other's sexual inclinations, said softly, 'Well, Elinka – why the smile?'

The big ex-doctor frowned. Let the others suspect what they liked but she did not wish them to know for certain. A Soviet woman was the equal of any man, hadn't Comrade Stalin far away in the Kremlin said so? But it was bad for partisan discipline, this familiarity. Besides, some of her women were bourgeois at heart; they were easily shocked. '*Comrade* Sonya,' she answered somewhat severely, 'it seems the Fritzes have left their Camp. It will make it much easier for us.'

'No wire to storm and no machine guns to be overcome, Comrade Commander,' Sonya snapped, obviously understanding the meaning of her tone.

'*Da, da.*' The woman partisan leader made her dispositions swiftly. She drew off her glove, licked her forefinger and held it up to the faint wind. 'The wind is coming from that direction.' She pointed to the east. '*Horoscho*, we will split up. Tania's section will swing out in that direction and feign an attack. The hounds will scent them early enough and make their damned racket. In the meantime, we shall come in from the west – over there – hopefully undetected.'

Sonya spoke up then, not wasting any time complimenting her lover, but then Elinka was a clever woman and not only on the battlefield – in bed, too. She knew how to bring another woman to the height of sexual ecstasy, perhaps because she was a doctor and knew such things. 'Your orders for the attack by Group West, Comrade Commander?'

The big woman didn't hesitate one instant. 'Liquidate,' she barked and then without losing another second, she cried, '*Davoi . . . davoi . . .* '

Hurriedly her women partisans scrambled back on to their carts. The drivers cracked their whips. A minute later they were rumbling forward once more. Two minutes after that, they had disappeared into the mist once again . . .

Now the three-sided, unequal race was in full swing, though apart from the baying of the guard-dogs which betrayed Mueller's presence, neither side knew of the other's exact whereabouts. Of course, the Three Rebels were at a disadvantage. The other two groups, heading unwittingly for one another on a collision course, had wheels. *They* had to rely on their feet. But Karl, panting leathern-lunged in the lead, knew they could use the mist to hide in, and possibly the wooded heights to left and right of the track when the pursuit came too close. Naturally the damned brutes of dogs wouldn't let up so easily, even if their masters lost the fugitives. The problem then was to lose the hounds. But how?

Even as he racked his brains, Karl had instinctively begun to toil up the nearest height towards the thick groves of spruce trees glimpsed briefly through breaks in the mist. Already he could quite clearly hear the grind of trucks moving forward in low gear, punctuated by the deep bass cries of the hounds. Mueller's men were really quite close now. His jaw tightened with determination. The bastards were not going to get him alive! Behind him, Ami tightened his grip on the sharpened tablespoon. He, too, intended to die fighting rather than be dragged back to that hellhole of a Camp.

Five minutes passed. The chase was coming ever closer. Now they were going all out, racing upwards to the cover of the trees, while the groan of the heavy trucks in first gear grew louder. Now their pursuers were flying flares into the sky at regular intervals, obviously realising from the excited baying of the hounds that the fugitives were quite close. Time and time again the flares sailed through the thick grey mist to explode in a glare of burning red, colouring the clouds a sinister, bloody hue.

Karl, his face lathered with sweat, his eyes wild and desperate, shouted, 'Keep going . . . comrades . . . we're nearly in the trees now . . . keep on going, friends!'

A ragged volley of rifle shots followed his exhortation. Tracer zipped crazily through the mist. Next to Polack a burst of slugs splintered the nearest tree and showered him with wood fragments. He cursed angrily and ran on.

Below, the noise of the motors had ceased now. Perhaps the drivers were not prepared to take the incline. But there were more voices behind the fleeing men shouting excitedly, and the baying dogs were fast approaching. In front Karl sought frantically for their cover, as they ploughed through the rolling clouds of fog, their breath coming in short hectic gasps, their lungs about to burst through their breast-cage with effort at any moment.

Among the trees they just might be able to dodge the guards. But what about those damned dogs? Could they escape them? Face contorted with fear, Karl panted on up the steep incline. Then suddenly he was stumbling into the trees, feet cracking the frozen snow that lay there among them, the branches lashing cruelly against his face as he, followed by the other two, plunged deeper into the grove. On and on they went, driven forward by that overwhelming fear of what would happen to them if they were taken again. The thick branches tore and ripped at their faces and clothes. They heeded them not; nor the pain. Already the hoarse shouting behind them had grown fainter. But the hounds had not given up. *They were still on their trail!* The fugitives could hear that frightened hoarse baying still. The four-legged bastards simply wouldn't give up. They were carried away by that primeval atavastic thrill of the chase.

Now they were stumbling and slipping down a small dried-out gulley, its sides glazed with ice, which burrowed its way through the trees and probably ran on across the downward slope beyond. As they fought their way onwards, Karl tried to reason out their position. Now he felt confident of tackling the first dog to catch up with them. They had managed that black beast outside the wire, hadn't they? But once they stopped and tried to deal with the dog, their two-footed pursuers would catch up with them. *What were they to do?*

One minute later, the problem was upon them as a great black shape sprang startlingly from the undergrowth to their right and dropped nimble-footed right into the centre of the gulley in front of them, barring all further progress.

111

They stumbled to a halt, sobbing for breath, chests heaving uncontrollably, mouths agape like a village idiot's, while to their front the great black beast crouched snarling softly, its evil brown eyes watching them, ready to spring at the first sign of danger.

'God!' Ami gasped and stopped, unable to say any more. But Karl knew what he meant. After all they had gone through, this evil hound had trapped them. Soon, if they didn't do something swiftly, the guards would be on the scene and that would be that; they would be finished.

Karl shook his head. With a hand that trembled violently he pulled out his sharpened spoon and held it, handle outwards. The hound sank back on its haunches, yellow teeth bared beneath that long decadent wet upper lip. A snarl started to rise from deep down within its throat. In a moment it would jump!

Commander Shimsk hesitated no longer. She had just glimpsed the fascists, drawn up in the trucks through a gap in the mist below. The drivers had remained in their trucks gunning their engines, obviously trying to keep warm while other men were milling around, quite unaware that they were in any kind of danger. Indeed, most of the Fritzes still had their weapons slung. Whatever had brought them out of the protection of their Camp clearly entailed no threat to them. She smiled. But there was no warmth in that smile.

Wordlessly she signalled with her hand. The drivers clucked their tongues and the column of *panje* wagons started to spread out virtually noiselessly to left and right, the partisans already unslinging the round-barrelled tommy guns with which most of them were equipped. She nodded her head in approval. They were well-trained. They knew their business as well as any regular male Red Army unit did.

Now they were in position: an extended column with the

flanks to left and right slightly in front of the centre, so that the attack formation resembled the spread horns of one of the oxen which the peasants used to plough their fields, with the points protruding beyond the brow. It was the usual partisan attack formation.

She raised her hand. In it she held the fat bulbous flare pistol. Without hesitation she pressed the trigger. A soft crack. Whoosh! The flare ascended into the misty sky, trailing bright white smoke behind it. It arched. Suddenly it exploded in a shower of bright silver stars.

The excited women waited no longer. '*Urrah!*' they cried shrilly like a battalion of Red Guards going into the attack. '*URRAH!*' The drivers whipped the rumps of their skinny steppe ponies and at once they were surging forward in a curved line, machine-pistols already chattering, the hooves of the *panje* horses thundering on the turf. '*URRAH!*'

Tinplate whipped round, caught completely off-guard. He raised his Schmeisser desperately. Too late! The burst of m-p fire ripped the length of his big chest, stitching blood-red buttonholes in it, searing upwards and ripping loose that silver plate on his big skull which had given him his nickname among the inmates of Camp Death. He fell, dead before he hit the wet turf, his brains splattering the ground in a mess of steaming grey and purple.

Howling Mad Mueller was caught by complete surprise, too. His mad face contorted, but not with fear. Instead it was animated by a look of absolute wild excitement. He was going into battle again. After these long sad years of inactivity, he was going to fight again. If he was about to die, he told himself, as he drew his pistol, he would do so as a fighting soldier on his feet in battle, not like some fat rear echelon stallion in bed. Carefully, with one arm placed behind his back, as if he were on some peacetime range, he peered down the barrel of the Mauser and slowly took aim.

CHAPTER 4

The survivors straggled by the Three Rebels' hiding place, next to the dead hound. There was something unreal, even eerie, about their progress. Not a word was spoken as they tried to escape that terrible wrath of the partisans. The only sound that came from these big well-fed guards who had once been so sure of themselves, was the harsh gasping of their breath. They did not even make an attempt to hide. It was as if they had accepted their inevitable end with lemming-like fatalism.

Face stricken with horror, Karl peered out of the hide of leaf-mould and branches, hardly daring to breathe. Down below as the mist rolled away to reveal that dreadful scene, the Russian women were massacring the survivors, accomplishing it like efficient workmen to whom this was just another job of work. They moved forward among the bodies slumped everywhere – a dead man with a thin wire bitten deep into his neck, face purple, tongue hanging out like wet leather; a guard rocking back and forth in utter misery, his empty eyesockets scarlet oozing pits – systematically putting their pistols to the backs of the wounded men's skulls, blowing the bone away in a welter of crimson gore.

Next to Karl, Ami retched and thrust his clenched fist into his mouth just in time. He started to vomit silently, skinny shoulders heaving as if he were sobbing. Beside him, eyes wide and round with horror, Polack mumbled his prayers in Polish.

Karl told himself that it was too late for prayers now. There was no God on high to show mercy to those poor wretches below, as the Russian women slashed, gouged, chopped and hacked at the few remaining guards still

114

standing, trampling them underfoot when they went down, screaming and begging for quarter, in their savage eagerness to get to the next man. He had never seen women like these before. They were like wild animals, cursing and shrieking, carried away totally by the blood-lust of slaughter, their eyes flashing, their hair streaming from beneath their fur hats as they dashed from one dying German to the other, deaf to the men's pathetic cries for mercy.

Howling Mad Mueller had fought them off until his pistol magazine was empty. Now, surrounded by the women he had killed during that first crazy charge, he stood bolt upright, despite the blood dripping down the side of his crazy-calm face, warding off his assailants with blows to left and right with his cane. Time and time again the harridans rushed him. But he always seemed able to fight them off in the very last moment. They were unable to use their automatics, too, for fear of hitting their own comrades.

'Great God in Heaven,' cried Ami, who had so often fantasised about slaughtering Howling Mad mercilessly, sadistically. 'They're not women . . . They're animals! I never thought that women could –' He stopped short. A large woman, looking even bulkier in her padded jacket, had stepped forward. She bawled something, her breath fogging on the morning air. The cries, the obscenities, the shrieks ceased, as if by magic, and the howling mob of women drew back from a panting, bleeding Mueller.

He staggered and seemed about to topple. In the very last instant he caught himself from falling, as the big bulky woman raised her pistol and took careful aim. Mueller lifted his hands, as if to ward off the bullet with his soft flesh. To no avail. At that range the Russian woman couldn't miss. Mueller shrieked with agony as his kneecap shattered in a welter of gore, through which the flying bone gleamed like polished ivory. He went down on his good knee, blood arching in a scarlet stream from his wound.

For a moment he tried to hold on to his cane. But he couldn't. Slowly it dropped to the ground and he was defenceless.

For what seemed an eternity he knelt there, panting heavily like someone who had just run a tiring race, gaze listless but without fear, while the circle of women stared down at him as they might have at a boxer fighting off the count.

Then Elinka, for it was she, turned and snapped something to the women. One, not dressed in the padded jacket and fur cap of the partisans, forced her way through the throng, her hair flying like that of some demented witch.

'Holy strawsack!' Karl cursed in surprise. 'You know who that is, don't you, comrades?'

Polack whistled softly and said, 'It's Howling Mad's woman!'

'*Jawohl*,' Ami chimed in as surprised as the others, wondering how she had got here, 'the piece o' gash who cleans - *cleaned*,' he corrected himself hastily, 'his quarters for him.'

Elinka whispered something to the maid and then with a sudden peal of laughter, her head flung back as if this was the greatest joke on earth, she handed the pistol with which she had just wounded Howling Mad to Aniya.

Hesitating for a moment, the peasant woman fumbled with the weapon, and then her face set, pale but determined, she advanced on the kneeling man, swaying violently now, as if he might relapse into unconsciousness at any moment, his head hanging.

She paused, while a sudden silence fell on the great crowd, broken only by the dry crack of pistols as further on they continued to finish off the remaining wounded Germans. Suddenly her free hand reached out. Grabbing Howling Mad by his lank blond hair, she jerked his head upright, a savage look on her pale face. He looked up at her, recognition beginning to dawn in his lack-lustre eyes. He opened his mouth to say something, but she shut him

116

off with a quick snorted retort. She fumbled with the pistol, still holding the German by the hair.

She rapped out something which the three comrades hiding up on the rise could not hear. Whatever it was, it brought a gasp from the watching women. Numbly, Howling Mad started to open his mouth, head tilted upwards so that it looked to Ami from the Catholic Rhineland like that of a churchgoer back home about to receive Communion from the priest.

But it was not the Communion wafer that Aniya began to slip into his mouth; it was the blue dull metal of the pistol's big muzzle. Slowly, very slowly, she slipped it in, millimetre by millimetre, ignoring the choking, gagging sound her one-time tormentor was now making, enjoying every second of it, feeling an almost-sexual tingling in her loins so that the nipples of her breasts were erect and her breath was suddenly coming in short hectic gasps. At her knees, Howling Mad's eyes bulged from his head. He choked for breath. Weakly he tried to escape her grasp, but she held him too tight. There was no escape. Nor was there from that rod of evil-tasting, oiled steel that was being rammed ever deeper into his mouth until it seemed to fill every space, right up to his tonsils and he was being strangled by the hard rigid tumescent enormity of it. Tears started to roll down his swollen cheeks. If he had been able to do so, he would have pleaded with her for mercy. But now the one-time cleaner, whom he had abused so often in the past, knew no mercy.

She no longer felt any rage. Her desire to kill, which minutes ago had burned within her with all-consuming, unreasoning hell-fire, had vanished, to be replaced by a yearning ache which she couldn't explain, but which turned her whole body weak with longing and desire. Between her legs she felt herself grow wetter and wetter. In a moment she must drop, she must, or she would explode. Her whole body was ablaze. She had to do something to extinguish that burning longing. *She had to!*

117

'What . . . what's she doing, Karl?' Polack stuttered helplessly, but unable to take his gaze off that eerie scene below, with the woman thrusting the muzzle ever deeper into the bulging mouth of the dying man kneeling in his own blood. 'What?'

Karl was too mesmerised himself to answer. Besides, what could he answer? His mind, in a turmoil by the events taking place below could not find the words to describe the perversity of the scene. It belonged to the world of the crazed sexual sadist.

Suddenly the woman's body went rigid. Her spine arched. A low moan started to come from between her wet slack lips. Her loins thrust forward. The finger holding the trigger of the pistol almost buried in Mueller's throat whitened. Her pelvis jerked as her head fell backwards, her face suddenly flushed a hectic red.

The burly woman shouted something in Russian. Later Karl thought it was some kind of encouragement. The woman with the gun did not seem to hear. She was shaking all over now. Strange hectic gasping noises came from deep down within her.

Karl, watching, felt himself sweating with fear – and something else he couldn't explain. God, why didn't she fire and have done with it? Let her get it over with. PLEASE! Now the sweat was pouring from him. Next to him, Ami crouched with his fingers tightly clenched, as if the strain was almost too much to bear.

Suddenly – startlingly – it happened. The woman pressed the trigger. There was a muffled explosion, followed an instant later by a great roar that made the watchers start up with surprise. The back of Mueller's head lifted right off. Next instant it disintegrated in a scarlet mushroom of blood and gleaming bone, and the headless torso flew backwards to hit the ground with a thud, leaving the woman, suddenly limp and weak at the knees, to stare down at the bloody red rod of steel in her

118

abruptly nerveless fingers, as if she could not understand how it had got there.

'I know he was a bastard,' Polack broke the heavy brooding silence, as below the big woman walked over and took the pistol from the cleaning woman's weak grasp, 'but I didn't want –'

'Shut up,' Karl hissed sourly. 'Don't even talk about it!' He took one last look at the murderers, unable to comprehend how women could behave like that. But it was the damned war. It changed all things, turning even women into sadistic ruthless killers, without one bit of mercy in their whole being. He shook his head like a man sorely tried, unable to comprehend the world any more. Unwittingly the women partisans had saved them, but the price of their freedom had been just too high.

'Come on,' he whispered, as the women began to spread out, starting the customary partisan looting of the bodies, occasionally kicking a body when they suspected someone was feigning death, 'let's get out of here . . . while there's still time.'

'Can't get out fast enough,' Ami agreed, his voice subdued, his normal Rhenish high spirits vanished. '*Jesus Maria an' Joseph!*' He shook his head and could say no more.

Wordlessly they set off once more. Their eyes, staring out from their emaciated, vulpine faces were blank of emotion. They could have been those of men already dead. Without a glance to left or right, they marched on to the railhead. Behind them the dead guards started to stiffen in the morning cold, while their murderers brewed looted tea and drank it round little flickering fires, chatting animatedly, for all the world like local housewives at some village *krug** . . .

Two hours later, the Three Rebels were on the heights

*Meeting place.

119

overlooking the railhead at Krasyna Voda. It was like all the other Russian villages they had ever encountered in their two years in that accursed country: a collection of rundown log shacks and straw-roofed *isbas* grouped around the only stone buildings in the place, the railway station, the 'house of culture' and the onion-roofed church, its faded gilt gleaming a little in the weak winter sunshine.

There were soldiers everywhere. Some were railway men and officials, striding to and fro self-importantly with clip-boards in their hands, but most were leavemen, laden with heavy packs filled with souvenirs and whatever they had been able to save from their rations for the people back home. They were easy to spot, for each one of them carried his rifle against the partisans on the journey into Poland and a neat little packet. This was the 'Führer Parcel', containing a pound of coffee, a ring of sausage and a can of meat, intended to convince the hard-pressed civilians back in the Reich that the *Wehrmacht* at the front had so much food that the soldiers could spare some to bring home as a gift.

The place looked the same as every other rail-stop on the Runway from the front, save for one thing. It was packed with patrolling chaindogs, working in pairs, their carbines slung over their shoulders, their silver plates of office slung around their necks sparkling in the sun's yellow rays.

'And you know why they're down there, comrade?' Karl said after he had finished surveying the place.

Polack nodded his cropped head. 'Yes, Karl, they're looking for us.'

'Yes!' Karl frowned. 'So we've got a problem. Somehow we must hide out till dark. If there *is* an ambulance train coming down from the front, it will come under cover of darkness as I've already explained. But how in three devils' name are we going to dodge those chaindog swine till then?'

Ami grinned for the first time since they had left the scene of that horrible massacre back on the steppe. 'I know,' he said, looking down at his begrimed nails with mock modesty.

'You would,' Polack growled. ''Cos you're a clever bastard, aren't you?'

'Shut up, Polack!' Karl snapped hastily. 'Get on with it, Ami. Where?'

By way of answer, Ami grinned slyly and formed a circle with the forefinger and thumb of his left hand. Then he proceeded to make a very obscene gesture. '*There!*' he said simply.

CHAPTER 5

The *pouf* was doing splendid business, although it was only ten o'clock in the morning. But in these railside brothels, which lined the route to the front at every stop in Russia, business always went on twenty-four hours a day. Day and night there would be noisy, excited, often drunken crowds outside the places, each man holding the prescribed three items they needed for entry: a contraceptive, five marks to pay for the whore's services and – in winter – a log of wood to heat the brothel's fire.

Of course, some of the leave-men, worried at the customary VD check at the Reich's frontiers, did not seek entry to get at the women. They used the place as a social centre, where they could drink, eat a plate of soup with their comrades and warm up. For the rearline brothels and hospitals were the only places in the whole length of that accursed country which were properly heated.

Now the Three Rebels, their faces washed clean with frozen snow they had found in the woods, their wooden holsters strapped to their belts, submerged themselves in the excited crowd of infantrymen, sappers, tankers, flak-gunners and the like who were waiting outside the local house of culture, which had been transformed into Krasyna Voda's *pouf*, as the soldiers called such places. Upstairs the off-duty whores lolled at the windows, displaying their ample if blousy charms, as they smoked or drank their daily ration of vodka; while the fat pastor, masquerading as a sergeant in the *Wehrmacht*, who was in charge of the place, rolled up and down the line, as drunk as the customers, crying 'Bless you my children . . . bless you all!'

Polack frowned. Religious as he was he didn't like drunken priests, even if they were heathen Protestant ones and not Catholic like himself. But Karl was pleased. The brothel suited their purpose perfectly as a hangout for the day. Here no one asked questions and there wasn't a chaindog in sight – they probably only turned up at night when things might get out of hand. Both the whores and their patrons were concerned with two things only: money and sex.

An hour later, their money handed over and their regulation three minutes upstairs already taken care of, the Three Rebels relaxed in the overheated fug in the large, low-ceilinged room below. It was packed with soldiers, smoking their pipes, taking slugs out of their 'flatmen', running lighted matches to kill the lice along the seams of their shirts, or simply sleeping it off in the corner next to the tiled oven which reached to the ceiling.

'Many a time I've counted hundreds of the filthy little beasts on my alabaster torso,' the old soldier opposite was saying, between puffs at his shagpipe, as he ran a lighted candle the length of his dirty vest, 'and when yer think the bastards can lay ten eggs a day, yer could have thousands of 'em nibbling at yer foreskin if yer don't keep 'em under control.' Next to him another grumbled, 'It's not as bad as them nags we have in the horse artillery, *Kumpel*. Yer average battery o' nags can produce a ton o' hoss-shit a day. So imagine how that attracts them Popov flies – as big as hornets the buggers are – and do they sting!'

Karl, his eyes closing in the heat, kept nodding his head routinely, only half-listening. It was the same old soldiers' talk he had heard in a dozen similar places in these last five years – 'subject number one' they called it: sex with a good old moan, thrown in for good measure.

But while he half-listened and fought off sleep, his mind worked on their problem. If, as he hoped, there were hospital trains from the front passing this way heading for the Homeland, two questions were raised. Did they stop at Krasyna Voda and if they did, how were the Three Rebels to get on board? They weren't wounded, were they,

123

apart from minor lacerations from the guard-dog at Camp Death.

But whey should they stop here? Wounded soldiers didn't need women and beer. Of course, the train, if it existed, might take on fresh supplies at Krasyna Voda, or it might stop to pick up wounded from partisan attacks; and as they had already seen, the partisans roamed the steppe in force attacking where and when they pleased.

Karl's mind wandered back to what they had seen at dawn and he puzzled yet again at the incongruity of human existence. Only hours before, German soldiers had been slaughtered like dumb animals, a mere dozen kilometres from this very spot. Here, other German soldiers caressed women's bodies, drank their schnapps and sat yarning in a warm comfortable fug, as if the world were at peace. It was all very strange . . . very strange indeed. Suddenly he couldn't keep his eyes open any longer. His eyelids felt like lead weights. Before he knew it, he was fast asleep . . .

'*Los, los, wirds bald?*'

Karl awoke with a start, frightened by that harsh official voice. He blinked rapidly and opened his eyes. Poised in the door of the room there was a mountain of an NCO muffled in a greatcoat with the collar raised about his ears, checkboard in one hand, pencil in the other. Around his arm he bore the armband of movement control. Obviously he was one of the local officials in charge of the *Reichbahn**.

'Come on, you bunch o' cardboard soldiers,' he bellowed in high good humour, 'your coach is without ready to take you back to those you adore, you bunch of poxed-up Popov-killers. Let's be having you!'

Behind the big NCO, as the leave-men started to collect their kit, the drunken sergeant-priest hovered, waving little bandages giving off a strange medical smell. 'Don't forget to put one of these on your thingies, men, if you've been upstairs with my good ladies. Wards off the old social

*German railway.

124

disease. We don't want to take the little lady wife or sweet-heart a nasty souvenir from Russia, do we now?' he smiled at the throng drunkenly, fat face exuding good cheer.

Ami shook his head in mock wonder. 'Now I've seen everything in the Greater German *Wehrmacht*,' he exclaimed. 'A priest in uniform running a knocking shop and selling pro-kits. *What frigging next?*'

'What frigging next indeed,' Karl echoed, waking up rapidly and wondering if they should go out with the leave-men and risk the chaindogs patrolling everywhere outside. It wouldn't be long before they were spotted, he reasoned, once the leave-men had boarded their train for the Home-land. Then the clock would really be in the pisspot!

Rapidly the room emptied, with one excited soldier pulling on his trousers as he ran after the others, crying, 'Stopped on the frigging job . . . Stopped on the job . . . Ain't there never no peace for a poor old ordinary frigging stubble-hopper!'

Then the room was empty, save for the Three Rebels and the fat pastor who was now swaying dangerously, his unsold pro-kits dangling uselessly from his fat fingers. He beamed at the three young friends. 'Are you not going on the leave-train, my dear young fellows?' he asked and Karl could have sworn he heard a kind of simper in the man's voice.

He took a chance. 'No, Sergeant, we were waiting for the hospital train tonight. We've got friends from our regi-ment – the Fourth Grenadiers – on it. Do you happen to know, Sergeant,' he added with apparent casualness, 'when it's due here?'

The fat NCO took the bait hook, line and sinker. Without a moment's hesitation or a question about how the three of them found time off from total war to go visiting wounded comrades in this arsehole of the world, he answered, 'After dark, of course. They're usually in about twenty hundred hours if there are no bandits' – he meant partisans – 'up the line. But it'll be after dark some

125

time.' He smiled at them drunkenly. 'It's going to be a long wait for you chaps and my good – er – ladies are about to go off-duty now. Perhaps,' he hesitated momentarily, 'you might like to come up to my quarters to relax and pass away the time till this evening.' He ran his plump hand over his balding head and gave them a significant look.

Next to Karl, Ami hissed out of the side of his mouth, 'Well, I *thought* I'd seen everything – a priest in uniform running a knocking shop and selling pro-kits. But I hadn't. *Now the frigger turns out to be a warm brother* as well!*' He rolled his eyes eloquently. 'Kiss me frigging good-night, Sergeant Major.'

Karl was just about to refuse the simpering priest's offer but then caught himself, in time. 'Will there be something to drink, Sarge?' he asked, smiling back winningly at the drunken priest.

'Of course, of course, my dear young friend,' the priest said eagerly. 'And hot food as well. You fellows from the front always have a hearty appetite, I know. I'll cook it myself, as soon as I've changed into my frock.' He giggled and pretended confusion, fluttering his eyelashes seductively. 'I mean my ecclesiastical robe, naturally. Ha, ha . . . Now come on, let us not waste any more time. Permit me to lead the way – er – upstairs . . .'

Polack looked aghast, Karl grinned. Ami, for his part, pulled a sour face and grumbled, 'The things I frigging well do for you, Karl. Just don't leave me alone with him, that's all. I don't trust the bugger, priest or not.'

'Don't worry, Ami, your virginity will be safe as long as I'm around . . . Now come on.'

Warily they started to mount the dark stairs after the homosexual priest . . .

Even as the white-painted train with the huge red crosses

*Homosexual.

126

on its side started slowly to enter the station at Krasyna Voda they could smell its unique odour: a mixture of ether, chloroform and human misery. There was no mistaking what this train contained – hundreds of gravely-wounded men heading for the blessed security of the hospitals in the Reich, though all too many of the poor pain-racked wretches aboard would be dead long before they reached the German border.

With a rusty squeal of brakes, the long train shuddered to a halt. Great clouds of steam bellowed from the hard-pressed locomotive. Stiffly, the guards in their leather face-masks to protect against the biting cold crawled down from their machine gun platform behind the cab and dropped gratefully to the platform. In that same instant the chain-dogs, armed with carbines, swept forward to seal off the train from prying eyes, carrying with them the bulky middle-aged women of the German Red Cross bearing their heavy jugs of steaming coffee for the wounded.

Someone gave an order. The doors were slid back. A cloud of warm fetid air swept on to the platform. Young nurses, shivering in the sudden cold, their white aprons flecked with drying blood, lugged heavy bodies, all of them bearing dirty bandages and shell-dressings, out of the carriages and dumped them unceremoniously on the platform to be picked up later. They were the unfortunates who had already died on a trip which would take them five days to reach the Reich. An orderly in a rubber apron started to march the length of the train, armed with a huge syringe. At each door he passed and pumped in a great cloud of white anti-louse powder. It was a primitive means of trying to combat typhus, for all the wounded were overrun with lice and on the Eastern Front an epidemic was already raging. No one wanted to take typhus back to the Homeland. The Party wouldn't tolerate it.

Now, all was hustle and bustle as the train crew prepared for the next leg of the journey – the long haul across Western Russia to Warsaw in German-occupied Poland.

Water gushed into the boilers from the canvas sleeves, more coal was loaded from the bunkers, the guards took on board more ammunition for their twin machine guns – they had already had one brush with the partisans further up the line – and all the while the chaindogs watched, their eyes under their gleaming polished helmets, hard, suspicious, and wary.

It was now that the Sergeant who bore the twin metal crosses of a military padre moved softly out of the shadows, one arm gripping, leading his two wan weak patients, while in the other he carried what was obviously a bundle of rations. The little group moved slowly and the bigger of the two patients moaned softly, clutching at intervals at his stomach, as if he were suffering intermittent spasms of pain.

The group approached the Sergeant in charge of the chaindogs, a big man, whose helmet seemed two sizes too small for his broad shaven skull so that it sat upon it like a child's toy. 'What is it, comrade?' the policeman asked easily, for the padre bore the same military rank as he and it pleased him to address a man of the cloth as 'comrade'.

'Two more unfortunates,' the padre answered solemnly, gaze fixed on the dusty platform in the humble manner of a trained priest. 'Dysentery,' he added.

'The thin shits – er – excuse my French, comrade. Is that what they've got?'

The padre nodded solemnly. 'They're to go to Warsaw to the hospital there.'

'Hm,' the Sergeant of MPs grunted. 'Paybooks,' he snapped.

Obediently the two sick men reached in their tunics' breast-pockets and proffered the documents to the NCO. The latter pulled back his hand hastily. 'Don't give 'em to me, you pair of piss pansies. I don't want to catch the trots as well. Just open them!'

Dutifully he peered at them in the poor light, cursorily

checking the photos. 'Yer've lost some weight,' he concluded and then spoke to the padre.

'What MO certified them sick, comrade? They ain't got no tags.' He meant the paper tags that all the wounded bore, giving details of their wounds, treatment, drug dosage and so on.

The padre coughed delicately into his fist. 'They were taken ill in my establishment over there, you know it?' He nodded towards the blacked-out house of culture.

A light dawned on the chaindog's hard face. 'Natch, you're the sky-pilot who runs the knocking – er – brothel for other ranks, aren't you? Heard of you.' He laughed. 'Your whores must really be ugly to frighten the shit out of yer customers, eh?'

The padre gave him a wintry smile and mumbled something.

'All right then, take 'em aboard, comrade. The coach for the dysentry patients is towards the end of the coach. The nurses don't like the pong up front.' He guffawed coarsely again as the two sick men shuffled forward towards the steps. 'And don't forget to stick a cork up yer arses. We don't want no accidents on this trip, do we?' And with that he was gone, leaving them to clamber inside and inspect their new quarters: a long open coach, with wooden seats at each side, decorated with a stencilled sign, reading: ATTENTION, RESERVED FOR DYSENTERY PATIENTS ONLY.

The smaller of the three men wrinkled his nose at the stench and looked at the bloody faeces and wads of used cottonwool that littered the wet floor. 'With this pong, who'd want to be in here 'cept poor bastards like ourselves. God almighty, what a frigging pong!'

The padre, who was reaching up to place his bundle on the rack above their heads shook his head in sorrow. 'My son,' he intoned, 'must you always use the language of the gutter? And you *are* using the name of Our Lord in vain, you know.' He tut-tutted and finished his task before sitting down very, very carefully next to the sick men.

129

Five minutes later there was the clatter of steel wheels on the rails, and a hiss of steam. The train jerked and they caught hold of the sides of the seats to prevent themselves from falling. A whistle shrilled. *'Abfahrt des Lazarettenzuges nach Warschau,'* the guard with his red sash called from outside. *'Alle zurücktreten, bitte!'*

With the wheels clattering almost angrily, the long train with its cargo of pain and misery began to move, slowly at first and then gathering speed at every second. The three men said nothing, listening to the haunting echo of the train as it began to leave the little blue-lit railhead, watching each light go by as if it were important to do so. Then outside all was darkness. They had left Krasyna Voda behind them – for good.

The padre let out a great fart and cried with sudden exuberance, 'We've done it, comrades. We've pulled it off!' Hurriedly he fumbled inside his pocket to produce an instant later a full flatman of vodka. He ripped off the cork with his teeth, raised the glass bottle as if in toast and cried, 'Home to Mother, lads . . . Home to Mother at last.' He took a mighty slug and sat back suddenly, as if overcome with emotion at what had just happened. *They had done it!*

CHAPTER 6

Next to him, Karl's comrades snored and for a while he dozed too in the comfortable fug of the dysentery coach, which so far had not been visited by any one of the hospital train's staff. Perhaps, he told himself, the smell put them off and he didn't blame them. But still the stench was better than being asked awkward questions.

Listening to the monotonous roll and beat of the train's wheels, his gaze trying now to penetrate the red-glowing gloom, Karl was lost in thought, finding sleep impossible. It seemed to him that they had been on the run for an eternity, though it was only a matter of two days. But so much had happened since they had crawled along the shaft to freedom. First the killing of the dog, then the chase and the massacre of the guards; then after that the brothel and the homosexual priest, still probably locked up in his own bathroom, naked. Karl smiled softly at the memory of the fat queer, crying his protests as they had shoved him in the bathroom and then had sat down to eat the great pan of fried potatoes and eggs – God they had eaten six of the precious eggs apiece! Somehow he doubted the padre-Sergeant would report what had happened. The penalty for homosexuality in the Greater German Wehrmacht was seven years' hard labour in Torgau.*

Karl yawned softly, while next to him Polack continued to snore open-mouthed, as if he hadn't a single care in the whole wide world. Lucky Polack, he told himself. But for a while at least all three of them could stop running, but *he* couldn't stop worrying.

He hardly dare think of what lay in front of them.

*A notorious military prison.

131

Security was tremendous in Russia and probably Poland, too. But it was nothing compared with the kind of police checks and the like they would surely face once they crossed into the Reich. '*If*,' a little voice at the back of his head grated warningly, '*if you manage to cross into the Reich!*'

Karl nodded his head sombrely, as if in agreement. Every man's hand was against them, that was for sure. Most civilians back home were solidly behind Hitler and even those who weren't were too scared of the Gestapo to ever say anything against the 'Greatest Captain of All Times', as the hairy-arsed stubble-hoppers mocked their remote Commander-in-Chief who never came to the front. Yes, once in the Homeland they would be able to trust no one.

Karl sighed and wished he could sleep like the rest. How blessed it would be if he could just curl up like Ami was presently doing and sleep away time – sleep until it was all over: the chase, the pressure, the whole damned miserable war! But he knew that wasn't to be. He had to keep planning, pursuing his aim until finally they could get there. '*And what then?*' that harsh little cynical voice at the back of his mind demanded. '*So you survive 1944, where will you be in 1954 – or 1984 – for that matter? You'll be some old bugger of a working stiff, who spent the best frigging years of his youth being shot at and trying to dodge being shot at!*'

Karl dismissed the insistent little voice. What had he said right at the beginning while they were still in Camp Death? Take it step by step, day by day. So that's how they would do it. He would worry about the Homeland when they got there. First they'd deal with the problem of Warsaw. He closed his eyes, his mind full of shadows and dark forebodings. It was in this frame of mind that he crossed the border into German-Occupied Poland. Now the Vistula and the one-time Polish capital lay only a couple of hours away, for the train would be scheduled to arrive there under cover of darkness so that the local civilians couldn't see the state of the Conqueror's wounded.

The curfew would be reigning still in the capital, at least for the Poles. So how were they going to remain undetected until life commenced once more in the great city?

'*Step by step* . . .' he ordered himself and then after a while he fell into a troubled sleep, his dreams filled with horrors and impending doom . . .

The long white-painted train, its coaches now covered with grime, soot and mud, started to steam slowly into the great echoing station, while the loudspeakers boomed out their messages metallically, and officious RTO officers doubled back and forth preparing to receive the wounded.

Karl pushed back the blackout and yawned, as he peered out. There were the usual women from the Red Cross waiting with their steaming cans of coffee and piles of sausage sandwiches, waiting on the platform in front of the line of ambulances, the drivers gunning their engines to keep them warm. They were the ones which would transport the wounded to Warsaw's numerous military hospitals.

Karl gave the ambulances a quick glance and then looked up the platform, craning his neck to do so. As he expected, there were half a dozen chaindogs waiting at the barrier, moodily puffing at cigarettes, half-hidden in the cups of their hands. Naturally they'd be keeping an eye on the train, just in case. So there was no way out – up there.

Ami must have read his mind for he said urgently, 'Well, the meat-wagons' – he meant the waiting ambulances – 'got into the station, didn't they?'

'So there's got to be another way out!' Karl beat him to it excitedly.

'*Genau!*' Ami began as the door to their compartment was flung open imperiously and a huge nurse filled the doorway, rubbing her massive left breast underneath the blood-splattered white apron, as if she were kneading dough for the oven.

Polack's mouth dropped open with shock and Ami hissed, 'God in Heaven, all that meat and no potatoes! I haven't seen that much meat since the days before rationing.'

The big nurse gave him a withering look. 'Shit-cases, aren't you?' she rasped in the accent of Berlin-Wedding. 'It smells like it as well. Now take them brooms over there in a corner and get this place swept out. It's like a pigsty in here! Then report over to the driver of the last ambulance. He'll tell you where to go. The seriously-wounded go first, not you pant-shitters. Now, don't let me have to come back here and find this place like this again.' And with that she swept out, still kneading her left breast.

'She knows what she can do with her frigging broom!' Ami snorted hotly, once the door was safely closed behind her. 'I'm not cleaning up this shitty place for her.'

Karl chuckled and said, 'Doubt if a broom pole'd do much good for that one, Ami, even if it went in *headfirst*. But those brooms are a good idea, though.'

'What do you mean, Karl?' Polack asked.

'Well, you know the old army drill? As long as you've got something in your hand, the big-shots never notice you. You're doing something, so you're all right.'

'But won't they have Poles to do jobs like that here in Warsaw?' Ami objected.

'Probably during the daylight hours. But not during curfew, Ami.'

'So, if we got off the train with them brooms,' Polack began in that slow ponderous manner of his –

Karl didn't wait for him to finish. 'Come on you two, grab the brooms and let's head for the ambulances before those stinking chaindogs finish their fly spit-and-a draw and begin heading this way.'

'But where are we going after we get out, Karl?' Ami objected.

'Let's –'

'*Let's take it step by step!*' The other two beat him to it.

Laughing like schoolkids just released from a boring lesson, they took the brooms and started to sweep their way to the door. Five minutes later, their brooms conspicuously displayed over their shoulders, the Three Rebels started to move along the length of the column of ambulances, where busy nurses were already snipping at bandages and arranging saline drips, as sweating stretcher-bearers hurried back and forth with their moaning bandaged cargo. Karl frowned as a couple of nurses went by leading a wounded man, both his arms enclosed in 'Stukas'*, his face a mess of black-pitted suppurating little wounds and his eyes covered by a thick bandage. Obviously a mine had exploded in the poor man's face and blinded him. Here was yet another victim of that brave 'New Order', which a mad dictator had inflicted on a suffering Europe.

Nobody noticed them, it seemed, as ambulance after ambulance was loaded with these ruined young men and drove away through the dark entrance; everyone was too busy with the wounded.

Karl nodded. Barring the exit there was a red-and-white striped pole, which was raised and lowered by a fat middle-aged soldier every time an ambulance went out. The other two Rebels got the message. Immediately they lowered their brooms and started sweeping towards the barrier, as if they had been ordered to do so. The man at the pole didn't even look at them. His whole attention was concentrated on the fleet of ambulances.

Outside, the street, still shrouded in pre-dawn gloom, was empty. Even the whores who always frequented stations such as this at all hours in search of customers in uniform were absent. Obviously the occupiers kept a strict curfew on Poles. Karl frowned. Somehow they were going to have to hide out for the next hour or so until the curfew ended, for he guessed the chaindogs would run all-night

---

*A plaster-cast named after the gull-winged dive-bomber because of the similarity in shape.

135

patrols specifically searching for people such as themselves – deserters, drunks and the like.

'*Alles in Ordnung?*' he said routinely to the fat man working the striped pole as another ambulance laden with groaning soldiers drew up for a moment.

'*Alles Scheisse,*' the other man grumbled.

Karl laughed sympathetically. Inside, he told himself the fat bastard didn't know how good he had it, working his frigging pole in the middle of Warsaw. He wasn't getting his fat arse shot off at the front, was he?

One by one they filed through the checkpoint, while the ambulance driver crawled forward in low gear, doing no more than five kilometres an hour. Obviously some sort of speed limit applied at the exit, Karl told himself, as he led them out into the city, nose twitching as he smelled that familiar Polish smell: a mixture of garlic, spicy sausage and sweet pickles. His stomach rumbled noisily and he remembered suddenly that they hadn't eaten a thing since the fat queer's *Bratkartoffeln and Spiegeleier* the previous evening. Suddenly he felt very hungry. He turned to Polack and said, 'Polack, you'll have to forage a bit and get us some fodder once the curfew's over. My guts are doing backflips and –'

'Hey, you!' a harsh official voice cut into his words and suddenly he was blinded by a beam of hard white light. 'What's yer game?'

Karl didn't need to be told that the speaker was a chaindog. Only military police cops talked like that. He reacted immediately. '*Run!*' he yelled urgently and flung his broom in the direction of the voice. There was a yelp of pain and somebody fell heavily on the wet cobbles.

A big man loomed up to their front. He bore the silver plate of a chaindog. Madly he was struggling to free the strap of his carbine from his brawny shoulder. Polack didn't give him a chance. He lunged with the broom as if thrusting home a bayonet. The man gasped mightily and went down like a suddenly-deflated balloon. Polack sprang over him and rammed his broom in the fat cop's face as he did so.

Then the three of them were running flat-out, with the whistles shrilling their urgent summons behind them. They had been rumbled. They had almost walked straight into a police trap. Now there was going to be all hell to pay . . .

One hour later, teleprinter operators everywhere in police stations, military police posts and Gestapo offices scattered throughout the Polish capital, were receiving the same message to be passed on to all officials and officers. WANTED FOR DESERTION, SUSPECTED MURDER AND PROBABLE COLLAB-ORATION WITH THE ENEMY IN RUSSIA, CARSTENS, KARL, ZIMANSKI, LUDWIK AND DOEPFGEN, ADOLF STEVEN . . . There followed a lengthy description of the wanted men's physical appearance and all identifying scars and then the message ended with the bald brutal words: THESE MEN ARE KNOWN TO BE DANGEROUS. IF THEY REFUSE TO SURRENDER IMMEDI-ATELY WHEN CHALLENGED, THEY ARE TO BE SHOT ON THE SPOT! The last three words were underlined to make sure that everyone understood.

Now the Three Rebels were no longer simply escaping – they were running for their very lives!

CHAPTER 7

Warsaw was dying. The Three Rebels could see that. On all sides in the streets, which were bare of vehicles save those of the *Wehrmacht* and ancient, wood-burning taxis towing steaming boilers behind them, there were sallow-faced, undernourished men and women, their heads ducked into the collars of their shabby coats, hurrying through the ruins to whatever work they had. There were beggars everywhere. Ragged women and children, some with only scraps of cloth covering their bare feet, held out their hands as the three fugitives passed, begging for bread in German and Polish, knowing even as they did so that these Germans were not going to give them any.

'What a mess,' Ami commented, their own problem forgotten for a moment. 'What a frigging mess.'

Karl nodded slowly and Polack, looking sad and pensive, dragged his eyes from an old woman who lay bundled up against the wall and who might well be dead, and said, 'My mother – God rest her soul – always told me how grand Warsaw was when I was a kid. The fine shops, the elegant women, the good food. Look at it now.' He shrugged expressively.

'It's the New Order,' Karl said. 'The benefits of the One Thousand Year Reich bestowed on the grateful natives.' He spat in the dust.

Ami looked at a ragged boy, belly swollen with hunger, eyes bulging large and glittering from an emaciated face, rummaging in a dustbin for whatever it might contain. 'Some people say they didn't have a pot to piss in before the war anyhow,' he said.

Polack flushed angrily. 'Don't say that Ami, even as a

joke. Now we've taken the very piss from them – even if they didn't have a *pot* before the war.'

'Peace . . . peace.' Karl raised his hands to appease Polack. 'Let's concentrate on our own problems, now, shall we? Look, it's my guess that they've rumbled us. That nasty little business at the station seems to prove that. So we haven't got a chance in hell of getting on that leave-train to Berlin. The chaindogs will be waiting for us, you can be sure of that.'

Ami nodded dourly and Polack said, 'You're right, Karl – as usual. But what are we going to do? We can't wander around here much longer in uniform with no papers – ' suddenly his stomach rumbled noisily '–and no fodder either to speak of.'

'Agreed, Polack. Our luck's running out. We can't chance our arm much longer. So the first thing we've got to do is to get out of Warsaw toot-sweet – and then somehow we've got to make it to the Homeland without the train, even if we have to hoof it.'

Ami groaned, but Karl ignored him, hurrying on rapidly. 'So let's see about doing a bunk from Warsaw first.'

'One thing at a time, Karl,' Polack said and grinned. 'Step by step as usual.'

'Step by step it is, Polack,' Karl agreed with a grin, though he had never felt less like smiling in all his life. 'Now, you see that?' He indicated a battered blue-and-white tram, packed with workers, some of them squatting on the vehicle's bumpers, which had come squeaking round the corner. 'That's going to be our magic coach to whisk us out of Warsaw.'

'But we haven't got no Polack green moss* – whatever they call it,' Ami protested.

'*Zloty*,' Polack said. 'That's what they call marks here – *zloty*.'

*Army slang for 'money'.

'*Schön gut*, so we ain't got none. So what are we going to pay the tram conductor with, Karl?'

Karl patted his shabby tunic. 'We're conquerors, aren't we? Do you think any hairy-arsed Polack is going to ask us – members of the victorious *Wehrmacht* – for the fare? *Nix*! Now then, Polack, you can read the lingo. Point us in the right direction. We want a tram that is west-bound. Doesn't matter where it's going, as long as it's heading west. All right, Polack, you're in charge now. As the golden pheasants' – he meant the Party officials – 'back home always say – "the Führer commands and we follow". Right, Führer, start commanding . . .'

Ten minutes later they were safely ensconced in one of the shabby trams, nicely seated in the front bench, *Reserved for Members of the Occupying Power*, and trying to ignore the evil looks being cast in their direction by the shabby Polish crowd which filled the antiquated vehicle. They had wheels again. They were moving.

The trouble started just as they were descending with the throng of Polish workers in their shabby black caps and clogs at the depot, which was located in what looked like an industrial district. Chimneys smoked all around and grim, red-brick factories were visible behind high barbed gates guarded by civilians carrying rifles slung over their shoulders. The Three Rebels had just got off the tram when a column of skeletons in earth-brown ragged smocks came lurching round the corner, the laggards being cruelly lashed by elderly guards on *panje* ponies.

'*Jeniec*,' Polack heard one of the Polish workers whisper and translated quickly for the others. 'Prisoners of war . . . Popovs, by the look of 'em.'

They nodded in understanding and halted as the column of misery came level with them, obviously heading for the factory opposite to start another day of slave labour. Their stench was awful. It reminded Karl of the filthy stink that

140

came from the monkey house at Hagenbeck* in his youth. Their eyes spoke of near-death, but here and there they burned with such hatred of their captors that Karl felt for one fleeting moment that his body could be consumed by it.

A big Russian, with a blood-stained bandage round his shaven skull, his bones sticking through his ragged tunic, staggered and went down on one knee. Immediately one of the *Wehrmacht* guards leaned down from his little pony and began flogging him with his whip so that the blood started to spurt from his lacerated back, while the Russian pleaded in his own tongue for mercy. Ami couldn't contain himself. Before the other two could stop him, he had darted forward, grabbed the whip from the elderly soldier's hand and flung it to the ground. A great gasp of both fear and surprise went up from the Poles.

'Why, you cruel bastard!' Ami cried, beside himself with rage, his skinny little face flushed crimson.

The elderly guard looked down at him, face registering complete surprise. 'But they're only Popovs, comrade,' he said chidingly. 'Not human beings like us Germans. Shouldn't worry about sub-humans like that.'

'Shut your damn fat lip!' Ami cried, fists clenched, eyes blazing, as the Poles gawped and the Russians simply stood there, shoulders hunched like dumb animals to be disposed of without protest just as their masters wished. 'Yer can't treat men like frigging that!'

'What's all this?' a superior-sounding, well-educated voice demanded, cutting into the exchange. 'Why is this column being held up?'

The other two turned sharply. An officer, mounted on a fine white charger, had cantered round the corner, reining in his horse when he saw the little scene and the stalled column.

'Who are you? Why are you interfering with my chaps?'

*Famous Hamburg zoo.

141

Karl saw the danger immediately. 'Run for it, mates!' he yelled urgently. 'Come on, *hoof it!*' He thrust himself forward into the crowd of Poles, pushing and barging through the surprised workers, heading for the maze of shabby little streets just beyond the factory.

Ami woke up to the threat at once, too. His rage vanished as soon as it had come. He flung himself forward, followed an instant later, albeit a little more slowly, by Polack.

'Apprehend those men!' the officer cried, rising up high in the saddle as his mount bucked and trembled with sudden fright. 'Stop those men running, will you? . . . Come on, look alive, you silly fools!'

Now Karl was clear of the factory, pelting all-out for the cover of the next street, with its line of one-storey, red-brick workers' houses. Ami was just behind him, skinny little arms flashing back and forth across his chest like pistons. But Polack was trailing behind. He was always slower than the others. But he reckoned that the guards on horseback wouldn't be able to get through the crowd of Poles. They wouldn't fire, either. After all, the fugitives were fellow members of the *Wehrmacht*. But Polack had not calculated on the swiftness of one of the elderly guards.

Right to the front of the column, one of them, a fat man with steel-nickel spectacles, whirled his heavy black whip around his head like some South American gaucho might do his *bola*. Next moment it was hurtled through the air, straight towards the running man. Polack heard it hissing towards him. Instinctively he turned, and the whip struck him full in the face. He yelled with sheer agony and felt himself falling to the cobbles, as back at the column the guards urged their horses forward, scattering the Polish civilians and heading straight for him. Desperately he tried to rise, blood squirting from his nostrils. That wasn't to be. A heavy boot smashed into his side. He grunted with pain and dropped once more, rolling himself into the foetal position. Not a moment too soon. The heavy, studded boots started to crash into his inert body over and over again . . .

*
142

'*Los, du Schwein* . . . Hurry up, you great horned-ox, open your eyes. Don't keep pretending you can't hear us . . . *Los*!' The cries seemed to Polack to be coming from far, far away. Perhaps he was dreaming. But a hard slap across his ashen face told him he wasn't.

He shook his head. It seemed twice its normal size. The red mist in front of his eyes vanished and he was aware suddenly of a rotten headache. He wiped his hand across his face. It came away smeared in blood, *his blood*! Abruptly he realised he was in trouble, serious trouble. He opened his eyes.

He was in some kind of an office. There was the usual office-style furniture with a picture on the wall of Hitler dressed as a knight, astride a horse and carrying a swastika banner. Polack frowned. He realised suddenly he had never seen Hitler on a horse yet.

Another stinging blow across his face sent his head slamming to one side. He gasped and his eyes focused on his tormentor. He was a big noncom with a brutal pocked face, standing next to the elegant officer who had commanded the column. The latter stood with his arms folded across his chest, smoking a gold-tipped cigarette in an ivory holder, looking as if he were bored rigid by the whole business. 'Ah,' the officer said, 'we have returned to the land of the living, have we?' His accent was upper-class and Prussian. Polack recognised it from the Junker landlords of East Prussia where he had once worked as a boy farm labourer. Instinctively he pulled a face.

'Shall I belt him one, *Herr Oberleutnant*?' the burly NCO growled, raising his right fist again. Polack saw the knuckles of the hand were red and bruised and he knew why.

'Hold hard, Neumann, not so hasty. Old lady is not an express train, as you common soldiers say.' The officer tapped his holder with his manicured fingers and the ash from his hand-rolled cigarette dropped neatly on to the carpet. 'Let us see if the peasant has a tongue.' He leaned

143

forward and said to Polack, 'I am going to talk very slowly and I am going to talk in words of few syllables. Do you understand?' He beamed at Polack, as if he were talking to a village idiot.

Polack nodded his head numbly and wished next moment he hadn't. It hurt like hell.

'Now, I want to know just who you are – and your two comrades too, naturally. The paybook we found on you isn't yours. That is obvious. Otherwise you have no other papers. So, my dear fellow, what are you doing in Warsaw, annoying my poor bunch of overweight, elderly gentlemen, eh?' He beamed at Polack again.

Polack said nothing. Next door there was a twittering of female voices in Polish. Obviously the clerks were watching the interrogation. God, Polack thought, if only they could pass on the word where he was to Karl and Ami, they'd come and rescue him. He knew that implicitly. The other two Rebels had not let him down yet. If *only* he could speak Polish to them!

'Did you hear what the *Herr Oberleutnant* said, you arse-with-ears?' the noncom said threateningly through gritted teeth, thrusting his face close to Polack's so that the latter had a whiff of his stinking, stale breath. 'Now don't fart about. Spit it out – *who are you?*'

Stubbornly, deliberately, Polack closed his lips. The NCO hit him. Polack's lips split like an overripe plum. Hot blood began to trickle down his unshaven chin.

The officer shook his head. 'Tut-tut, aren't we stubborn. But my dear fellow, don't you realise you are making it worse for yourself by remaining silent like this? If you are *Wehrmacht*, which by the look of you I think you are, spit out what you know and we'll pass you over to the chaindogs. If you *don't* speak there is only one course open to me - to hand you over to the Gestapo. And let me tell you this, the Gestapo don't work with their hands in kid gloves. They tell me they can even get a mummy to talk.' He tittered at his own humour. 'So what are you going to do?'

The NCO frowned.

Polack looked at his hands. They were bound with some kind of wire to the heavy chair in which he had been placed. The sight offended his Slavic soul. What kind of world was this? What right had these Junkers to tie him up like some dumb animal being led to the slaughter! His face hardened and although it hurt like hell, he closed his lips stubbornly.

The officer sighed. 'God, *Feldwebel*, what a bore! Oh, do hit the silly chap again, will you and see if we can change his damnfool mind.'

'With pleasure, sir,' the NCO replied. He hauled back his arm and clenched his fist, his jaw hard, eyes gleaming. Polack could see he was enjoying this. He was another pig of a damned sadist like Tinplate Head had been back at Camp Death.

'*Arschloch!*' the NCO grunted and slammed his clenched fist right in the centre of Polack's face. It exploded in a flare of bright red stars. Polack felt his nose crunch, as the bridge went and blood started to spurt from his nostrils. His mouth suddenly flooded with blood, his cry of pain smothered in it.

He realised that he couldn't stand much more of this and the NCO was showing no signs of flagging. After all, this was obviously a change from the boring routine of guarding a lot of half-human Popovs ... He had to act fast. God in Heaven, he wished Karl were here. He *always* knew what to do in situations like this. He, Polack, was a stupid peasant whose brain seemed to work at half the speed of Karl's.

'I'll tell you,' he pretended to quaver, 'but please don't hit me again. I'll tell you ...'

'Now that's much better,' the elegant officer said happily. 'Now we can get this unpleasant business done and finished with, can't we, *Feldwebel?*'

The latter grunted something. He was obviously not particularly pleased to be cheated of his pleasure.

145

Polack opened his mouth deliberately and allowed the blood to dribble down his chin. 'Do you think I could be freed, *Herr Offizier?*' he said humbly, keeping his head lowered so the other two couldn't see the sudden determination in his blackened eyes. 'So I can clean my face. I've got a handkerchief in my pocket, sir.'

'Of course, of course. But please hurry up. There is a reception at eleven hundred hours at the General's house. Can't miss that, can I?' He nodded to the NCO and grumpily the latter started to untie the wire which bound Polack's wrists.

Polack waited, his head bent as if in defeat. But his mind was racing. He was trying to identify the direction from which those Polish voices were coming. Finally the NCO grunted and straightened up. 'All right shitbag,' he commanded, 'clean yersen up and a bit sharpish, as well!'

Polack drew a deep breath. Suddenly he launched himself forward. The NCO slammed against the wall, caught completely off-balance. 'Oh, I say!' the officer cried and fell backwards. Next moment, Polack was diving through the glass partition which divided the office in which they had held him from the one next door.

Girls screamed. The German director yelled something. A telephone slid from a desk with a jingle of bells. A typewriter overturned. Polack hit the floor with a thud. '*Je jestem polacki, kolega**,' he cried in one last desperate effort to the circle of shocked faces staring down at him. Next moment he fainted.

*'I'm a Pole, mate.'

CHAPTER 8

The Pole was a striking-looking little man with a grizzled goatee beard and bright blue eyes which danced with suppressed energy and excitement when he spoke. Since their arrival in Warsaw that dawn, he was the first Pole Karl had seen who had any fire about him. Now, as the rough-looking crowd in their shabby blue overalls and peaked black workingmen's caps, edged in around the two of them in that mean back street, which smelled of stale cabbage and defeat, he demanded, 'Now then – who are you? Deserters from the *Wehrmacht*, eh?'

There was such a natural air of authority about the man that Karl automatically came to attention and said, 'You might call us that.'

'*Pan Comendant*,' one of the rough-looking men growled threateningly. 'You call him by title.' His German was terrible, but comprehensible. Suddenly Karl realised that they had fallen in with the Polish partisan movement and he shivered. They were as good as dead.

The small bearded man saw the shudder and said, with a cold little smile, 'We are not murderers, German. We are soldiers in mufti, members of the *Armja Krakowa*. The Home Army you would call it in German. All disciplined men acting under military law, in other words. Now then, you are deserters. Why and from where?' He rapped out the question, as if he were used to asking questions and having them answered.

Somehow Karl felt confidence in the little bearded Pole and as swiftly as he could, knowing the danger Polack was in now, he told him their story: how they had escaped from the Camp, travelled right across Western Russia into

147

Poland and how they hoped to escape from Germany altogether.

The little man listened impassively, while one or two of his unprepossessing followers translated into Polish in an undertone for those who did not understand German.

'And so, as you say, one of your comrades who is of Polish descent, was taken outside the factory?' the leader snapped when Karl was finished.

Karl nodded and bit his lip. He hoped against hope that the little Pole could suggest something. Without their help, Polack was lost.

'You know, of course,' the Pole said after a moment's consideration, 'that the factory is a big place and it is guarded by Poles in the Germans' pay' – for a fleeting second his dynamic face registered contempt – 'and we do not know where exactly they are holding him. But we still have a chance.'

Karl's heart leapt with relief and Ami beamed.

'But once the Gestapo or your Field Security Police have him, there is no hope. Their headquarters are in Central Warsaw and we would not dare to tackle such places. Is that clear?'

'Yes, I know . . . er – *Pan Comendant*. But will you try to rescue our comrade?'

'Yes.' There was no hesitation. 'For two reasons. One, he is of Polish descent and two,' he allowed himself a little smile, 'one more German deserter like you two is one fewer German to fight.'

Karl smiled with relief.

'So it's got to be the factory.' Hastily he turned to the others and started speaking to them rapidly in Polish, while they nodded their heads at intervals and dutifully repeated one word over and over again, '*tak . . . tak . . . tak!*' Karl knew it meant 'yes' so he assumed that their leader was giving them orders. A moment later this was confirmed when the Poles began to remove parts of a strange-looking

148

weapon from beneath their shabby jackets or from down the inside of their trouser legs.

It came in three parts – a barrel, a metal stock, and a long magazine filled with nine-millimetre slugs which was clipped on to the side of the handy little weapon. 'Sten,' the leader informed Karl when he saw him look in the direction of the funny-looking machine-pistol. 'It comes from London,' he added proudly. 'The English Mister Churchill sends them to us personally by his aeroplanes at night.' Then he was very businesslike again. 'We've got to get into the factory before your people arrive to take him away. We have friends in the place, of course. If they know where your friend is, they will tell us. Then we must move quickly.' He slapped his hip hard in a strange gesture. 'Let's go!'

Without another word, the little man swung round, went straight through the door of the nearest worker's house, down the short passage and quickly out into the tumble-down yard. With a grunt he clambered up the wall which separated it from the next house and vanished. Hastily his men, with a bewildered Karl and Ami following, did the same.

'Christ on a crutch!' Ami panted, as they blundered through yet another miserable hovel, reeking of poverty, with barefoot blond children in rags staring at them open-mouthed and a mother sucking the edge of her dirty apron with fright, 'these buggers do just what they like, don't they?'

Karl, gasping for breath, for the little man kept up a cracking pace, nodded his agreement. He knew why. These Polish partisans from – what had the little man called it – 'the Home Army' – were in complete control of their own people. They could, indeed, do just what they liked. Suddenly he felt a surge of new hope. If anyone could free Polack, it would be the little leader . . . They plunged on, over yet another wall.

*

149

'I suppose we really should see that he's taken to hospital,' the elegant officer was saying in the background, as the Polish secretary leaned over Polack on the glass-littered floor, dabbing his bloody face with her delicate handkerchief and making soothing little noises.

'No, sir!' the NCO who had struck Polack replied. 'That big bugger's tough. Full of piss and vinegar.'

'What curious expressions you other ranks use,' the officer drawled, as the Polish secretary leaned a little closer and whispered into Polack's ear: 'They know you're here . . . We got a message to them.'

Polack, still in a daze, didn't know who 'they' were. But he did feel a new sense of hope. Someone was prepared to help him.

'All right,' the NCO snapped gruffly to the secretary. 'Enough of that! He's not hurt that bad. You,' he growled down to Polack, as the secretary moved back to the other Polish women, standing a little scared in the corner of the outer office, 'on yer feet! There's a car on the way to take you to HQ.' He brought back his cruel-nailed boot and slammed it into Polack's ribs. The girls gasped with shock.

Slowly Polack lumbered to his feet staring at his tormentor through puffed up eyes.

The NCO glared back at him. 'Don't look at me like that, apeturd. Or I'll really give you something –'

'Stop that!' the elegant officer cut in quickly. 'Let's be on our way. Time is running out.'

The NCO dug Polack in the side surlily. '*Los,*' he snarled.

Reluctantly, or so it seemed, Polack moved towards the door, followed by the officer who smiled politely and gave a little gallant bow in the direction of the secretaries and the typists, while the NCO gripped his pistol holster suspiciously.

'I kiss your hand, ladies,' the officer said and then they were out, moving down the long corridor which echoed hollowly to the sound of their boots. On both sides there were thick, soundproof glass partitions through which they could see shabby workers moving back and forth between apparently noiseless lathes and drills so that it seemed to Polack that he was viewing some ancient silent movie. Indeed, the whole business appeared to him unreal and remote, as if it were happening to someone else. Although the danger to him was clear, he could not quite take it seriously.

They turned a corner. Another long echoing corridor. At the far end there were two Poles in the dark blue uniform of the renegade police service which worked for the German occupiers. Both of them had big service revolvers in shining leather holsters at their hips. For Poles they looked well-fed and efficient.

The officer beamed when he saw them. 'Escort for us till we get out of this place, *Feldwebel*,' he commented. 'Funny feeling it gives me. Glad when we're out of here.'

'Polacks!' the NCO sniffed contemptuously. 'That'll be the day when a shitty Polack puts the wind up me!' As if to emphasise his contempt, he dug his pistol into Polack's sore ribs and muttered, 'Come on, slime-shitter, we haven't got all frigging day, you know.'

Polack stumbled on, rage beginning to well up in his bruised, broken body like a blood-red tide.

They neared the Poles. The taller of the two stiffened to attention and touched two fingers to his cap in the Polish fashion. 'The car is outside, *Herr Oberleutnant*,' he reported in good German. Automatically the two of them fell into step with the others, flanking Polack on both sides.

The NCO flung the big glass door open. A wave of cold air came wafting in. Outside, the cobbled factory yard was empty save for the elderly guards, holding their ponies and looking boredly at their miserable Russian prisoners. There was no sign of the car.

The officer frowned. 'The car?' he queried.

'Just beyond the gate, sir,' the taller Pole answered smartly. 'This way, sir.' He flung out his right hand like an attentive waiter ushering a favourite customer to a choice seat.

They started forward again. One of the elderly guards yelled, '*Hab acht!*' The prisoners stiffened to attention, gaze fixed on some remote horizon, as the officer came level. Casually he raised his leather-gloved hand to the gleaming peak of his cap. '*Bitte weitermachen,*' he said in the very same instant that with startling suddenness, the siren on the factory roof began to shrill its urgent warning.

Immediately all heads went up. Why the air-raid siren? Who was to bomb Warsaw? Not the British. They were too far away and as for the contemptible Russians, they wouldn't dare!

But the Poles seemed to be taking the warning seriously. All of a sudden there were half a dozen of them, dressed in the usual shabby clothes, sprinting across the yard, blowing their whistles and twirling their rattles frantically. In a flash, all was confusion. The *panje* ponies, startled and frightened, reared up on their hindlegs and flailed the air with their hooves. The tightly-packed column of Russian prisoners started to break up, as they sought for cover. Hastily the elderly guards began to unsling their carbines, crying angrily, '*Stehenbleiben . . . Stehenbleiben, ihr russische Schweinhünde!*'

One moment later there was the first shrill of a machine-pistol. A fat guard clawed the air, red holes stitched the length of his chest, as if he were climbing the rungs of an invisible ladder. The Russians panicked, then bolted. Helplessly the other guards tried to stop them. They were swamped by the sheer number of the POWs. The officer yelled out an urgent order. Next to Polack, the NCO clicked off his safety. One of the blue-uniformed Poles slammed his boot into the German's leg. He howled with pain and began to double up, pistol still in his hand. Polack yelled something in Polish and jammed his elbow into the NCO's pain-racked face – hard. The latter's nose burst, as if pulped and he went down, spitting out teeth that showed gleaming white against the bloody gore.

'*Ide, kolega!*' the taller of the two Polish 'policemen' cried urgently, as the guards started to fire wildly into the mêlée.

Polack needed no urging. He started to move – and quick.

'Hey, you!' the elegant officer began. His cry ended in a shriek as a little man with a beard and bright blue eyes appeared from nowhere, or so it seemed, his machine gun chattering frenetically. The officer's legs gave way beneath him like the legs of a newly-born foal. He collapsed somewhat stupidly on to the cobbles, looking at his shattered legs as if he couldn't believe this was happening to *him*.

The little man with the beard paused only to grab the pistol from the officer's hand and then the whole group was running madly for the gate, kicking and punching their way through the confused mess of guards and Russians.

They sprinted through it, with the siren on the roof still howling wildly. A black Horch was hurtling down the road towards them. Polack took his gaze off Karl and Ami who were crouching there next to the wall with a bunch of armed civilians. '*Gestapo!*' he yelled urgently, for he needed no crystal ball to identify the hard-faced men in the front of the big open tourer.

A heavy-set civilian leaned out of the side of the speeding car. He had taken in the situation at the gate in a flash. A pistol barked. The taller of the two Polish 'policemen' yelped with pain. He clapped his hand to his shoulder. The fingers flushed red with his blood immediately. But the dynamic little man with the beard reacted at once. He raised the strange little machine-pistol he carried and his knuckles, gripping the trigger, whitened. He fired. A stream of slugs shattered the windscreen of the Horch. It disappeared into a gleaming spider's web of broken glass. Desperately the driver, half-blinded and his face streaming with blood, tried to control the big car. He fought the wheel crazily. To no avail. The Horch reared up on to the

153

pavement, totally out of control. With a crash that made the road shake, the car smashed into a gas-lantern. Whoosh! There was a tremendous explosion. In an instant the gas-lamp was burning fiercely, as the trapped Gestapo men fought frantically to get out of the wrecked car before it was too late.

It was no use. The engine started to burn. The trickle of petrol that ran from the ruptured tank ignited into a tremendous flash of white blinding incandescent flame. Next moment the chassis of the car was sailing leisurely into the air, while one wheel bowled crazily down the cobbles, as they all stared at the sudden holocaust in awed silence. Then the little man was crying urgently, 'Come on, you stale pisspots – run for it . . .' And they were pelting frantically into the myriad of back streets, with the siren still shrieking like the howl of a demented banshee.

CHAPTER 9

'*Germany*,' Szwagier said and pointed with his stick to the hills beyond the river. 'Well, once it was Poland . . . Now it's Germany.' He gave them a faint smile as if the thought pleased him for some reason or other.

It was now a week since the little man with the goatee beard had spirited them out of Warsaw so dramatically, and they had been taken over by the Home Army. And real army it was, too, with its own structure, newspapers, radio broadcasts, even books, existing under the very noses of the German occupiers. Laws were promulgated, courts held where collaborators and traitors were dealt with, so that the real masters of rural Poland remained the Poles themselves.

On the second day of their flight the Three Rebels had been passed on over the artificial border between German-Occupied territory and the 'Central Government', a Polish enclave run by collaborators – in theory, at least. By means of wood-burning trucks, horse-drawn carts and a couple of times by bike, the three fugitives, accompanied by ever-changing guides from the Home Army, had progressed steadily westwards. Now on this seventh day, guided by Szwagier, a tall humorous man, they had reached the border of the Reich at last.

Now Szwagier*, for that was how he had been introduced to them by their previous guide – the Home Army worked very hard to protect the identity of its members – ordered them to squat in the cover of a patch of oaks, overlooking the border river and began to instruct them on the next stage of their journey. 'Your clothes', he indi-

Szwagier is Polish for brother-in-law.

155

cated the shabby workers' suits they had been given in Warsaw, 'and identity documents of volunteer Polish workers for the Reich should stand up to a routine check. But as you Germans,' he looked pointedly at Karl and for some reason the latter felt himself blushing, 'regard us Poles as third-class citizens, even a teenage fart of a Hitler Youth will feel he has the right to challenge you as a Pole. Best thing is to get German ID as soon as possible. But for a day or two . . .' he shrugged and left the rest unsaid.

'Now, there are two bridges across the river, ten and six kilometres respectively up and down stream. They are guarded. We think, therefore, that your best bet is to cross the river here. At this time of the year, with the snow gone, it should be fordable. Soon you will find out if we're right or not.' He chuckled softly.

'But I can't swim,' Ami protested hotly.

'Well, this is a good time to learn, eh,' Szwagier replied.

Now it was Polack's turn to chuckle. Karl for his part stared at the blue-grey hills beyond and told himself what a crazy world this was: he, a German, smuggling himself into his own country with the aid of a Pole. The world had gone totally *meschugge!*

'Now, you Germans are not complete fools, of course,' their guide continued. 'The border guards realise anyone trying to get in – or out – of the Reich illegally won't take the bridges. So they run patrols at *irregular intervals,*' he emphasised the words, 'between the two. Usually they cover that area of scrub and trees some two hundred metres beyond the river. Do you see?'

They nodded. 'Do they run them at night too?' Karl asked, rapidly absorbing the information.

'Officially we poor third-class citizens are not supposed to be out after curfew which is at dusk,' their guide replied. 'But we have watched them and, yes, they do patrol at night. But you'll take the cover of darkness, of course. With their glasses in the daylight, they can see for kilometres. It would be too dangerous to attempt to cross then.'

Again the Three Rebels nodded in agreement. Once they had established whatever routine the patrols had, Karl told himself – and in the Greater German *Wehrmacht* there always had to be some sort of routine – they would cross immediately.

'As soon as you're through,' Szwagier went on, 'start walking due west till you reach Neustedt. It is a small town used by miners who work in the pits all around. There you take a tram. Don't be afraid. There are no checks on the workers' trams and you,' he indicated Polack, 'speak Polish. Most of the border folk are what you Fritzes call "water-Poles", who speak both Polish and German. But be careful,' he raised a dirty finger in warning, 'trust no one – Pole or German. Regard everyone as a potential spy or traitor who would turn you in to the Gestapo for a loaf of bread. Once you reach a big city, you can relax. What is it you Fritzes say? *Stadtluft macht frei**. In the city people are more concerned with their own affairs than they are in the countryside.'

'But we have no money,' Ami objected, making the German gesture of counting coins with his thumb and forefinger.

'Don't worry about that,' the Pole said airily. With a flourish he produced a thick wad of blue-green *Reichsmarks* from his inside pocket and handed them ceremoniously to a surprised Ami. 'There are two thousand marks there, donated to you courtesy of the Home Army.' He winked. 'But don't look at them too carefully, will you?'

'What do you mean?' Ami asked puzzled.

'Well, those notes never came from Berlin, you see.'

'You mean they're blossoms?' Karl interjected.

The Pole understood the German word for 'fakes' and grinned. 'Yes, they're *blossoms* all right, but fairly good ones. Wrinkle and dirty 'em up and you'll be able to pass them without too much trouble. Now, here you are.' He

*Town air makes free.

157

passed over the parcels he had been given at their last stopping place. 'There's bread and meat in there. Should last you for a couple of days. After that you're on your own. As you know you can usually get a bowl of soup at a station restaurant and the like without coupons. But don't go begging at any houses,' he added swiftly in warning. 'That'll be a sure sign you're on the run because you're without ration coupons.' He looked at the three young men solemnly and searchingly, as if he were seeing them for the very first time. 'Remember, if you are caught, it will be your death sentence. You have been aided by the Polish underground. In the eyes of the Gestapo that makes you not only deserters but *traitors* to your unhappy country. It will mean the axe.'

The three of them looked grim, for they knew the Pole was right. Capture *would* mean the frock-coated public executioner in his top hat and mask, wielding that razor-sharp gleaming axe. From now onwards they couldn't afford to be caught.

The Pole saw the look. He forced a smile and said, voice warm and encouraging, 'Comrades, you have come so far and experienced so much that God must certainly be with you. So why should He desert you now?' He stretched out his hand. 'As you say in German – *Glück auf* . . . good luck!'

Swiftly and solemnly he shook each one of them by the hand, his grip firm and encouraging. A minute later he was on his way again, striding off swiftly back into his own clandestine life of which they knew nothing.

Suddenly the three of them sensed a feeling of loneliness, even abandonment, as they watched him disappear. For a whole week now someone else had taken over their lives, fed them and housed them, protected them from the police and the Gestapo, and generally made the decisions for them. Now they were on their own again, having to make their own way. As they viewed the distant hills which were Germany, they felt a tingle of fear . . .

The first patrol, four soldiers under the command of a

Corporal, passed through the rough terrain to their front just after midday. The Three Rebels watched the soldiers, middle-aged reservists by the look of them, plod in single file to a copse of winter-bare trees, where on an order from the Corporal, they fell out and smoked a cigarette before returning the way they had come. The Rebels guessed that meant that another patrol covered the area to the right of the copse. What now remained was to find out the intervals between this first patrol and the next. Once they knew that, they could work out the time they had at their disposal to cross the river, pass through the trees and reach the hills, where they supposed they'd be able to hide out safely until the dawn.

But all throughout that long afternoon another patrol stubbornly refused to appear. Once, at about three o'clock, as their limbs began to stiffen in their hiding place with the long wait, they spotted a lone soldier on a bike riding slowly along the path on the far bank of the river. But he was unarmed and they supposed he was just out for a ride in his off-duty time.

By five o'clock their nerves were beginning to fray and Polack, normally so solid and quiet, twice snapped angrily at Ami over the division of the sandwiches that Szwagier had given them. Karl, too, found himself looking at the old watch the Poles had given him more than necessary, feeling a vein at the side of his brow beginning to twitch out of control. Soon, he knew, they had to make a decision one way or the other.

An hour later, as night was beginning to fall and there was still no sign of a second patrol, Karl said, 'Well, Polack and Ami, what do you think?' There was no need of any more explanation; they knew exactly what he meant.

Ami spat drily. 'I'm for trying. If I don't move soon, I'll frigging well take root.'

Polack nodded. 'Me, too. I'm for going, Karl.'

Karl sighed with relief. He was glad they had made a

joint decision. 'All right then, give it another fifteen minutes and we go . . .'

In the end they did not even wait that long. The tension was just too much for them. As if to some unspoken agreement the three of them rose and began to filter to the river, their stiffness gone now, as they tensed for action, their nerves jingling with pent-up excitement and apprehension. Karl gasped as he went into the icy water. But there was no turning back now and this was, he knew, the spot where they were most vulnerable if a patrol came along. They had to get across as quickly as possible.

The others followed. Puffing and shivering at the same time, they waded ever deeper into the slow-moving stream until the water reached their chests and Ami groaned *sotto voce*, 'For God's sake, don't leave me, comrades. I'm shit-scared of deep water.'

But even as he spoke, the water was beginning to grow more shallow and two minutes later they were wading ashore on the muddy bank opposite, blue in the face with cold and shivering violently. Now as the shadow of night started to sweep across the countryside like the wings of some sinister great black bird, they clambered up the bank and into the open ground beyond. Instinctively they crouched, hearts thudding wildly, trying not to step on twigs which would snap noisily under their weight, exerting all their willpower not to run, just in case they were being observed by someone with glasses.

Ahead the trees loomed up out of the evening gloom. They were big ancient oaks, well spread out and still bare from the winter. Karl bit his lip with worry. The damned things wouldn't present much cover, if a patrol *did* appear. The sooner they were through them and moving into the hills beyond the better.

Now they were only a few metres away from the trees and their confidence started to return. It seemed quite easy. Like the rest Karl began to wonder why he had been scared in the first place. Everything was going smoothly.

160

Slightly in the lead Karl pushed into the trees and paused for the others to catch up, wiping the sweat from his forehead. Now to clear the wood. His policy right from the start of taking it step by step was paying off. 'Come on,' he whispered hoarsely and waiting no longer, he set off through the dripping dank oaks, as the other two followed.

They pressed on eagerly, feeling the ground rising under their feet, knowing they were getting ever closer to the safety of the hills beyond; sure that easier times were ahead. Karl, in the lead, felt that a great burden had been lifted from his shoulders. Why, they need not have wasted the whole afternoon waiting for the second patrol which didn't turn up. This was as easy as falling off a log.

The trees began to thin out. Beyond, the hills were outlined a stark jagged black against the lighter gloom of the descending night. They were nearly there now. Karl summoned up more strength. They were nearly through the danger zone. It was working . . . it was working.

'*Halt!*' The sharp command cut into him like a knife.

He stopped, as if petrified.

To his horrified amazement, a tall thin youth in a dark uniform, an air-rifle slung over his skinny shoulder, stepped out of the trees to his right.

Caught completely off-guard, Karl seemed rooted to the spot, as Ami and Polack stumbled to a halt behind him. Out of the trees more youths, all unarmed save for their daggers at the waist, were appearing, some of them in black shorts, their knobbly knees pink with cold.

'The . . . the Hitler Youth!' Ami stuttered in total, absolute amazement. 'It's the Hitler Youth!'

'Hold your mouth, you insolent Polish dog!' the tall blond youth, who looked about sixteen, commanded haughtily. '*Rottenführer* Hartmann,' he snapped, as if he were on a parade ground, 'Commander of Border Patrol, Auxiliary Ten. What are you doing here? You know it's forbidden for Poles to come across here.'

Surprised as he was and shocked, Karl almost blurted

out they were German. But he caught himself in time and, hoping that Polack's accent might fool the cocky Hitler Youth leader, he nodded to his comrade.

'We are Poles, coming to Germany to work,' Polack stuttered hastily. But as always he was not a convincing liar and he actually blushed as he said the words, and reached for the document their guide had given them.

Rottenführer Hartmann did not deign to look at it. 'You know this is not a legal crossing point,' he barked, while his band gazed at him in awe, something of which he was well aware. 'You should have crossed at one of the two bridges where there are proper German authorities to verify your identity.'

'I'm very sorry, *Herr Rottenführer*,' Karl said rapidly, hoping that he hit the right servile note. 'We won't do it again. We'll just go back and –' He turned and seemed about to go, but *Rottenführer* Hartmann was quicker. '*Stehenbleiben!* Do not move from the spot!' he commanded icily, obviously enjoying this moment of triumph. 'In our New Germany, we do not do things like that. You must come with us to Neustedt. *Kontrolle!*' He barked the word, as if it were explanation enough in itself. 'Krueger and Hurwitz – form up left and right of the prisoners. The rest of you to the rear. *Marsch . . . marsch!*'

Dutifully the little boys in their short pants, hands on their Hitler Youth daggers, doubled off to take up their positions all around the 'prisoners' before a bewildered Karl could react.

For one wild moment he thought of attacking the silly little boys, playing soldiers with their toy weapons. But what would they do with them? In order to silence them, the Three Rebels would have to kill the lot of 'em – and he knew they wouldn't be able to do that.

Karl did not know what to do and numbly he surrendered to events. Thus it was that after two years of total war the Three Rebels returned to their homeland, prisoners of a bunch of little boys in short trousers.

BOOK THREE

In the Reich

CHAPTER 1

The Three Rebels sat miserably on the wooden bench to the front of the rickety old bus which was taking them to the county jail. Behind them the Polish-German miners, setting off for their morning shift, remained huddled in silence or talked in undertones, shooting constant glances in the direction of the 'prisoners', as they were now named ever since their proud schoolboy captors had handed them over to the local policeman at Neustedt.

But the big heavy-set Gestapo man who had been sent to guard them on the way to the county jail for questioning heard neither the whispering nor saw the covert looks. He sat next to the driver near the door, muffled in his ankle-length green leather coat, puffing at his stump of a cigar and obviously feeling very full of himself. He was Gestapo, wasn't he? This Polack border-pack were scared of him, weren't they? As for the dejected young prisoners, he'd seen plenty of their kind in these past few years - yellow-bellied cowards, trying to dodge the column, while in Russia their pals were having their turnips blown off by the thousand. No, *Kommissar* Dirkmann had nothing to worry about; and if there was any kind of trouble, which he strongly doubted, he had a nice little neat Walther pistol in his pocket. It was only a seven millimetre, but it'd blow a big frigging hole in anybody fool enough to tangle with it. No, Dirkmann thought, he'd have no trouble on this particular early morning. He had taken one look at his prisoners in the driver's mirror and they had been suitably subdued and crestfallen. The cowardly young swine had no fight left in 'em, he concluded.

But while Karl's face presented a picture of resigned depression, as if he had already come to terms with his

165

fate, his mind raced desperately. He knew that once the Gestapo man delivered them to the county jail at Neustedt, they were finished. A regular German prison would be virtually impossible to break out of.

So, if they were going to do anything, it would have to be done before they reached Neustedt, wherever that place was. He was confident that the three of them could handle the middle-aged, self-confident Gestapo man even if he were armed. After four years at the front they knew a few tricks he had not even dreamed of. But what would the reaction of the civilians be, if they tackled him, that was the question. Most of them were 'water-Polacks', normally scared of their own shadows. But the miners were big burly men, who might well spring to the aid of the Gestapo man in order to save their own skins . . .

Karl tried to reason their problem out. Would there be mines inside this place Neustedt, he asked himself, as the dreary Silesian countryside rolled by outside, flat, featureless and unlovely? Hardly likely, he told himself, hope beginning to well up slowly inside him. The nice stuffy citizens of the average German town with its highly-polished windows and spotless streets wouldn't particularly welcome a dirty coalmine in their midst, would they?

But if the mines to which these men were travelling were, as he now hoped, located on this side of Neustedt, what chance would there be of getting rid of the driver and Gestapo man before they reached the town itself? Little, he concluded, unless they worked very fast and had a plan already prepared to be put into operation once the bus had started up once more. He bit his lower lip with worry and felt his palms beginning to grow greasy with sweat despite the cold interior of the bus. God Almighty, he told himself a little bitterly, there are too many 'ifs'!

Time went by. Now they were beginning to pass dirty white little cottages, with smoke coming straight from the chimneys into the still grey sky; skinny pigs rooted in the fields round about. One-time Polish territory, Karl told

166

himself, before the Reich had incorporated this part of Silesia into its lands back in 1939. Although their guide back at the river had told them not to trust anyone once they passed into the Reich, he felt that the locals, if they were originally Polish, would not betray them deliberately. That was some consolation. He craned his neck. To their front and right he could see the typical stork-legged tower surmounted by a great wheel, of the winding-shafts. They were entering the coal-mining zone. He tensed.

Behind them the miners started to stir. He heard a couple of them say in Polish '*gruba*'. It was almost identical to the German word '*Grube*' – and it meant 'pit'. Were these the pits that employed the miners on the bus? He began to pray – *hard*.

Packed next to him in the tight wooden seat, Ami nudged Karl carefully and nodded slyly in the direction of the front. The Gestapo man's head had fallen to his chest, revealing the rolls of fat on his bull-neck beneath the black felt hat, which was as much the uniform of his calling as the leather coat. He was dozing off. Karl nodded back. If only the miners would get off soon and leave the three of them with the driver and the big Gestapo man! It was their last chance. He prayed even harder.

Polack cocked his head to one side to listen to the miners' conversations, then he turned to Ami, eyes fixed on the Gestapo man's fat neck, and whispered something. Ami did the same, moving his head almost painfully slowly, as if it were worked by rusty springs. He didn't want to rouse the Gestapo man's suspicions. 'Polack says,' he whispered as they had once done back at Camp Death in what now seemed another age, 'the lot of them are getting off here – it's the main pit.' Karl breathed a fervent sigh of relief. His prayers had been answered. There *was* a God after all!

A minute later the driver started to double de-clutch, the gears of the ancient bus protesting noisily, and they began to slow down. In front of them the pit complex loomed up large: a collection of shabby buildings, great

167

heaps of coal glistening in the morning dew, and all dominated by the great wheel of the haulage cage.

Behind them the miners began lighting their last cigarettes before they went underground, pulling their gear and sandwiches from the racks, a few of them tugging down little cages with a wildly-protesting canary inside.

'*Grube Erika*,' the scrawny unshaven driver announced. '*Alle aussteigen – Endstation – Grube Erika!*' Then with a quick look at the Gestapo man who had woken from his doze, he repeated the same information in Polish. Karl shook his head in mock disbelief. Why had everyone to be so damned self-important? Surely all the occupants of the rickety bus knew where they worked? Then he dismissed the matter and concentrated on the task at hand.

One by one the miners filed by them, avoiding looking at the prisoners as if the latter were stricken by some illness that might infect them, while the Gestapo man at the door tugged up his collar grumpily at the sudden blast of icy air.

Barely had the last miner passed by, when he cried to the driver, '*Mach' schnell*. Close the shitting door! That wind's enough to freeze up yer outside plumbing!'

'*Jawohl, Herr Kommissar*,' the driver quavered, for he too was a 'water-Polack' and was scared. Hurriedly he turned the handle at the wheel which closed the door. Next moment he thrust home first gear and released the clutch. The bus began to draw away slowly.

The Gestapo man flung his prisoners a quick look in the rearview mirror and settled more comfortably in his seat once more. But this time he didn't doze off and Karl knew why.

On the horizon, silhouetted a stark black by the first thin yellow rays of the winter sun, he could see the outline of a small Silesian town: a long spread of one-storey houses centred on a green sheathed church steeple. That would be Neustedt, he guessed. There was no time to be lost. Even at the thirty kilometres an hour the bus was travelling, they'd be there in ten to fifteen minutes. It was now or never.

He nudged Ami and, indicating he should watch the Gestapo man, Karl bent down as if casually, though his heart was thumping like a trip-hammer with suppressed excitement. He fumbled with his right boot . . . The Poles had removed their old *Wehrmacht* dice-beakers. The man with the beard had explained that they would have given them away: Polish civilians wearing German jackboots would have been immediately suspect. In their place the Three Rebels had been given typically Polish boots. They were scuffed and well-worn, but possessed good leather soles and leather laces, white and untreated on one side, which one tied by winding them round the metal studs that ran right up the boots' front.

Now, hardly daring to breathe and aware that the Gestapo man could turn at any moment and demand to know what he was doing, Karl started to unwind the right lace, his fingers trembling and without sensation, feeling like clumsy sausages.

He finished. In dumb show he indicated to Polack at the far end to watch the driver when he moved. Polack nodded his understanding. Ami flashed Karl a frightened look. Karl was twisting the leather boot-lace between his hands, pulling it hard to tense its strength. It held. Ami swallowed. To have to do something like that in cold blood! He thanked God it was Karl and not he who was going to do it.

Now they were rumbling along a wooded stretch, the driver changing down to second gear as they began to take an incline. Karl flashed a glance behind him. The winding rural road was deserted. He darted a look at the tightly-packed firs on both sides. There were no hunters about or toffee-nosed foresters in their green uniforms. It had to be now. He drew a deep breath and launched himself forward. In the mirror the skinny little driver had spotted him. He opened his mouth to yell a warning. Too late. Karl had slipped the leather thong around the Gestapo man's fat neck and tugged hard. His sudden cry of surprise was stifled abruptly, as the lace dug deep into his throat.

The Gestapo man stiffened at once, hands clawing at the thong, his spine arched, as he exerted all his strength to loosen that terrible killing grip. Desperately Karl held on. His knee slammed into the back of the seat so that *he* could exert more pressure. Horrible gurgling noises started to come from the demented man. His face began to grow crimson as his eyes bulged.

Now Polack had seized the driver's right hand. 'Keep on driving,' he commanded in Polish, while Ami sneaking beneath Karl had felt in the official's pocket and found the pistol which was hidden there. He had noticed the bulge as they first entered the bus.

'*Karl!*' he cried desperately, as the Gestapo man's eyes started to turn upwards, a sign that he was passing out. Death was not far away. 'Karl, for God's sake.' Frantically he grabbed at Karl's arm and tried to break that murderous grip.

'I've got his pistol . . . It's all right . . . *Let go of him!*'

The Gestapo man gave one last sigh, and then his struggles ceased. He went limp in the same moment that Karl gave a kind of convulsive shiver like a man in the last throes of a fit and croaked in a voice that Ami could barely hear, 'Is he . . . is he dead?'

Ami listened at the man's chest for a moment. 'No,' he said straightening up. 'But he damn well nearly was, thanks to you, you crazy –' He stopped short. Karl wasn't listening; his gaze was fixed on some remote horizon, known only to him.

For what seemed an age, they froze in position like bad actors at the end of some melodrama, while the bus rumbled on through the woods, the driver blubbering to himself in absolute terror and praying for mercy in Polish.

Then the spell was broken. With fingers that shook badly, Karl eased the lace from the unconscious Gestapo man's swollen throat. It wasn't a pleasant job. The lace had bitten cruelly into his soft flesh and there was a livid crimson weal there now.

Meanwhile Polack rapped out an order for the driver to slow down, as Ami began to remove the Gestapo man's belt and use it to strap his hands behind his back. It seemed the obvious thing to do. But he avoided Karl's gaze as he did so, for he knew just as Karl did that they should have killed the fat cop there and then. It would have solved a lot of problems. Now they had to find some means of disposing of him, where he wouldn't be able to talk for a while.

This was the quandary which occupied Karl's mind, as the town of Neustedt came ever closer. So even as he started to formulate his plan, he acted. With the butt of the cop's pistol, he smashed the rearview mirror so the driver couldn't see what was going on without turning round. He indicated to Ami to watch the badly-frightened man and motioned to Polack to follow him to the rear of the bus where the emergency door was located. Quietly he turned the handle to Open.

'Listen, Polack,' he whispered, 'I am trying to trick the driver. In a minute I want you to speak – in Polish, which we know he understands – and say that after we reach Beuthen, we'll head south for Bavaria by train. From Munich we'll have a crack at the Swiss frontier. Got that?'

'Got it, Karl. Train from Beuthen to Munich . . . crack at the Swiss frontier.'

'Exactly. Of course, we'll be going in the opposite direction but when they question the driver, *that* might set them off on a wild goose chase – for a while at least. Right, here we go. Do your bit!'

As Karl walked back up the aisle, Polack repeated what he said in Polish and Karl hoped that the driver wasn't too frightened to take it in. He waited. Then he snapped to the driver, 'How far is it to Beuthen?'

'A hundred kilometres, sir,' the man replied.

'Have you got enough petrol to get there?' Karl demanded.

'To Beuthen?' the man asked stupidly. 'But I'm not authorised to use my petrol ration for that. My trip ticket doesn't allow it.' He looked at the unconscious Gestapo man slumped in the next seat, as if expecting confirmation of his statement from him.

'Can you make it to Beuthen?' Karl asked menacingly, flourishing the little pistol.

'Yes . . . yessir . . . naturally,' the driver quavered, his face turning even paler.

'Right. Then if you value your life, you miserable swine,' Karl, remembering the dialogue from the pre-war gangster movies he had liked so much as a kid in Hamburg, talked rough and tough, though he felt a fool for doing so in order to frighten the poor wretch, 'you'll get us there. *Clear?*'

'Clear, sir,' the man said hastily.

'Then drive straight through Neustedt and don't let anything or anybody stop you, if you know what's good for you.' He emphasised his threat by digging the driver in the ribs with the pistol. The poor fellow looked as if he might have a heart attack at any moment. 'Put the *Private* sign up.'

Hastily, with his free hand, the driver started to turn the handle that altered the display unit outside on top of the cab, while Karl, grinning despite the tenseness of the situation, made threatening noises at the back of his throat.

Five minutes later they were rattling through the little Silesian market town and heading north-west towards Beuthen. Karl relaxed. Next to him on the seat, keeping an eye on the still-unconscious Gestapo man, Ami said a little wearily, 'So far so good. But what next?'

Karl forced a grin. 'Must I say it, Ami?' he answered.

Now it was Ami's turn to grin. 'I know . . . I know . . .' he said. '*Step by frigging step . . .*'

CHAPTER 2

'Heil Hitler, Herr Oberkriminalrat,' the Gestapo man, his throat now muffled in a thick bandage, said hoarsely and flung out his right arm in salute.

Hans Meissner, the head of Beuthen's *Kripo**, smiled sardonically, flipped up his own arm from where he sat behind his big square desk, and said, 'Bullshit, Horst! Sit down and take the weight off your feet.' He thrust the silver cigarette box across the desk towards the other official.

'Have a lung torpedo – and puff the smoke out hard so that I can enjoy it, will you. The sawbones say I can't smoke or I'll snuff it five years earlier than normal. Some crap like that.'

'Yes, Hans.' The other man hesitated a little about the familiar form of address to such an exalted official, but after all they had been young detectives together before 1933. He took the cigarette and lit it, as commanded. He exhaled noisily.

Hans Meissner's thin clever face beneath the thatch of snowy white hair broke into a slight smile as he breathed in the cigarette smoke. What a fool he was to take any notice of the sawbones and stint himself of such exquisite pleasure. No cigarettes, no alcòhol, probably soon they'd insist he stopped bedding Lise. And what did it all matter? None of them would survive the damned war anyway. He saw the big fool opposite him was looking at him expectantly, so he said, 'Well, old house, you've certainly been to the wars by the look of you. Your local branch telephoned a report through to me two hours ago. But please tell me again what happened.'

*German CID.

173

The Gestapo man drew a deep breath and began, 'I was duly carrying out the orders of my senior officer to escort three prisoners . . .'

Hans Meissner sat back, eyes closed as if he were absorbing the information with all his faculties. In reality, he was bored stiff with the plodding fool and his police jargon. Why couldn't cops talk like other people? They were always 'proceeding' instead of 'walking' in the 'pursu-ance of their duty' – what else should they be doing? They were paid for it, weren't they? – and all the rest of that pseudo-legal claptrap. God, had he once really talked like that when he and the plodding fool had been young officers together before '33?

Upstairs he could hear Lise using the vacuum cleaner in his private quarters and he allowed himself a moment's indulgence as he thought of her dark, hairy Jewish body underneath the black silk overall she wore on such occasions. He concluded yet again, as he dismissed the lovely image, that he was a very lucky sixty year old, to be able to bed a twenty-two year old woman, even if she was Jewish.

'So that was it, Hans,' the other man was saying. 'When I came to, here I was in Beuthen and the swine had hopped out of the bus's emergency exit without that fool of a driver noticing them go. *Himmel, Arsch und Wolkenbruch,*' he snorted, suddenly furious. 'If I could get my hands on the young bastards, I'd . . . I'd . . .'

'Well, the way you're going at it, my dear Horst, I'm afraid that possibility is definitely remote,' Meissner said urbanely. He rose and smoothed down his elegant black tunic. He turned and stared out of the window at the street scene below.

Beuthen was busy. Since the war the place had really prospered. Standing in the middle of the coal, iron and zinc industries of Upper Silesia, which were always crying out for ever more workers to feed the booming armaments industry, there was plenty of money in Beuthen these days.

174

And plenty of new people, too, he told himself, adding to the hundred thousand citizens who had lived here before 1939. Not only Germans, either, but Poles, Russians, French and Belgians. There was a whole sub-stratum of foreigners, black marketeers, petty crooks and the like in which three deserters, if they were smart enough, could 'take a dive', as the inhabitants of the *milieu* called it.

Somehow, he mused, as he watched the streetwalker across the way pounding the pavement on the lookout for some male ready for a quick hectic five minutes in the *Bahnhofshotel* opposite, he did not think these particular three would stay in Beuthen. No, they'd be too smart for that. Even crowded as the city was these days, they'd be found sooner or later.

He swung round on a waiting Horst. 'Nebe* in Berlin called me an hour ago and told me I was in charge of the investigation. Himmler has agreed to it personally.'

His visitor was suitably impressed and Meissner smiled softly to himself. Horst had always been impressed by names and titles. It made him a bad cop. Outward show should never impress a policeman. 'Apparently,' he went on, 'your three fugitives are connected with the killing of a Camp Commandant at the place they originally escaped from – and that particular, unfortunate officer was once received and decorated by the Führer himself. So,' he shrugged his thin shoulders, 'when the Führer is involved in anything, things start to move.'

'Nothing should distract the Führer from his task of leading us to victory,' Horst said routinely, using the current slogan.

Meissner looked at him pityingly, as if he were not altogether right in the head. 'Now then, Horst,' he said briskly, 'let's cut the crap and get down to cases. These three young men are not your average deserter. They have made their way through Western Russia and Poland – both parts, and

*Head of the *Kripo*.

have succeeded in reaching the Reich. Quite an achievement without money, documents and so on. So it will not be a matter of just carrying out routine raids and document checks until we find them. I feel they are too shrewd for that.'

'Well, we know where they are headed for, Hans,' the other man said with renewed brightness. 'As I have detailed in my report the driver heard one of them say in Polish they would proceed to Munich and from there –'

'Horst,' Meissner interrupted the sudden flow of words firmly. 'If you believe that kind of shit, you'll believe that *Reichsführer* Himmler's grandmother was a Kiev Jewess called Sarah – and that his father had his dick docked by the chief rabbi!'

Horst looked shocked as if he had just uttered a grievous blasphemy. For his part, Meissner grinned. He didn't give a damn what Horst – or anyone else for that matter – thought of him. He was a doomed man and he knew it. Once the Russians came – and they would – they'd string him up from the nearest lamp-post without asking too many questions. That was the price he was going to have to pay for the fancy black uniform with its Swastika badge, the big salary and all the rest of the trimmings which went with being a police officer in the service of an empire whose leader had boasted it would last one thousand years.

'It was a plant, you big booby, a very obvious plant,' Meissner went on swiftly. 'Those three boys are smart. They'd know they wouldn't have a chance in hell of getting over the Swiss frontier. No, they will be heading in a totally different direction – and which direction will that be?' It was a rhetorical question, which he answered himself. 'As they can't go east and want you to think they're heading south but aren't, that leaves us west and north, doesn't it?'

'Yes, Hans,' Horst replied uncertainly, obviously confused now.

'From what you say the one said in Polish, it is clear

that they intend to cross into a neutral country. So what other neutral country is left in the west?'

Horst pouted his lips, as if thinking hard, though in reality all he wanted to do was to get away from Meissner, the prick, have a stiff drink and go to bed to rest his sore throat. 'There isn't one,' he said after a few moments.

'Exactly. That leaves us the north – and Sweden.'

'Of course – *Sweden!* I never thought of that.'

'Exactly. That, my dear Horst, is why you are a simple *Kommissar* and I am *Oberkriminalrat*,' Meissner said, smiling at the other man's discomfiture. 'And how does one get to Sweden?' Again he answered his own question. 'Why, one takes a boat and boats sail from ports.' Now he had had enough of toying with his dim-witted, former colleague. 'So that means three ports come into the question, the ones which service the traffic with those fat Swedish cats across the Baltic. They are Rostock, Wismar and Lübeck.' He ticked the names off with his elegantly-manicured fingers. 'Now it would be a tall order to run special security on all three ports. The local security people have enough problems on their hands with all those damned English POWs playing silly buggers and running away to the ports all the time only to be caught.' He sniffed. 'Those Tommies really do think this war is one big game of cricket or whatever the thing they play is called. So we have to decide on one of three on which to concentrate our effort. But which, Horst, *which?'*

Horst pretended to think once more. Now his neck really was hurting like hell. He wished he could just go to bed.

Meissner tapped the dossier in front of him on the desk, and quoted from it from memory. He was good at this. In the old days when he had been ambitious, his virtually-photographic memory had always impressed superiors. *'Carstens, Karl. Born 1920,'* he recited, *'Hamburg-Billstedt. Education Billstedt Volkschule. Occupation: Slater and Tiler. Mustered for the Wehrmacht 1939*, blah, blah, blah. Hamburg-Billstedt – that's a real red working-class district, my information tells me, and where did little working-class boys from Hamburg-Billstedt go for their holidays before the war? Why, Horst, they went to the seaside at Travemünde, an hour away from Hamburg by train. And where is Travemünde located?' He paused and waited like a schoolmaster for some reluctant, not too bright pupil.

'In the Bay of Lübeck,' Horst answered hesitantly.

'*Genau.* So what is my guess, Horst? It's this. They'll head for the port that is familiar to one of them – this fellow Carstens. They'll head for Lübeck. Now I want you to do one thing for me, Horst, before you get off to bed.'

The other man brightened up. He was being released at last. 'What?'

'Tell your office to inform their local Gestapo branches in Hamburg-Billstedt and Koblenz-Guels, where the other one Doepfgen was born, to check out the families. They might go there first for money, food, clothes – you know the sort of thing. I shall take care of the rest.'

'What will you do, Hans?'

'Why, I'll go to Lübeck, Horst, and take over personally. It'll be a little jaunt for me, get me out of the office.' He smiled winningly, but his clever, faded eyes didn't light up and Horst told himself Hans Meissner had always been a clever bugger – look where he'd got with his poor education! But he was getting old and too cocky by half. As for what he had just said about *Reichsführer* Himmler, Christ, he had slapped a lot of people behind Swedish curtains for saying much less than that about the *Prominenz*. One day, Meissner would open his big mouth a bit too wide and then the clock would be really in the pisspot.

So they chatted for a few more minutes about old times, before shaking hands and wishing each other '*Hals und Beinbruch*'*, as they had done in the old days when they had been rookie detectives together. Then the fat Gestapo man with the bandaged throat left, but before he went out

*Literally 'Break your neck and bones'. Roughly, 'happy landings'.

178

Meissner called to him from his desk, 'Oh, there is one other thing, Horst.'

'Yes, Hans?'

Meissner was quite serious. 'If I were you, I'd get out of the service this year, while there's still time.'

It was only later when he was outside in the busy street that Horst remembered that he should have asked what Meissner had meant by 'while there's still time'. But he hadn't. Instead he'd said, somewhat puzzled, 'But I haven't got enough years in for my pension, Hans.'

Then Meissner had laughed for no reason that he could account for and said, waving his hand in dismissal, 'Oh yes, that precious pension. Naturally, you can't afford to lose that, can you now?'

But as it turned out *Kommissar* Horst Dirkmann never did get that pension which undoubtedly was his right after so much loyal service to Kaiser, President and Führer. In February 1945 when the Russians came he was denounced and crucified, spreadeagled to the door of his own office in Neustedt. One of the crowd of drunken Red Army infantrymen stuck one of his own cigars in his mouth before he staggered off to the front, leaving the policeman to die with it still alight and smoking.

If *Oberkriminalrat* Hans Meissner had been alive to hear of the incident he would undoubtedly have been amused and saddened by it. But by then he was long dead himself. Now, however, as only a handful of kilometres away the Three Rebels lay buried deep beneath a load of coal in one of the railway trucks which would bear this Silesian 'black gold' to Berlin's fuel-hungry war factories, and waited impatiently for the goods train to commence its journey, Hans Meissner prepared for his.

As always he was meticulous, for Meissner's rise from detective to head of Silesia's CID was due not only to his sharp mind, but also to the care and thoroughness with which he operated. He called his deputy and gave him his instructions for the next few days. That was followed by a

179

call to the public prosecutor to inform him of his coming absence. No doubt Dr Klaus von Eberhardt, the official in question, was curious as to why such a senior man should absent himself on a relatively trivial case. But Meissner's own private archive contained some interesting episodes in the public prosecutor's personal life (as it did on most officials with whom Meissner dealt) which he would not want disclosed and so Dr Klaus von Eberhardt kept his thoughts to himself.

Within the hour, all was prepared and well-pleased with himself, Meissner crossed to the window again and gazed out. The 'pavement-pounder' had vanished. Obviously she was giving some lusty young serviceman his five minutes inside the *Bahnhofshotel*. He smiled at the mental picture and then thought of Lise upstairs, naked beneath the black overall. Lust stirred faintly in his loins. He looked at his image in the glass of the window and told himself that despite his snowy white hair and that heart condition the sawbones said he had, he wasn't doing so badly for a man of sixty. What better way to start his jaunt – his little holiday – than by dancing the mattress polka with Lise, even though it was only just on noon?

He crossed swiftly to his desk. He unlocked the secret drawer at its bottom and took out the little bottle of ether which she needed on such occasions. Why, he had been too delicate to ask. Even at his age he required no such stimuli, no booze, no black stockings, no little perversions – nothing. His mind and body did everything for him.

He smiled at the thought and tucked the bottle away carefully in the pocket of his elegant black tunic. He took one last look round his office to see everything was in order. It was – as always. Then he left, striding down the corridor which led to the stairs briskly, seemingly a happy man.

CHAPTER 3

Even in the brave winter sunshine, Lübeck didn't look too good, Meissner thought. It had never recovered from the Tommies' devastating fire-raid back in '42 and since then the 'air terrorists', as the radio now called the English Air Force, had attacked the port regularly once a month. There were great gaps in the medieval, half-timbered houses which made up the centre and even as the ancient wood-burning cab started to creak its way up to their hotel, he could see shattered ruins still smouldering here and there from the last attack.

But if Lübeck looked as if it was on its last legs, the streets were bustling and busy with young fit men in the uniform of the *Kriegsmarine* and the dark blue of the Merchant Marine and the fleets of half a dozen Baltic nations. Here and there he could pick out the blue and yellow emblem of the Swedes. They, too, were well-represented in the streets and obviously sought-after by the whores who were standing at every corner. 'Fat cats,' he muttered to himself a little resentfully at the sight. The young sailors would have the real bean coffee and silk stockings that the girls wanted more than money.

At his side, Lise took in the sights without interest. Her dark unpretty face was set in her usual sulk. He smiled, slightly amused. Here she was, probably the last surviving Jew in Lübeck whose fate lay completely in his hands – he could send her to the camps at the drop of a hat if he wished and no questions asked – yet still she sulked. It was as if she were some rich spoiled society beauty instead of a gawky, quite plain fugitive from National Socialist justice – if there were such a thing.

When he had first taken up with her in 1941 – she had

181

been betrayed to him by a water-Polack who had been hiding her for a price – he had told her, when she asked why he protected her, that she was his 'insurance, just in case'. For quite a while he had called her *'meine Versicherung, meine süsse kleine Versicherung'*. It had amused him to do so.

But after his wife was killed in the great raid on Cologne in '42 and Erich, his son, had vanished in the East – 'missing believed killed in action' – he no longer called her 'my sweet little insurance'. No insurance seemed of any importance any more. Besides, he was in too deeply now to be saved, whatever he did. He had forgotten that old adage which he learned at his grandmother's knee, when he had been a God-fearing tame little choir-boy, 'Hans, you know what they say – if you eat soup with the devil, you need a long spoon.' Unfortunately for him now, he *had* eaten soup with the devil for too long, and he hadn't used the right kind of spoon.

But Lise suited him. Despite her moods, her virtual ugliness, her unfortunate perversions, he got on well enough with her. Just as he was cut off from what went on all around him through his knowledge of what was soon to come, she was separated from that same world on account of her race. This meant that neither of them indulged in the silly small talk with which most people waste ninety per cent of their time. Both lived in cocoons of their own making and when they spoke to each other what they said was direct enough and seemed to be of some importance.

The taxi swerved to avoid an old woman in a rusty-black coat, wearily shovelling the 'horse-apples' left by a lean-ribbed old nag pulling a cart laden with sailors, heading back to their ship. It then started to slow down as they approached the hotel *Zum Holsten Tor*, named after the port's most famous landmark. Though at this particular moment the Holsten Tower did not look very impressive. Its roof had gone in some fire-raid or other and now the

182

place was covered with tarpaulins, while all the upstairs windows were bricked up.

'Dump!' Lise said as the taxi came to a halt. 'What are we doing in here? Dump!'

He didn't answer. She had already made up her mind. Instead, he got out first and opened the door for her gallantly, while the ancient porter, minus his collar, shuffled forward in carpet slippers to collect their cases. Five minutes later they were in their room, one with both windows intact and looking out over the dock area. It was busy with small naval craft and battered merchant ships, and next to the lean grey dangerous shapes of two U-boats, lay a large merchantman with a Swedish flag painted prominently on its rusty sides.

For a moment or two Meissner stared at the ship thoughtfully. Then his gaze ran along the dock itself. It was, of course, sealed off with the old pre-war brick wall, surmounted now with high concertina wire, and there were armed guards from the *Kriegsmarine* at the main gate. But there was a tramline running straight into the place to the left from the direction of the suburbs, which he suspected would be wide open when the dockers and harbour personnel went on and off-shift.

There had to be hundreds of civvies working on the docks, too, he calculated. Everywhere down there cranes were rattling, riveters busy at their task, carts trundling back and forth bringing in men and supplies. It was like one huge factory with the roof taken off to reveal the human hustle and bustle below. He concluded that the port of Lübeck would not be too difficult to penetrate for three determined men.

Meissner turned to Lise, his clever face thoughtful. She was already lying on the bed moodily puffing at yet another cigarette, the cases untouched, her stockinged feet resting on his uniform coat. She hadn't even bothered to take off her hat, which he had insisted she should wear for the hotel reception. He was still oddly embarrassed to be seen with a woman so much younger than himself. He thought a hat made her look older. Not that he had any cause to be worried by what receptionists – or anyone else for that matter – thought. The sight of his police uniform either made people shut up like a clam or turned them into sycophantic toadies.

'Why?' she asked suddenly, as outside a tramload of drunken sailors rattled by, all of them singing *Wir Fahren Gegen Eng-geland** at the tops of their voices. He smiled softly. They'd never 'sail against England' again.

'Why what?'

'Why this stupid jaunt, as you call it, to Lübeck to try to capture your three deserters? Why is the *Herr Oberkriminalrat*,' she emphasised the title contemptuously, 'interested in the fates of three common deserters?' She puffed at her cigarette and looked at the peeling, bomb-cracked ceiling above the bed.

'I've told you already. The Führer is interested, Lise.'

'I don't believe you. You could have sent one of your stooges. Nobody would have known.'

He hesitated a moment, wondering yet again at her directness. Most Jews he had known since 1933 had been craven people, frightened by the enormity of this thing which was happening to them. She, on the other hand, was not scared one little bit. He smiled and said, 'Yes, you're right. What I just said was bullshit.' He rubbed his chin thoughtfully. 'Why should I concern myself with the fates of three common deserters? Perhaps Lise, it's because I don't want them to escape our coming – well, whatever's going to happen to us sooner or later. Why should they get away with it – and live happily ever afterwards, as they used to say in the fairy stories when I was a kid?'

She stubbed out her cigarette almost savagely, then lit another one. 'A miserable little motive, don't you think?

---

*Nazi marching song 'We're sailing against England'.

184

Why shouldn't they have a chance if they can get away with it?'

'They're German and if you're German, you are a condemned man, I know it. One day we Germans are going to change places with you Jews. We'll be pariahs, the outcasts, the victims. So why should they dodge it? Let us all swim – *and sink* – together.'

'Nice philosophy of life, even for a cop and an old man like you,' she said, retreating into her own private world once more, the subject apparently forgotten. 'Hm!'

He waited a moment before saying, 'All right, I'm going down to the Harbour Police and other places. I'll be back for the evening meal. I'll take you out somewhere special. A place like this is sure to have some sort of black market restaurant where they don't require food coupons.' He chuckled. 'I'll ask the local cops – they'll know.' He picked up his cap and pulled his coat from beneath her. She made no response. But as he reached the door she called, without taking her dark gaze off the flaking ceiling, 'Bring some more ether . . . I'm out . . .'

Hauptmann Brandt was a big, hearty, confident man with a red face, the product of too much schnapps and the fierce north wind which seemed, to Meissner at least, to be coming right down the Baltic straight from Siberia. Brandt had been in charge of harbour security ever since he had left the *Kriegsmarine* to join the Water Police and he thought he had it all tied up. As the two of them strode along the jetty, with the waves whipping up white and angry against the stones below, he said loudly and proudly, 'Never had a deserter or Tommy POW get through yet, *Herr Oberkriminalrat*.' He tugged the dewdrop off the end of his swollen red nose and tossed it expertly into the Baltic. 'They'd have to get up pretty early in the morning to catch old Bernard Brandt with his knickers down about his ankles. Of that you can be certain.'

'Yes, of course,' Meissner said, only half-listening, his

eyes taking in the big rusting Swedish merchantman which he had especially asked to see. 'What's their usual ploy?'

'Pretty routine. They don't show much imagination. Two ways. They try to brownass Swedish sailors in the bars where they hang out. Buy 'em plenty of firewater – and by God don't those Swedes like their firewater – and then try to get them to take them aboard their ships. Or they go at it directly and smuggle themselves aboard. Sooner or later they're discovered by the crew or they surrender themselves to the Captain and ask to be taken to Sweden.'

'Both seem pretty easy ways of getting on a neutral ship to me,' Meissner murmured.

'Of course they are,' Brandt agreed easily. 'But the Swedish Captains are not going to risk their tickets hiding our deserters or the Tommies, are they? We ban them from any further trade with the Reich. So,' he shrugged, 'they turn them in to us every time.'

Meissner nodded, still eyeing the Swedish ship, calculating how he might get aboard unseen if he were a fit desperate young man on the run.

'To make sure,' Brandt went on, 'I mean a Captain could be bribed . . . The Water Police do spot checks on all neutral ships just within the Reich's six kilometre zone out to sea. So if they had taken a bribe to hide a fugitive, they could still be caught out. No Captain is prepared to take that risk.'

'So in theory then,' Meissner said slowly, formulating his words as he thought them, 'the only chance a fugitive has of escaping on one of those Swedish tubs is by hiding himself on the ship without the knowledge of the Captain and crew?'

'Exactly.' Brandt beamed at him. '*In theory*! In practice they haven't got a cat's chance in hell. My boys know every nook and cranny aboard those Swedish tubs. After all, all of my boys have been seamen themselves at one time or another. They know from their own experience

186

where a sailor-boy stows his bit of extra baccy or some firewater – the usual sort of contraband sailors try to smuggle through customs. No, *Herr Oberkriminalrat*, your tame deserters haven't –'

'*Herr Hauptmann . . . Herr Hauptmann!*' an excited voice broke into his words. They swung round.

A fat policeman pedalling away furiously was coming down the wet jetty towards them, waving his free hand excitedly.

Brandt cupped his big red hands to his mouth and yelled, 'Have a care, Otto! Not so fast . . . You're going to bust a gut in zero comma nothing seconds, if you go at it like that . . .'

'But it's for the *Oberkriminalrat*,' the fat cop yelled back excitedly, while a group of drunken sailors from the *Kriegsmarine*, the ribbons of their caps flying in the breeze, laughed and clapped and jeered, 'Now what are you up to, officer, don't you know you're breaking the speed limit?'

The fat cop ignored them. With a great flourish, he braked in a curve in front of the two police officers and stumbled to attention. 'Beg permission to report, sir?' he gasped, noting Hans Meissner's high rank.

'Oh, come off it, Otto,' Brandt snapped. 'We're not back in the frigging police depot now, you know. We're too old for that kind of bull.'

'Yessir. I agree, sir,' Otto said dutifully and turned to Meissner.

'Beg to report, sir – er,' he corrected himself hastily while one of the drunken seamen pulled out a *Kielersprotten** and stuck the yellow-smoked fish in front of his flies, crying, 'Oh, look at me, girls. I'm a frigging smoked mermaid!'

The others fell about with wild laughter while the fat policemen cried above the noise, 'Message just come in for you, sir, from Gestapo, Hamburg.'

Meissner nodded. 'Well, fire away, man. What is it?'

*A smoked sprat caught in the Kiel Bay.

'The suspects have been located, sir.'

'In Hamburg-Billstedt?'

'Yessir.' Otto looked a bit surprised at Meissner's knowledge.

'And what is being done about it?'

'Gestapo Hamburg reports that they are proceeding with the apprehension of the suspects forthwith, sir. Just wanted to inform you, sir, as a matter of routine procedure.'

At any other time Meissner might have pulled the fat, self-important policeman's leg on account of his excess use of police jargon. But this day he didn't. Somehow he felt a sense of let-down that the three deserters had been caught already. His 'jaunt' was over before it had really commenced. What a shame!

CHAPTER 4

'*Polente!*'* the skinny blond boy on the bike gasped, as he slammed open the door of the little working man's cottage at the end of the lane, gave his information and then started pedalling off again as fast as he could.

'*Oh, God in Heaven,*' Karl's mother quavered, throwing her apron in her face with fear just as Karl remembered her doing when the Gestapo had come to take his father away before the war. Karl swallowed the rest of the soup his mother had prepared for them in the tiny kitchen which smelled of boiled cabbage, poverty and defeat and said hastily, 'Don't worry, *Mama.* They won't get us – and don't forget you thought we were on leave.'

'But Karl,' his mother began, twisting her work-worn hands with anxiety, tears flooding her eyes, 'Karl –' She could say no more and even in his state of near-panic, Karl felt his heart go out to the poor old woman, who was alone now that his father had gone. He knew if they could get away this time, he would never see her again. God knows what would happen to her!

'There's a car at the top of the lane,' Ami whispered as he peered out from beneath the blackout curtain. 'The headlights are off and it's not wood-burning. The kid was telling the truth. It's the law all right.'

Karl nodded his understanding, brain racing, as he said a silent prayer of thanks for the kid's warning. Here in Hamburg-Billstedt, the working class was still solidly Red even after over ten years rule by the Nazis. They were no longer active in their opposition to Hitler – that would

*Cops.

189

have been too dangerous. But they would not lift a finger to help the brown-shirted bastards.

By now his mother had recovered from her first shock. She had been through this kind of raid often enough before the war when the old man had still been active in his beloved SPD*. Now she was hurriedly packing the sand-wiches which would have been their supper after the soup into a piece of newspaper for them to take with them, saying to herself, 'Growing boys can't go hungry . . . Growing boys have got to eat a lot . . .'

Karl half-smiled and made his decision. He knew the cops. They would have sealed off the other end of the dusty lane that ran down this double-line of working-class houses, expecting the fugitives to make a break for it that way in case they ran. For the typical policeman's mentality, that would be the obvious thing to do. So they would break out of the trap in the direction of the car. They wouldn't be expecting that.

Once they were through, all hell would be let loose. The cops'd raise the alarm. But Hamburg was big and he knew it like the back of his hand. With a bit of luck they'd get away with it and be on their way to Lübeck and freedom at last.

Hurriedly his mother reached up and gave Polack a kiss and thrust the sandwiches in his hand. Then followed Ami, the Three Rebels' tough guy, who suddenly was embar-rassed by the kiss for reasons known only to himself. Finally it was Karl's turn. He clutched the frail old woman to him, feeling her ribs, telling himself she lived off nothing but boiled potatoes and white cabbage – she had no money for the black market. 'Don't worry,' he whispered, a lump in his throat. 'Don't worry. We'll get through, Mama. Now turn off the light. We're off.'

'*Alles gute, Karl*,' she quavered and now the tears really began to flow down her wrinkled cheeks.

*Social Democratic Party.

190

Karl was glad when the light was switched off and suddenly they were in total darkness. He sensed the atmosphere of the poor little cottage where he had spent his youth – the smell of tobacco leaves the old man had grown in the garden drying under the eaves, that of the winter potatoes stored in the cellar, the shape of the wooden handcart in the passage with which he had fetched briquettes for the stove from the local factory . . . and then the three of them were slinking out into the night, fugitives in their own country.

On the tips of their toes they stole down the lane, keeping to the shadows. Somewhere an owl hooted. Otherwise there was no sound save that of the wind in the skeletal trees and a radio in one of the cottages, muted by the thick blackout curtains. It seemed as if they were all alone in the world. But Karl knew differently. Already he could smell the odour of a cigar coming from his right. Someone had got out of the car and taken up his post there, smoking quietly in the night, just waiting for the three tame little victims to walk right into the police trap.

Karl's jaw tightened angrily. Well, they'd have another think coming. They weren't going to do the cops that favour. With a hand that was beginning to sweat slightly with tension, he gripped the sock filled with sand more firmly. It was the best substitute for a blackjack, he knew. In the old days of the street fights with the brownshirts, his father had used a similar homemade weapon.

He paused and gestured to the direction from which the smell of cigar was coming. They nodded their understanding and went on as Karl opened the gate of the nearest cottage almost noiselessly. Like thieves in the night, they stole after him, as he tiptoed up the path between the dying rows of brussels sprouts and leeks. Somewhere a dog started to growl menacingly. Hastily Karl hissed, '*Lux – it's me. Quiet, boy.*' Evidently the dog recognised his scent for the growling ceased almost immediately and Karl said a silent prayer of thanks. They moved on.

Now they had almost reached the top of the lane where the main road which ran from Hamburg to the nearest town of Bergedorf lay. Peering through the heavy darkness, Karl could just make out the car. Its nose was pointing in the direction of Bergedorf – the way they didn't want to go. If things went wrong, they'd be running in the direction of Hamburg before the driver could turn the big thing round and be after them. That was something, at least.

Suddenly he halted. His heart began to beat furiously. Behind him the other two blundered to a stop. 'What is it, Karl?' Ami whispered fearfully.

'Look!'

In the last cottage before the road, a blackout curtain had been thrust slightly to one side so that a yellow shaft of light sliced the darkness and fell on to the bedraggled winter garden. The man hiding there thought he was concealed. But he was looking out from light into darkness, and Karl didn't need spectacles to see the steel helmet revealed thus. 'Chaindog,' he hissed. 'They've posted a chaindog there.'

'What now?' Polack asked, standing behind Ami.

'Can't go on that way. He'd spot us crossing the garden. We've got to get round the back of the house.' Karl's brow creased in a worried frown. The cottages weren't detached – they were linked to one another in rows. So there was no way of dodging behind them to the road; nor could they go forward. What now?

Ami supplied the answer, as to the rear there was the sound of solid, heavy boots. The cops had got sick of waiting. They were advancing on the cottage rented by his mother. In a few moments they'd find the birds had flown the coop. Then all hell would be let loose. 'Over the roof of that shed and down the back that way,' he hissed.

Polack cursed. He was a heavy clumsy man. He might just fall and alarm the cops. But there was no time left now to worry about Polack's mountaineering abilities. They had to act – and act fast. Karl darted forward. He bent and hissed, 'On my back, you big Polish clodhopper and up you go!' He grunted with the strain as Polack stepped on his back and then hauled himself on to the slippery slate roof. Ami followed a second later. Karl, the most athletic of the three, pulled himself easily up after them. For a moment they perched there like awkward great birds, listening. Nothing!

Hardly daring to breathe they started to cross the tiles, praying that they wouldn't slip. One by one they advanced up the slates, grasping out to secure a hold on the top. Karl managed it first. Polack followed, doing quite well for such a clumsy man. Surprisingly enough, it was small, wiry Ami who slipped. Perhaps he was too nervous, too excited. Suddenly he was slipping and as he fell, he cried out in alarm.

'*Wer da?*' a gruff voice demanded.

Next moment someone else shouted, 'There's somebody over there!'

Hastily, Karl grabbed Ami's outstretched hand and heaved. 'Come on,' he yelled urgently as below torches began to flicker on and there was the sound of heavy nailed boots running. 'The buggers are everywhere!'

With a gasp, Polack dropped to the ground on the other side of the shed. Karl and Ami followed an instant later and were running all out, even as they hit the ground.

'They are over there, I tell you!' an angry voice repeated. 'Turn your shitting torch in that dir–' the rest of the words were drowned by the sharp crack of a rifle firing. Just above their heads a tile shattered and inside the house the radio went dead abruptly.

They zigzagged madly down the little path that led behind the cottages. They knew the chaindogs were shooting to kill. 'Shot while escaping,' their report would read. It had happened before. It would save the middle-aged cops the bother of writing out a full report and a tribunal of kinds.

A dark figure loomed up from the house to the right.

Karl shouted in alarm. Polack, the nearest to the figure, didn't hesitate. It could only be a cop. His boot lashed out. The figure went reeling back, clutching at his shattered testicles.

Now the road to Hamburg-Bergedorf was immediately ahead of them. There was no traffic, not even a bicycle. Nobody had any petrol these days, only officials.

'Across the road and into those trees,' Karl gasped. '*Dalli . . . dalli, Kameraden!*'

A sudden throaty roar. A big engine sprang into life. It was the police car waiting at the top of the lane. Twin beams cut the darkness with their cold white light. They were outlined perfectly. '*Stehen-bleiben!*' an official voice yelled.

For a moment they simply stood there, transfixed like a moth blinded by a sudden light. They couldn't move.

There was a crash of gears. The big car lurched forward, still pinning them down with those sinister twin beams. Karl realised suddenly that the Gestapo were going to run them down. He acted instinctively. The sand-filled sock flew from his hand. He knew it couldn't make any impression on the windscreen whatsoever. But it was the only weapon he had.

Twack! The sock slammed into the windscreen and burst on impact. Frantically the driver, momentarily blinded, tried to keep control. To no avail. He screamed and flung up his hands as the big car slammed right into an oak tree. There was the heavy tearing and rending of metal. With startling suddenness the ruptured petrol tank exploded. *Whoosh!* The angry cherry-red flames seared along the road like a giant blow-torch.

The three running men reeled to a stop, the heat striking them in the face like a blow from a hot fist. 'God in Heaven!' Karl gasped, as one of the Gestapo fell out of the car on to the road, writhing crazily, as the greedy blue petrol flames devoured his body, his flesh already visibly shrinking and turning black in that tremendous heat. '*God!*'

But there was no time to waste on the fate of their pursuers. All around in the outer darkness whistles were shrilling urgently and angry men were shouting orders and counter-orders. The police were closing in rapidly!

Ami grabbed Karl's arm. 'Come on, Karl!' he yelled above the crackle of the flames and the moans and whimpers of the dying man. 'We've got to keep going. *Los, Mensch!*'

They began to run again. There was a scarlet stab of flame as a burst of tracer fire zipped towards them from the right. They ducked. Next instant, they were showered by stone chippings and mortar, as an excited voice cried, '*There the bastards are . . . Come on, lads . . . They're over there!*' There was the sound of heavy nailed boots pounding down the cobbled road.

A wildly-gasping Karl flung a frantic glance over his shoulder. Their pursuers, perhaps half a dozen of them, were only fifty metres behind. They had to shake them off – and soon. Somewhere, one of the bastards of policemen would be on his radio signalling ahead to the next police station – Barmbek, Rotenburgsort, somewhere like that – for them to put up barricades, traps. Time was running out fast. What in three devils' name was he going to do?

A fat lumbering figure sprang out of a doorway to their front. The distinctive square shape of his leather *shako* gave him away even in the darkness. He was a cop all right, and he had his hand raised as if he were stopping traffic. 'Hey you there,' he commanded. 'Stop running! Stand where you are. Let me see your papers!'

Now Karl could dimly see the object he was holding in his right hand. It was his service pistol.

'Well!' the lone policeman cried. 'Are you going to stop?'

Distinctly Karl heard the metallic click, as the cop snapped off his safety-catch and prepared to fire. In a minute he would shoot. There was no doubt about that. Under the Nazis, German police had long learned they could shoot first and ask questions afterwards; there would be no repercussions for him if he'd made a mistake.

'Shit,' Ami cursed. 'I'll go and piss up my sleeve, Karl!' He faltered to a stop.

'Keep on running – ' Karl commanded with a sob in the very same instant that the air-raid sirens began to sound their shrill warning of impending doom. As the flak further ahead along the River Elbe started to fire with a hollow, resounding boom, there was the heavy sinister drone of massed formations of heavy bombers. *The Royal Air Force was directly over Hamburg!*

CHAPTER 5

The hundreds of incendiaries came whistling down in great showers. They ignited at once in bursts of brilliant white flame, which turned into an eerie unreal glowing scarlet. The fat cop with the pistol, blinded and shielding his face from the sudden burning glare, staggered back as all along the road which led to Hamburg, roofs burst into flame.

The Three Rebels didn't wait for a second chance. Polack lashed out at the blinded cop. He slammed against the wall and Karl grabbed his pistol as it fell in the same moment that the shrill awesome whistle, which cut through the drone of massed motors and the bark of the flak along the Elbe, heralded the approach of high explosive.

Boom . . . boom . . . boom . . . The sledgehammer blows rocked the very earth beneath their flying feet, almost flinging them off-balance. The ground slid and trembled like a live thing. To their front, the tall nineteenth century villas swayed back and forth as theatre backdrops do when caught in a sudden breeze.

In a flash all was death, destruction, awesome chaos. Men, women, children came screaming from their houses, some armed with shovels, buckets of sand and water to fight the raging fires which were consuming their houses. Others had simply panicked and were fleeing, mindlessly carrying their pathetic bits and pieces, driven by an unreasoning terror.

Despite his own fear, Ami whooped with joy. He turned his skinny face to the sky, laden now with huge 'Christmas trees'*, and cried, '*Thank you, England! Thank you, Tommies!*' But Karl and Polack remained silent, as they fought and

*Slang term for aerial flares.

clawed their way through the refugees heading for the country. Both of them knew the RAF had saved them, at least for a while, but the cost in human life and misery was going to be colossal. For now the RAF was thrusting home its attack and the bombs were dropping in huge numbers with a devasting effect.

Screams came from all sides. The earth shook and trembled as fire-gutted buildings started to collapse, showering the burning tar of the streets with falling masonry. Hot burning winds seared down the roads, forcing them to hold their hands in front of their faces and eyes, gasping and choking for breath, as it tore the very air from their lungs frighteningly.

On and on they stumbled, fighting the flames, the crowds, the constant, ever-new detours where streets had been blocked. Horses bolted from burning breweries, their manes on fire. A naked woman fled by them, ripping off the last of her burning clothes as she ran. Still the white phosphorus pellets from the incendiaries embedded in her skin continued to burn.

All was horror now. Amputees from the Eastern front crawled through the streets on their stumps, whimpering piteously. A blind man was being towed with a broom by a man with no hands, holding it in his teeth. A crazy woman cradled the charred skeleton of a baby in her hands. A dead woman lay in the gutter, suckled in death by her baby. Horror upon horror . . .

But as Hamburg burned, the stream of panicked refugees with their bundles, handcarts and prams swept the Three Rebels with them past the desperate firemen fighting a losing battle with the flames hissing over the Alster* itself, making the water bubble and steam, through the cordon of middle-aged policemen trying to stop the exodus.

For the city was dying and even the most demented of the refugees reasoned that they would die with it if they

*Central lake and landmark in Hamburg.

did not flee at once. And all the time the RAF bombers came streaming in from the North Sea in waves to drop their deadly eggs. Here and there one was caught by the cones of converging searchlights, pinned like a trapped insect on a card, so that the flak guns could shoot it mercilessly out of the sky. But there were always more of them and in the end the flak guns ceased to fire, knocked out one by one or running out of ammunition and Hamburg lay ablaze and defenceless, completely at the mercy of those killers from the sky.

Twice the Three Rebels escaped death by a miracle. More than once they were bowled off their feet by a wave of blast as if they had been punched by some giant invisible fist. But coughing and spluttering and gasping for breath they were back on their feet again, impelled by that same unreasoning fear which animated all those hundreds – thousands of people – all about them in the stricken city . . .

Then it was over. Somehow they were outside Hamburg. To their rear the great city burned, silhouetted a stark black against the lurid scarlet sky. But no one in that great throng escaping from Hamburg looked back. Their eyes were set almost hypnotically in front of them as they moved, a vast army of sleepwalkers, without a word being spoken. Even the babies in their prams were hushed, as if they had exhausted all their cries or as if they could cry no longer.

Indeed, all of them – young and old alike – were drained of emotion, all energy virtually spent, feeling no more, reasoning no more, animated solely by the need to keep on walking and escaping that dying city. To an observer from another world, they would have seemed like weird creatures who bore little resemblance, save for the physical one, to what he had heard human beings should be. And all the while to their rear Hamburg burned . . .

But as dawn came, flushing the sky an ugly white, bringing with it a wind that filled the air with charred paper and the acrid stench of burning, they started to collapse with exhaustion, simply falling out of the long columns and slumping into the ditches or on to pavements to be stared at by the villagers of the hamlet through which they were passing with wide, unbelieving eyes. What had happened to them, the gaze read? Were these really Germans, the conquerors of all of Europe from the Channel to the Urals? Who had had the temerity to inflict whatever they had suffered on these shocked, ashen-faced sleepwalkers.

But as the first of the exhausted refugees began to fall out, the Three Rebels started to wake from their own daze. In the hamlets and villages which lined their route heading north beyond the Elbe, they started to encounter village gendarmes, who as yet were as shocked as the rest, watching this great procession of misery passing through and doing nothing to help or hinder them. Soon, however, the realisation began to dawn on them that these village policemen would commence reacting. The refugees would be guided into camps. The *Frauenschaft** would appear. There would be soup and coffee and bread. *But there would also be questions and demands for papers*.

Of course, for a day or two, they would be able to bluff it out. They had lost all their documents in the great blaze, that would be the first easy excuse. But someone, somewhere would eventually ask what three able-bodied young men like themselves were doing, not serving in the *Wehrmacht*? They could pretend to be men with reserved occupations, working in the war industry. Where, the question would be posed. *Weren't you needed again back at your factory?* *Bloehm and Voss* would be asked; *Krupp* would be telephoned. They'd gain another day or two before the factory authorities, back in business once more, would report, '*No, we don't have a Carstens, Karl working for us.*' And then the shit would really be in the shoe.

*Nazi women's organisation, equivalent to the WVS.

It was when Karl spotted the sign along the roadside, stating '*Marinelazarett, Geesthacht – 2 Kilometres*'* that the idea came to him. Soon, as he'd already realised, they would be spotted as men who should be in the armed forces. But as long as they were in uniform – even if they didn't possess the correct documentation, leave and travel passes and the like, they would be all right. In the general confusion of the day, which was being spread by the fleeing refugees, no one would ask too many questions of men wearing the uniform of their country.

'So where to get a uniform?' he asked the other two a little later, after he had explained some of his idea. 'Why,' he answered his own question, 'a naval hospital where there is always a floating population of sick matelots coming and going who are not known to one another.'

'*Einverstanden* – agreed –' Ami said. 'But even naval hospitals have guards. How would three civvies manage to get by them without papers, tell me that, old house?'

Polack nodded agreement. 'Yer, Karl,' he echoed. 'How?'

'Right ray of sunshine you are, Ami,' Karl snorted, his energy coming back to him as the urgency of their situation forced him to throw off the numbing shock of that great raid on Hamburg. 'Three civvies they might question – I agree with you on that. But what if *hundreds* of civvies started rolling up to the gates – civvies obviously in need of food and help?'

'You mean this lot?' Polack queried, staring about him at the pathetic blank-eyed refugees, still trudging on wearily, carrying their poor belongings.

'Yes,' Karl whispered, lowering his voice in case one of the civilians was still in possession of his faculties. 'They're hopeless sheep – look at 'em. All we need is to give them the word and they'd follow like those dumb sheep over

*Naval hospital.

201

there,' – he indicated a field – 'being sorted out by a shepherd's dog.'

Ami's eyes lit up. 'You're right, Karl,' he hissed. 'You're dead right. They are a bunch of zombies. Point them in the right direction and they'll just plod on, no questions asked. But say we do get those uniforms, what then?'

Karl grinned for the first time on that terrible day. 'Do I really have to say it?' he asked.

'Yes, Karl,' Polack prompted.

Karl shot him a look. 'You great horned Polish ox!' he snorted. 'We'll worry about that eventuality when the time comes. For the time being, we'll take it step –'

'*By frigging step*!' Ami, grinning too now, beat him to it . . .

The young ratings manning the gates of the *Marinelazarett*, overlooking the slow flow of the River Elbe, were swept aside as the hundreds of refugees poured into the courtyard, watched by the many silent sailors in the striped pyjamas of the wounded and sick. The Three Rebels allowed themselves to be carried forward with the tide. But while the eyes of those all around them were resigned, devoid of hope and emotion, theirs were quick and sharp, as they searched swiftly for the best source of a naval uniform.

But in the end, they didn't find the uniforms they needed. In a way, the uniforms found them. For as the mob pushed its way into the centre of the great courtyard, a voice boomed out above the racket, 'This way . . . Over here, ladies and gentlemen . . . Come on, there's hot soup and nigger sweat – *coffee*!' the voice corrected itself swiftly, 'for everybody.'

The three comrades turned. A huge fat man, face greased with sweat as if he had just come from the tropics, stood there a ladle in one hand, a soiled towel in the other, beaming a welcome at the refugees.

'A kitchen bull!' Polack said.

'A real live hash-slinger,' Ami joined in.

'A cook,' Karl complemented the others' comments and

grinned suddenly, 'and where cooks go to work they change –'

'– their uniforms,' Ami said swiftly. 'So what are we waiting for, comrades?'

Five minutes later or thereabouts, the three of them, now clad in the uniforms of the *Kriegsmarine*, stolen from the cooks' locker room, pushed their way boldly through the mob of civilians busy wolfing down plates of steaming pea soup, complete with 'one sausage, per person, *per-haps*', as the fat chief cook had bellowed to them happily, beaming at them like a mother proud of her children's good appetites.

They knew, of course, that they couldn't go out of the front gate. The sailor guards would ask them for a pass. But old soldiers as they were, they knew, too, that there were other ways of getting out of a barracks than through the front gate. Any place as old as this navy hospital would have another exit, used by countless generations of sailors 'going over the wall'. Now leaving the mob of civilians behind them, they set out to survey the high wall, topped with barbed wire, that ran round the back of the place.

'The trick is,' Karl explained, as they moved with apparent casualness, 'not to have any trouble getting out. For all the chaindogs know at this moment, we could have been killed in that raid on Hamburg. We don't want a fresh search to commence, looking for three matelots on the run in stolen cooks' uniforms, do we?'

The other two agreed, as they surveyed the wall, which was decidedly high and could be overlooked from the rear windows of the nearest ward. It was definitely something they couldn't chance going over in broad daylight; they would have to go through it.

But again luck was on their side. A minute later they spotted the gap through which a sailor on crutches, being led by another with one hand swathed in a thick pad of bandages and plaster, were crawling. They saw the three comrades and the one with the crutches whispered conspiratorially, 'You after a bit o'the other as well, shipmate?'

He grinned cheekily and without waiting for an answer, hissed, 'Shit on the shingle, I've got so much ink in my fountain pen, that I don't know who to write to first, matey!' With a mock groan he grabbed the front of his hospital pyjamas to emphasise his great need. 'Come on, the knocking shops in Geesthacht are already open!'

The Three Rebels needed no second invitation. Hastily they joined the two wounded sailors in their jaunt to the little town's brothels. But as Karl kept pace with the crippled one who hopped forward eagerly, detailing his sexual needs in joyful anticipation, his mood became serious. The Three Rebels had been lucky much too often. Surely their luck had to run out soon?

CHAPTER 6

Lise lay naked on the rumpled, sweat-soaked bed, her face ugly and damp, her hair matted to her head. She was conscious again in a day-dreaming sort of a way, but not aware of her circumstances: the hotel bedroom, with the jingles of the trams outside in the street and the strange flickering glow on the flowered wallpaper, which though she didn't know it was there came from the great conflagration in Hamburg, sixty-eight kilometres away.

For Lise was concerned solely with her own personal horror, as she had been ever since 'it' had happened. She had slept fitfully after Meissner had left for the port and dreamed that horrible dream, which had plagued her all these last years. In her dream she was crossing the border again into Poland, carrying no luggage, her money and jewels stuck to her body by tape. She could have been a walker, perhaps a mushroom-gatherer, for the wood mushrooms were plentiful on all sides, save in her dreams when they were enormous and spotted red like the *Teufelspilz**, with huge sickly white, thick stems. But that had been her hope back then.

However, she had been out of luck. The two Polish guards might well have been waiting specifically for her, as they stepped out of the trees, grins all over their evil slavic faces beneath the peaked caps. They even addressed her in German straightaway, '*Papiere . . . Ausweis, bitte.*'

Of course, she hadn't had papers and they'd known it. She was a Jew fleeing for her life; her German passport had long been taken away from her. She had offered them money. They had taken it without thanks. Then they had

*A species of deadly poisonous German mushroom.

205

wanted the jewels, threatening to dose her with castor oil to check whether she had swallowed them.

In the end she had given in, rolled up her skirt and pulled them from the tape attaching them to her upper thigh. They had followed with greedy eyes, especially the bigger of the two men, who wore his black moustache swept upwards in the fashion of a cavalryman from the nineteenth century. Then she had had nothing and her fear and apprehension had begun to grow by the second, as the wood started to grow darker and they had continued to stare at her in that direct greedy way. Now she knew they were were no longer just greedy for money.

'*Zhid*!' the one said after a while.

It wasn't a question; it was a statement of fact. She had denied it hotly.

'No, not a Jew, I am a German,' she had cried. 'I must have crossed the border by mistake – from Danzig,' she had lied glibly, her body trembling with fear. Were they going to sell her to the German border guards? She had heard of that being done before!

They had both grinned and again the one said, '*Zhid*.'

Some time after that they had marched her off, with the two of them behind her, talking to each other softly in Polish, their words punctuated now and again by laughs which sent shivers down her spine. For they boded no good.

But they hadn't taken her back to the German border. Instead, they had penetrated even deeper into the woods, so dark now that the taller of the two had to switch on his torch now and again to find their way. Finally they had brought her to a stork-legged wooden tower with a cabin on top of it higher than the trees all around; it was the kind German foresters used back home to spot game. This one she guessed was used by the Polish customs men to spot game of another type – human beings on the run from Hitler's Germany such as herself!

They had forced her to climb the ladder and for the first

206

time one of them touched her – 'Cavalryman', as he would become later in her nightmares. He had run his big hand up the length of her thigh. Just for a moment and he had not done anything indecent. But it had sufficed. That brief touch had told her what was going to happen to her tonight.

It did, Many times, with each one – the Cavalryman and Ludwik, for that was the other's name – taking turns on the rough bed of coats and blankets set up in the corner. They had accepted her virginity without comment. Her tears, her cries of pain and fear roused them only to greater orgies. They had shown no mercy, no remorse, no compassion. It seemed almost as if because she was a *Zhid*, as they called her, she were less than human, not worthy of their pity.

But when Ludwik had gone towards dawn, leaving her huddled and sobbing in the corner alone with the Cavalryman, things had changed a little. He had offered her a drink from the bottle of vodka they had been using during the night-long rape and when she refused he had produced a thermos of cold coffee and gave her a drink from that. Some sandwiches had followed and he had smiled and nodded his head with approval when she had eaten one of them.

By midday she had recovered a little. He had left her alone a while so that she could tidy herself and use the bucket in the corner. When he returned he had asked her to tell him her story – how she had fled Berlin the day after the Gestapo had come for her widowed father, making her way to the Polish frontier on foot and in local buses with the police on the lookout for escaping Jews such as she was in every large town she had to pass through. She had even warmed a little to the rapist when he had declared at the end of her tale that he would see that she was taken to Cracow as long as she kept her mouth shut. She had promised she would; her life, she had reasoned, was more important to her than her lost virginity.

It was about then that the second ordeal had commenced. She had seen, of course, that he was becoming sexually aroused again. His eyes had taken on that same glistening sheen, an animal-like gleam, a totally naked lust, and he constantly licked his thick red lips as if he were thirsty. The bulge in his loins was naturally all too obvious.

This time, however, it had been different. He had produced a little bottle from the rucksack in the corner and pulled out his handkerchief. 'This will make it easier for you,' he had said, his voice husky and barely under control, as if he were suddenly out of breath.

'What is it?' she asked in sudden fear as he came over to her, deftly uncorking the bottle as he did so.

'Don't be afraid,' he said. 'I have used it before with other young girls like you . . . It is good . . . Harmless . . .' His accent was becoming thicker and he seemed to be having difficulty in getting out the words in German and all the time those animal eyes had devoured her body, as if he could barely stop himself from reaching out and ripping the blood-stained frock from her battered body.

Suddenly she caught a whiff of the bottle's contents. It smelled of hospital wards. 'Why,' she had stuttered, alarmed and puzzled both, 'that's . . . *that's ether!*'

'Yes . . . Yes . . . *Tak, tak, Zhid* . . . Don't be afraid, please. Good . . . *Dobro* –' Suddenly he had lunged forward. He clapped his big hand with an ether-soaked handkerchief over her mouth. Her scream of fear had been cut off abruptly. Like a wild animal trying to free itself from some trap, she had struggled, writhing back and forth desperately. But then a strange dreamlike lethargy had overcome her. She felt herself go limp, on the verge of losing consciousness, but still aware of what was happening. And what was happening was – *pleasurable!*

What orgies of sexual love – for by the end she had loved him, even though she had never even learned his name – had taken place there in the woods and the little dwelling in which he had lived by himself, before she had finally been taken to Cracow, as he had promised. He had plunged her into the depths of depravity, corrupted her beyond her previous imagination, humiliated her in ways she had never dreamed possible – and she had loved it!

Screaming and biting, she writhed back and forth in a kind of demonic frenzy, mouthing crazy obscenities, enjoying every wild second of it, arching her spine as she rode him, her head rolling in absolute ecstasy, digging her nails into his buttocks till he had yelped in pain, pressing her legs high above her head in total abandon, wanting only pain and pleasure. Pain and pleasure – that was all she wanted, had ever wanted. But first there had to be the bottle. Yes, it made all things possible – *the bottle*!

Now lying there, her forefinger already automatically searching for pleasure in that dark, wet mound, she remembered and felt anew that old surge of disgust and desire.

Suddenly her eyes flicked open. She withdrew her hand from the mound, dark ugly face suddenly contorted with self-disgust. She turned her head and saw the bottle, that damned bottle around which her whole existence now centred, standing on the night-table. Dearly would she have loved to have reached over and smashed it. But she knew she daren't. She wouldn't be able to function without it.

Meissner had warned her often enough that it would kill her in the end. 'I've asked the sawbones. They tell me it softens the brain. First you go crazy, then you croak.' He had told her when she had first come to him and she had demanded ether the second night, to use it for their love-making. But what had she cared about Meissner's warnings? What did she care about anything?

She thought about the night before the nightmare had come. The ether session, the weight of his old body descending into the cradle of her upraised legs, the grunting brutality of the way he had thrust into her loins, her own gasps of pain and pleasure – all over in so many minutes. *Was that all life was about?*

209

Outside, millions of men and women were engaged in total war, being killed in their thousands daily all over the world, fighting, suffering, dying for causes which they felt were heroic, worth dying for. And what did she do? Why, she lived for the depravity and momentary pleasure that the bottle brought! It was disgusting! What good was she contributing to humanity? Wasn't she merely a parasite, living outside the time in which she existed, pandering to an old man who had saved her, but probably had the blood of other Jews on his broad capable hands. God, what a hopeless, helpless creature she was!

Lise was crying softly when he came in. As always, he took in the situation immediately. He could never cease being a cop, even when he was off-duty. 'The nightmare,' he said. 'The Cavalryman again, eh?' He had got it all out of her in the end, after she had asked for the bottle. He shook his head and glanced at the ether on the bedside table. 'You can't go on much longer like this,' he said softly.

She stopped crying. She could do so without much effort. 'Are we leaving?' she asked, ignoring his remarks.

He sat down in the chair opposite the rumpled bed. 'No. I suppose I should, but I'm not. The three of them escaped from a Gestapo trap at the home of one of them. Apparently they really did a job on one section, killed their driver, injured the rest. Tut-tut,' he made the appropriate sound, but he didn't look one bit sad. She knew why. Meissner didn't like his colleagues of the Secret Police. 'They reason in Hamburg that the three deserters could well have been killed in the Tommies' terror raid on the place last night. But I don't think so. They've been too shrewd for that so far. To my way of thinking, they'll have got away and Lübeck's only an hour's journey by train from Hamburg.'

'So you're staying?'

'Yes,' he answered, taking his eyes off the bottle.

Suddenly, on an impulse for which she could find no reason, she said baldly, 'Let them go.'

He looked at her hard with those cop eyes of his. 'When I was a young detective,' he said, 'our chief once called us in to complain about the force's over-indulgence in what he called "cereals, the kind you drink." *Firewater*, in other words.'

She nodded, but said nothing. She knew his oblique approach to things; it was part and parcel of his police training.

'He said to us, "Gentlemen, I don't mind an eye-opener at eight in the morning. Everybody needs that. I can understand the need for a pick-me-up around ten and nobody's going to hold a few drinks about lunch time against you. I know you'll need something to keep you awake mid-afternoon, or thereabouts. Of course, you're entitled to a few drinks before dinner and a schnapps or two afterwards. But, gentlemen, this constant *sip, sip, sip* all day long has got to stop!" ' He smiled softly and for once she did, too. It really was quite funny in a tough-cop cynical fashion.

'So what does the story illustrate? I'll tell you. Just like our poor old chief, who sip-sipped himself all day long till it did for him, I've got to have that constant burn going all day long, too, so that I can keep going. It's an addiction,' he paused and stared at her hard, his look penetrating and strong for such an old man, 'just as your bottle is. The other day I said to you that I wanted to catch those men because I didn't want them to get away with it and live happily ever afterwards. But that was only part of the story. I need this chase like my old chief needed his sip-sipping. It keeps me going, makes me forget the awful tedium of life, its purposelessness – the inevitable fate of those of us who are German.' He gave her a weary smile.

'We could make an end of it,' she said in that old direct fashion of hers, wasting no words. 'We're no good . . . no use. Why not get it over and done with now?'

He shook his white head. 'You mean the suicide pact, the bottle of schnapps and the rubber hose-pipe leading from the exhaust into the back of the car? Oh, no, not that.

211

Couldn't bear the thought of someone like me pawing over the mess. I want to go in a more dramatic way than that. Fancy hanging around for hours, boozing and waiting for the gas and the pills to work!'

'You've got a service pistol.'

'Messy. Seen too many of those. You miss and you're a blind, senile cripple for the rest of your days, dependent on someone else. No, for me, Lise, suicide is out. But why all these classy chats about the cosmos and the future?' He rose to his feet a little stiffly in the way old men do, supporting himself by placing his hands on his knees to lever himself upwards. 'Get dressed. I'm going to take you for a walk. Then we'll have breakfast in that black market place. I think we'll even make it a champagne breakfast.' He smiled at her. 'You deserve it after the Cavalryman.'

Slowly she raised herself from the bed, an idea beginning to form in her head.

'*German* champagne,' he added as she moved. 'Can't afford the black market frog stuff on my salary.'

But she was no longer listening. She'd even forgotten the bottle for the moment. Now her mind was full of death . . .

CHAPTER 7

The three of them pretended to be casual as they lounged next to the shed door behind the big derricks and cranes moving back and forth along the jetty on their rails, loading and unloading the merchantmen. In reality they were exceedingly alert, their eyes absorbing every detail of the *SS Volta – Stockholm* which lay to their front, taking in coal from one of the high bunkers, a huge Swedish flag decorating its side.

From their perspective the merchantman looked vast, with great rusting metal sides and a bridge which towered above them several storeys high. At the gangplank there was an armed sailor of the *Kriegsmarine* together with one of the ship's officers, carrying a check-board. Obviously it was his function to approve anybody and anything which went aboard, with the assistance of the helmeted sailor. There was no hope of getting on to the ship by that means.

Otherwise, the only connection the merchantman had with the jetty were two slack steel hawsers which led from the bollards on the land up to the ship's rear. As fit and as tough as they were, the Three Rebels would find that slack cable a difficult thing to climb.

'What about the ship's dinghy?' Polack whispered, nodding slightly in the direction of the little boat, its top covered with tarpaulin, which bobbed up and down cheerfully to the rear of the ship.

Karl shook his head doubtfully. 'My guess is that's the first place they'd search for stowaways,' he said softly in return. 'Nor is there any chance of getting up that gangplank. I bet it is guarded day and night.'

'Yes, you're right there,' Ami agreed. 'But what about the other side?'

'What do you mean?' Karl asked.

'Well, we don't know if there aren't more ropes and hawsers hanging down from that side. Perhaps even some open portholes. What do you think, Karl?'

Karl rubbed his chin thoughtfully. They had all used the razor stolen in the cooks' quarters back at Geesthacht to shave in the cold water of a lavatory – and it hurt. 'Could be, could be, Ami. But how are we going to get round to the other side of the vessel –'

'*The law!*' Polack cut in suddenly.

They swung round. A battered black car was bumping and lurching its way across the littered jetty in their direction, the name *Wasserschutzpolizei* painted on its bonnet. 'The harbour police,' Ami said as the car started to pull up in front of the Swedish merchantman.

Two officers got out while the third occupant, a skinny ugly woman, remained seated, puffing moodily at a cigarette. Perhaps she was a prisoner of some kind, Karl told himself, as the two officers paused, returned the sailor guard's salute and began to talk to the Swede.

The three of them watched, already guessing what the two elderly cops were doing there. They wouldn't be hanging around the dirty jetty, getting cold and mucking up their clean boots, unless they had something specific in mind – and that was the Swedish ship and the problem of stowaways such as themselves.

There were plenty of gestures and nodding of heads, as if the Swede didn't understand German too well and needed help. But there was no mistaking the gesture he made when the taller of the two cops, a white-haired man, who was obviously of high rank to judge by the gold braid on his tunic, pointed on deck and the Swede shook his head firmly. There were going to be no stowaways on *his* vessel – that was very clear.

There was an exchange of cigarettes and much scraping of matches as the little group lit up. Casually the white-haired cop turned round and began to survey the surrounding area. For a moment he looked at the three sailors standing there and Karl felt a little shudder of fear and apprehension. There was something strangely wilful and determined in that gaze – so unusual in a man of that age. The white-haired cop was someone to be greatly feared, he realised that instinctively. Out of the side of his mouth, he whispered as they had done back in Camp Death, 'Come on, comrades, let's slope off. I don't like the look of that old cop one little bit.'

The other two needed no urging. They had seen his eyes, too. Affecting that casual lazy roll of a sailor off-duty, his mind concerned solely with women and booze, they 'sloped off', watched by the ugly girl in the car, still puffing moodily at her cigarette and wondering why the three sailors had been watching Meissner so intently . . .

Most of that day, eyes peeled for any naval shore patrol, the Three Rebels scouted around the harbour, trying to find some means of getting on board the Swedish vessel. For they reasoned that if she was already loading coal, her cargo – whatever it was - was already aboard and soon she would be sailing. For a start they took a 'trip round the harbour', together with a group of drunken merchant seamen and a party of schoolkids in Hitler Youth uniform, who had eyes only for the 'grey wolves of the sea', as they called them. But the old steamer which did the job didn't approach close enough to the *SS Volta* for them to see anything of the other side in great detail. What they did see, however, was a large sign attached to a post stuck in the dirty swirling oily water of the harbour, proclaiming *'Passengers who take these boats need special permission from the Harbour Police to enter the dock area proper.'*

That meant, as Karl told them, that it was forbidden to approach the *Volta* from the other side and that there was only one way open for them to get on board – up the steel ropes which connected the Swedish merchantman to the jetty.

'When?' was the simple reaction of the other two. For

215

they both knew time was running out. They couldn't wander around Lübeck for much longer without being picked up in the end. Besides, the Swedish ship would sail soon.

'Tonight,' Karl answered, equally laconic, saying the word with more confidence than he felt . . .

After an interminable wait, darkness fell at last. They had spent the last few hours moving from one waterfront inn to the other, fighting off sleep – for they were utterly weary – and moving on immediately they suspected a shore patrol was on its way to check papers. By now the blackouts were going up everywhere in the bomb-shattered streets and what few vehicles were about were driving cautiously, the road illuminated solely by slits of blue light from their headlights.

But here and there at the docks as the work continued of loading and unloading there were still circles of light at strategic spots and they dodged from one to another carefully, making their way ever closer to the *SS Volta*. They passed the red-and-white striped sentry box which housed the sentry guarding the entry to the jetty and smelled the heady odour of Virginian tobacco. The guard was enjoying a sly smoke, dragging at some foreign cigarette or other. The knowledge gave them more confidence. It meant that no patrolling, officious Guard Commander was in the offing; otherwise the sentry wouldn't have dared. They pushed on.

Now the ugly shape of the Swedish ship's superstructure loomed up out of the gloom to their front. Here and there on the rusting deck small blue lights glowed. But there was no sign of any movement on the upper deck. The crew, they concluded, would be in the harbour's brothels or inns or in their bunks. It seemed a good time to attempt the long climb.

But the sentry was still at the gangplank, his features outlined by a solitary light above his helmeted head. Karl opened his suddenly parched lips and whispered, 'Now!'

Obediently the three of them started to pull their socks over their boots in an attempt to deaden the sound. Now without another word, they crept towards the steep hull, crouched low, hardly daring to breathe. At the gangplank the naval sentry didn't move. For a moment they hunched at the base of the hull. It rose high above them – so high that they could no longer see the upper deck – like a steel mountain. Karl told himself it was going to be a bitch getting up there without making a sound. A real bitch!

But there was no time to be wasted. He spat on his hands and nodded. The other two nodded back. Wordlessly Karl gripped the hawser and began to climb, while next to him, Polack did the same on the other cable. The very last stage of their escape had commenced.

Like a monkey, glad of the shadow now cast by that steep cliff of metal, Karl started to shin upwards, praying that Polack would be able to keep up with him – he was much heavier and less agile. Now and then he looked up to see how far he had progressed. But after a few attempts he gave up. The damned thing seemed practically vertical. Still he was making good progress, though his shoulder muscles were already beginning to burn murderously, as if some fiend were sticking the tip of a red-hot poker into them. He persisted doggedly, his breath coming in harsh gasps. The sweat started to pour from him. To his right, he could hear Polack labouring away, too, occasionally cursing softly in Polish, as a loose strand of wire in the hawser cut into his palms.

Now Karl was getting ever closer to the side of the ship – he could smell the typical stink of diesel, salt-water and waste – and the cable was becoming progressively tighter. He was below the level of the deck still, probably level with the cargo holds. He climbed on, his progress getting slower now, as the cable edged increasingly closer to the body of the Swedish vessel. It was becoming more and more difficult to wedge his hands in between it and the metal side.

217

Still he persisted. He had got this far; he was not going to turn back now.

He came level with the first of the portholes. The curtains were drawn and no light emerged from the cabin beyond. Perhaps someone slept in there; perhaps it was empty. For an instant he was tempted to try to crawl through. But that would be too risky – yet. There was still Ami down below. He climbed on, the drops of sweat dripping from his forehead and threatening to blind him.

Now his muscles ached like hell. His whole back was ablaze with the strain. He knew he couldn't hang on much longer. He had to reach the upper deck *soon*, or he'd let go and plummet to the hard concrete of the jetty below. He willed himself to carry on. '*Another metre,*' he pleaded with himself through gritted teeth. '*Just another metre – please . . .!*' The strain was impossible. Still he climbed. Now, although he couldn't see it, he guessed he was parallel with the upper deck. It could be only a matter of another couple of metres. '*Come on, you soft bastard,*' he urged himself on. '*You're nearly frigging well there now . . . Stick to it!*'

His head slammed against a metal plate. In the very last moment he controlled his cry of pain. Now he hung there, the hawser biting into his burning bloody palms, his shoulder and upper arm muscles racked with agonising, almost unbearable pain. He raised his head. In the gloom it was hard to see, but there was a cone-shaped metal plate all around the cable, barring any further progress. Cautiously, he freed one hand and began to feel around it. He stretched as far as he dare, but still could not find the plate's outer edge.

Next to him, and cursing fluently under his breath, Polack did the same. But although his arm was much longer than Karl's, he, too, failed to discover the full extent of the strange metal cone.

Then Karl had it. This time it was his turn to curse fluently, overwhelmed by a sense of utter despair. It was the one thing they hadn't taken into their calculations. The metal cones on the cables were to prevent rats from the shore entering the ship. They would be shaped so that the point of the cone would be directed at the land, while the V of the cone flared up on all sides. Now these two-legged landrats, which they were, were effectively trapped by the device.

For what seemed a long time, he simply hung there, fighting off the almost-overwhelming desire to simply let go and plummet to the concrete below. That would be the end of it all. They had tried so bloody hard and had had so many near-misses. Hell, their luck had been too damn good to be true. Now it had run out for good. *They'd had it*!

'What we gonna do, Karl?' Polack hissed. 'I can't get no further.'

It took all that remained of Karl's willpower to force himself to answer. 'Nether can I,' he choked, near to tears.

'I can't hang on much longer, Karl!'

Karl swallowed hard. 'We're going down again, Polack,' he said. 'There'll be another way,' he lied.

'Bet there will, Karl. Nothing ever gets you down, Karl,' Polack agreed.

Karl could have burst out sobbing. Why did the other two have so much confidence in him? Christ on a crutch, he'd fucked the whole thing up – right at the very last minute, after they'd come so very far. But instead of sobbing, he concentrated on getting down the cable, for his strength now was ebbing fast.

Taking risks, knowing that his arm muscles wouldn't last out much longer, he began coming down the hawser too fast. Polack fell behind, taking his time, but then he had the strength of an ox. The ground started to loom up. The pale blob of Ami's face looking up at them appeared. God, he must be wondering why the hell they were coming down again! Somewhere he could hear the whistle of a train. Why couldn't they be seated comfortably in some nice warm train taking them to the end of the world? Why should they be here in the night, risking their necks, every man's hand against them. It wasn't fair!

The loose strand of wire stabbed down beneath his nail with startling, excruciating, red-hot pain, as it ripped deep into the nerve end, tearing off the nail. He yelled with the agony of it. Next moment he was falling. He couldn't help himself. Madly he gyrated and rolled his body. He must hit that concrete!

'*Wer da?*' an excited young voice called from below. It was the sentry. A torch flashed on. Karl caught a wild glimpse of it, as he contorted his crazily-flailing limbs, the light flashing from left to right as he spun round and round.

The water struck him an icy blow. He gasped and went under. The light vanished. He came up, spitting out oily dock water, gasping for breath. An explosion stabbed the darkness in a scarlet flash. There was the sound of heavy running nailed boots. A voice cried out something in a foreign tongue. High, high above them, an arc light was switched on and someone yelled, 'Watch that shitting light . . . The blackout . . . the Tommies!' and then Karl was calling desperately, 'Jump, Ami! I'll grab hold of you. *Swim*, Polack! We must SWIM FOR IT, COMRADES!'

CHAPTER 8

'*Jawohl, Brandt. Hab verstanden,*' Meissner said excitedly, holding the telephone in one hand and a good cigar in the other, for they had just finished a late supper in the black market restaurant. 'And they escaped?'

Brandt at the other end said they had.

'It just *has* to be them,' Meissner snapped, suddenly in high good humour despite Lise's sulks all evening. 'First there's three of them, dressed in sailor's uniforms. Then they pick a Swedish tub. Yes, it's them all right.' He paused and puffed away at his cigar, listening hard as *Hauptmann* Brandt continued his report from the docks.

Lise listened, too, though anyone observing her might have thought her mind was at the other end of the world. So these three unknowns who had the courage to put a stop to it by voting with their feet had attempted to get aboard the Swedish vessel – and somehow she guessed they were the same three young men whom she had seen lounging on the jetty this very morning. She didn't know how she knew it – she just did.

On the phone, Meissner was asking Brandt when the Swedish vessel was supposed to sail. He listened attentively to Brandt's reply before saying, 'So if she is to sail on the dawn tide, you will search in about – ' he glanced swiftly at his watch, 'ten hours, say around four o'clock tomorrow morning?' Again he listened.

Then he rasped out some words, forgetting to knock off the long crust of white ash from his cigar in his excitement, so that it dropped unheeded on to the bedroom carpet. Lise frowned. She knew Meissner. When he was after someone, everything was thrown to the winds, even his personal comfort. Nothing had to come between him and the chase.

221

'As soon as the search is over, withdraw the sailor-boy guarding the gangplank. Make a show of it so that if our three rogues are watching they'll be able to see easily that the coast is clear.'

Brandt said something. 'No, don't put on any special guards,' Meissner ordered a moment later when Brandt was finished speaking. 'I don't want them to grow suspicious. Just the normal complement of guards on the main gate to the harbour installations.'

He paused and listened. 'Yes, I will be there *personally*, Brandt. One hour before the *Volta* sails.' He grinned at his own image in the dressing table mirror. 'If they're on board by then, I want to have the personal pleasure of cuffing them. Naturally,' he added hastily, as if it were important, 'you and your fellows will have all the credit.' His grin broadened. 'Why, old house, there might even be a bit of tin' – he meant a medal – 'from the All Highest personally in it for you. Right then, get some shuteye, while there's still time. We're not getting any younger, are we?'

Brandt must have echoed the sentiment, for Meissner said happily, 'As long as we can get the old pecker up in the position of slope arms, we're not finished yet, Brandt. *Gute Nacht. Bis morgen . . .*' He put down the phone with a flourish.

Hastily, Lise looked up again at the flaking ceiling, as if she were bored by the whole silly business. Meissner was almost feminine in his awareness and sensitivity to moods. She didn't want him even to start thinking about her and her motives because she seemed to be showing interest in the fates of these three common deserters.

Meissner ripped off his tight stiff collar and walked over to the bottle of schnapps in the corner. He looked at her inquiringly. She didn't respond. He shrugged slightly and poured himself a finger of the fiery northern gin, downed it in one go and shuddered pleasurably.

'I think I've got them,' he announced when she didn't speak, squeezing the two long metal hooks into the uppers

222

of his gleaming jackboots and beginning to tug them off in this manner. 'By dawn we'll know.'

'I see,' she said listlessly, feigning boredom. 'How do you know?'

He told her what Brandt had told him just now and said, 'They're determined young men. They'll have another go to get aboard that tub, I'll bet a month's pay on it. Besides, there isn't another Swedish ship due in Lübeck for more than a week. If they don't get on this one, that's it. Tomorrow we'll pick them up whatever they attempt to do, that's for certain, and *they* will probably know that.'

She took her time as his face went red with the effort of tugging off the first boot. Fortunately his head was bent while he was doing it so he couldn't see her eyes. 'But they might be able to discover a place on board to hide that *you* can't find. And once the vessel has been cleared by *Hauptmann* Brandt's police, you can't really delay the ship long enough for it to miss the dawn tide, can you? It won't look good to the Swedes who think you Germans are so *terribly* efficient.'

He looked up at her and grinned, still in a high good humour. 'We're only efficient, my dear Lise,' he lectured her, 'because we're so damned chaotic in reality, totally without order. Elbows - here come I,' he made a gesture with his elbows bent of thrusting his way through a crowd, 'that's your real German. So we have to be disciplined and ordered and told what to do – smartish.' He paused for breath and began to occupy himself with the other boot. 'You're forgetting the Captain of the tub and his crew. If there is a really good hiding place on board her, they'll know it and anyone trying to hide there will be handed over to us – *toot sweet*!'

'You are always so shitting confident!' she blurted out.

He looked up again, in no way offended. Indeed, she could not remember one single time when he had ever been offended with her, even when she was half-mad with the 'bottle'. 'You're getting nervous,' he said. 'It's too tight in

223

this hotel bedroom. But tomorrow afternoon we'll be on our way back to Beuthen and the flat, don't you worry.' He leaned across and pressed her skinny knee. 'Why don't you use some of – well, you know what! Might calm you down. Besides, I want a good night's sleep tonight if I'm going to be up at the crack of dawn.' He winked. 'What I just said to old Brandt was a typical piece of male boasting. You know, the pecker at the position of slope arms and all that. Getting old, you know.'

She did not seem to hear him. Instead, she had turned and was looking at the full bottle on the bedside table nearest her side of the bed.

He took off his clothes, put on his pyjamas and then walked to the blackout curtains. 'I'll open the window,' he said. 'It's airless in here. The light.'

She leaned over and clicked out the light. He drew the curtains and opened the flap. The soft muted noises of the night filtered in: the drone of a night fighter flying in circles high above, the metallic striking noise from the dock; the raucous singing of a couple of drunks.

With a grunt of pleasure he sank into the big bed. He didn't say anything. Neither of them ever did, not even 'good night'. They were like two strangers stranded on a desert island, who, due to the circumstances, know absolutely everything about each other, down to the most intimate details, yet remain essentially strangers.

Softly, she removed the stopper from her bottle and took a slight sniff. On nights like this, the ether became her sleeping pill. Slowly she started to drift off into a fitful sleep. Beside her, his mind full of the morrow, Meissner remained awake. He knew a good cop should be able to switch off at night; he never could.

He tried to make his mind wander, to think of other things which would make him sleep . . . Gertrud, his wife, killed in the terrible night raid of a thousand English bombers on Cologne. Now he no longer missed her – she had been too much of a fat fussy *Hausfrau* in the end. His son . . . now he could only remember him as an open-faced boy in short trousers that seemed too tight for him always . . . '*Papa, can I have a look at your pistol, please*' – that had been his standard request. God, why hadn't he let him join the police? He had tried to save him from the corruption and what had to come by making him join the *Wehrmacht* and he had vanished into the nameless wastes of Russia before he was nineteen . . .

But try as he might, Meissner's mind always came back to those three young men on the run – Carstens, Doepfgen and what was the other one's name? Yes, Zimanski, obviously some kind of water-Polack. How were they going to do it? *How*?

His thought processes became vague, less exact, slower. He felt his inner eyes begin to grow smaller and smaller. He was drifting off. Outside in the bomb-damaged cathedral, a clock chimed twelve. In five hours he'd have to be up on his feet again. He needed the sleep. But if they were the kind of men he suspected they were, would they simply try again and fall right into the trap?

He visualised the rusting Swedish merchantman once more. In his mind's eye it wavered and trembled like a mirage seen through the shimmering blue air of a desert heat haze. There was no place they could successfully hide on the old tub. Nowhere . . . Suddenly it came to him, revealed in total one hundred per cent clarity and certainty, as if in a vision from Heaven. Why, of course, that's how they would do it. '*The dinghy,*' he whispered drily, already half-asleep now. '*The damned dinghy* . . .' And then he was gone, asleep at last. Outside, the cathedral clock chimed the half hour in grave metallic inexorability . . .

The mattress creaked slightly, as she turned to look at him, her mind still woozy, bedded in thick cottonwool from the ether. Asleep, he looked very old and shrunken as he lay on the pillow, the *Federdecke* pulled up high around his hunched shoulders, so that only his face was visible in the cold spectral silver light of the moon. Frail, too, even

225

fragile, as if one hard blow to the back of that white-thatched skull would shatter it easily like a soft-boiled egg struck by too hard a blow from a spoon.

'*The damned dinghy*', those were the last words he had muttered before he had fallen into this deep sleep, and she knew why he could sleep now. He had solved whatever problem had been troubling him. Instinctively, she realised that he had come to a conclusion; he knew now how to capture those three young men on the morrow. Soon, in a few hours, they would be trapped as she had once been trapped by 'Cavalryman' and Ludwik, and would now remain trapped until the day she died by that damned bottle.

The thought reminded her. Softly, very softly, for now it seemed important not to waken him, she removed the stopper and took a small sniff of those heady fumes which she loved and hated. She replaced it and returned to her old position, one hand supporting her head as she gazed down upon him in the cold rays of the spectral moon, which now hung above Lübeck.

They'd be out there, too, somewhere, waiting like she waited – for what? They'd be tired, hungry, frightened as she had once been in that Polish forest when they had trapped her and she had first heard that Polish word, which would forever symbolise awesome menace and impending violence to her – *Zhid*!

Time passed. Outside, Lübeck had grown silent. Even the noise from the docks had ceased. The only sound now was Meissner's gentle breathing. Like all old people he slept without movement, gently, hardly making a sound so that often when she gazed at him in the night she thought he might well be already dead. But he wasn't, of course. The *Federdecke* moved up and down slightly as he breathed in and out.

Her mind drifted and drifted. Occasionally she took controlled sniffs of the ether. Not too much, just the right

226

amount. Once, all the *Oberprima**, just before the *Herr Direktor* had kicked out all the Jewish pupils, had been taken to see what he had called a 'typical piece of decadence – Jewish Modern Art'. He had spat out the last word as if it had been poisonous. It had turned out to be an experimental film made in the twenties, full of crazily distorted scenes heaped one upon the other without any logic. One scene had stuck in her memory particularly.

It had depicted a knife – no, an open cut-throat razor – being stropped by a man unseen. In between the movement of the gleaming razor back and forth on the leather belt, the camera had flashed to an eye: a larger-than-life eye, bloodshot and protruding, as if the owner suffered from a thyroid condition. Back and forth . . . back and forth . . . eye . . . razor . . . razor and eye . . . until suddenly, terrifyingly, the razor had flashed out and sliced right into the eye, from which a disgusting scarlet substance had oozed with horrifying slowness.

Now she remembered that razor, and was again fascinated by the oozing of blood from that dreadful wound, in slow motion. She licked her lips, which were cracked and parched. Meissner had a razor, one of the old-fashioned open ones. 'I'm an old man,' he often declared when lathering his face and preparing to shave himself. 'I stick to old-fashioned ways.' He liked to draw attention to his age, as if it were an achievement to be old. But in fact, he had the quickness of a much younger man, *and* he took the young man's attitude to sex: cocky and a little boastful.

She licked her lips again and thought of that eye. At her side he breathed shallowly. Somewhere in the trees that lined the street beyond the cathedral, an owl hooted solemnly. Dimly she felt it strange: an owl in the middle of the port? She thought of the razor – no, *his* razor. She knew its position in the bathroom next door exactly. It rested, unwary fingers protected from its sharpness by

*Sixth Form.

wadding, in a kind of ivory sheath on the glass ledge beneath the mirror, next to his old-fashioned shaving cup and battered brush.

The eye . . . a razor . . . three young men out there in the darkness. She took another careful sniff of the ether. Not too much, not too little . . . just enough to keep her in her present mood. Next to her, he breathed out and mumbled something in his sleep which she couldn't understand. The dinghy, he knew how . . . The eye, oozing blood and gore like lumpy thick tomato sauce. Back and forth . . .

At the back of her head, the little voices had commenced again, hammering at her consciousness, urging, telling her to do things, *evil* things. She started to sweat. She could feel her whole body suddenly bathed in prickly heat. The blood drummed in her ears. But still she could hear those cunning, persuasive voices.

Razor . . . blood . . . back and forth . . . ticking to and fro like the heavy slow pendulum of a clock. *Zhid*, the Cavalryman had said. The devil's mushrooms were huge, reaching to the sky with thick white stems, exuding menace and evil! God, how they would hurt her . . . *Razor . . . blood . . . back and forth* . . .

Hardly aware of what she was doing, Lise rose noiselessly from the bed. Like a sleepwalker, the damp soles of her feet sticking a little to the lino, her ugly face set and crazy, she started to move towards the bathroom.

CHAPTER 9

'*Alles klar, Herr Hauptmann?*' queried Captain Svenson of the SS *Volta*, a big man with a rugged face and bushy eyebrows, as he passed over the bottle of aquavit.

Brandt, an old hand at this sort of thing, took a swig, although it was a bribe in a way. '*Alles klar, Herr Kapitän,*' he answered, wiping the back of his hand across his lips. 'My boys have looked the ship over and found nothing.'

'My boys as well,' Svenson said in good German. 'None of them damned RAF men. Like boys, they are. They think this is a game. Don't they realise I'd lose my ticket if I took them to Sweden?'

'A German skipper would probably lose his turnip,' Brandt said, rubbing it in. He didn't like the Swedes much. They played both sides of the field. Once the Western Allies really started winning, they'd be pro-Allied. When he saw that the rugged Swedish Captain didn't understand the slang word, he indicated with his big paw the act of chopping off someone's head. 'Turnip - head,' he said.

'*Tak,tak,*' Svenson nodded.

Brandt looked at his watch, as his middle-aged policemen and the young, weary sailors of the *Kriegsmarine*, who had assisted them in the search of the neutral vessel, started to form up on the deck below. He frowned. He would have thought that Meissner should have been here by now. He was supposed to be a real hot-shot cop. His sort were normally never late. He wondered what he was supposed to do next.

'Like a pound of coffee?' Svenson whispered furtively, misconstruing his hesitancy. 'Real *bean* coffee?'

Brandt grinned in the darkness. The old bugger was

trying to bribe him. Svenson wanted no more delays; the
tide wasn't far away.

'A true German needs nothing, old house,' he answered,
mimicking the tone of a hundred per cent Nazi, which he
wasn't. 'Not even *real bean* coffee.' He stuck out his hand.
'You're cleared, Captain. You can sail on the tide.
Remember there'll be the normal check somewhere in
German territorial waters.'

Svenson returned the grip and said, 'Won't forget, *Herr
Hauptmann*. Till next time.'

'Till next time.'

They exchanged salutes formally and then Brandt
nodded to his Sergeant. The latter rapped out an order
and the mixed search-party of policemen and sailors began
to file down the gangplank, past the unshaven, weary
Swedish officer, armed with his usual check-board.

Brandt followed and strode over to his waiting car,
parked in the lone circle of light cast by the blue-covered
arc lamp. Behind him the signal telegraph rattled immediately and there was the answering throb of engines starting
up. The Swede couldn't get away soon enough, he told
himself. The fuckers were scared shiteless every night that
the RAF would get them while they were still in Lübeck.
Sometimes he wished the Tommy terror fliers would. It
would teach those fat cats of Swedes what the frigging war
was all about.

He leant inside the driving compartment. 'Any word
from *Oberkriminalrat* Meissner?' he asked.

The driver hastily put out his cigarette end and snapped,
'*Nein, Herr Hauptmann*.'

Brandt's nostrils wrinkled. The bugger had been
drinking aquavit. The Swedes were liberal with their
bribes, he told himself. They'd even nobbled his driver.

He clambered in the back, as the searchers marched
away, vanishing immediately into the blackout. He
slumped there and yawned wearily, wondering what he
should do. He knew Meissner's orders. The Swedish vessel

should be left wide open between now and when she sailed to give those three deserters – poor sods, whoever they were – a chance to crawl aboard. But where in three devils' name *was* Meissner? This was supposed to be where he took over and directed the rest of the operation. Jesus H. Christ, how he wished he could close his eyes and sleep!

For a little while, Brandt debated with himself, as the dockyard came slowly to life. Here and there the rusty rattle of chains commenced. A generator burst into life, frightening away the gulls which rose in hoarse plaintive protest. From the Swedish vessel came a clatter of pans, and the smell of good bean coffee wafted across the jetty. Brandt's big stomach rumbled noisily. He could have done with a mug of that strong nigger sweat himself, he thought. He looked at his wristwatch. It was nearly six. Meissner should have been here by now, he told himself.

'All right, driver,' he commanded, making a decision. 'Start up.'

'Where to, sir?'

'To *Oberkriminalrat* Meissner's hotel,' he ordered. 'Something must be wrong. He might be sick.'

Brandt flashed one last quick look at the bay. Steam was beginning to pour from the *SS Volta*'s funnels. It wouldn't be long now before they left. Over at the exit to the harbour a lone rowboat was making its way slowly to the barrier. A pilot perhaps, he guessed, or possibly someone checking the boom before it was raised to let the Swede out. Then he dismissed the boat and waited impatiently until the driver had reversed in the direction of the city.

'No, *Herr Hauptmann*,' the unshaven under-manager said, looking worried. 'According to the night porter, he hasn't left.'

'Well, I've knocked and I haven't got a reply,' Brandt said grumpily. 'And the door's still locked!' He eyed the harassed undersized manager sourly.

'I'll get the pass-key, sir. One moment, sir.' The civilian hurried round the back of the reception desk, pushing past the sleepy night porter, whose job it was to check identity cards of visitors and watch out they didn't bring whores up to their rooms - without greasing his dirty palm first, Brandt thought.

Led by the manager, the two of them mounted the creaking stairs to where Meissner's room was situated. From the unblacked-out window, Brandt could see that it was completely light now. It could be only a matter of minutes before the Swede sailed. He waited impatiently as the civilian fumbled with the key in the lock, muttering to himself as he did so. Finally there was the soft sound of something falling on the inside. Brandt told himself the key had been in the lock there. What was going on? Why had Meissner locked himself in? Or was it that woman of his who had done it? Anyway, Meissner couldn't 'give him a cigar' for missing the Swede. He had done his duty.

Next moment the manager turned the key and opened the door slightly.

Brandt knocked discreetly on it. He didn't want to catch the boss's wench with her drawers down. Not that he fancied her himself; she was too skinny. He liked women with big lungs, something a man could get his paws on. No answer. He thrust the manager to one side and clearing his throat noisily in warning, he pushed the door completely open.

Next to him, the civilian gasped with shock and his hand flew to his mouth in the gesture of a woman when she is caught by surprise. '*Grosser Gott*!' Brandt exclaimed and with a bound he was inside the room.

From the window hook a naked body was hanging, the rope cutting deep into the skinny neck, the tongue hanging out like a piece of purple leather, the thighs stained by the liquids forced out of the woman in those last cruel moments.

But it wasn't his superior officer's mistress which caused Brandt to halt in mid-stride – he had seen suicides enough in his lifetime. He was used to them. It was the body on the rumpled, blood-soaked bed, the thrown-back *Federdecke* slowly dripping a congealed dark-red blood, its consistency like thin wartime jam.

It was *Oberkriminalrat* Meissner, his throat cut like a jagged red mouth with the blood-smeared razor which lay next to his head on the pillow. But that wasn't all. There was yet another horror.

At the door, the manager saw the direction of Brandt's gaze, as the latter stood there as if transfixed in that room of death. 'In God's name,' he quavered, 'why did she go and do –' He couldn't finish. His voice broke off suddenly and holding on to the doorpost for support he started to retch violently, his skinny shoulders heaving.

Brandt wiped his big hairy paw across his mouth and quelled his own heaving stomach. Murder victims he had seen often enough, but never one like this. Not only had she used the razor on Meissner's throat, but she had *emasculated* him, too. In his mind, Brandt could not bring himself to use the other words; they were too terrifying!

But that wasn't the end of it, either. After she had cut his throat and done the other thing to him, she had stretched out the old man's hands so that he lay there like some latterday Jesus on the Cross. In one hand she had carefully placed the piece of gory flesh which she had excised from his loins and in the other, a small, nondescript bottle . . .

Five hundred metres away, Captain Svenson gave a last look around the deck to check if the deck-cargo was correctly secured. It was. So he bent down to the voice-tube and pulling out the plug, growled to the engineer down below, 'Both ahead . . . dead slow!'

The merchantman shuddered and the deckhand threw away the last line connecting them to the shore. Slowly, very slowly, the heavily-laden ship started to edge its way into the channel, nosing through the cans and condoms and the usual waste that floated in harbours. Svenson heaved a small sigh of relief. Business was good with the Germans and his company was making a fortune supplying them with the ball bearings that were essential for their booming war industry, but still he was always scared when he was in a German port. It was not only the bombers, but also the police. In good old socialist Sweden, the police were a bunch of incompetent comedians; here they were ruthless killers. He was glad to see the back of them for a week or two till the next trip.

He bent again and commanded, 'Half speed ahead – both!' The telegraph clicked metallically and the ship picked up speed. The screw vibrations settled down to a steady rhythm. This was the speed he would keep until they cleared the boom and then he'd order full speed ahead and not reduce it until they came to the port of Kalmar, that is unless he ran into one of their damned spot checks.

Svenson lit a cigar and strode over to the other side of the bridge. The *Volta* seemed to be the only ship sailing on the morning tide, which surprised him a bit. The Norwegians should have been moving out, too, but then now that they were occupied by the Germans, Norwegian and Danish skippers did what the Germans told them to do. Nothing moved save for a small rowing boat next to the boom. He eyed it for a few moments and hoped the fishermen – or whatever they were – would stay where they were next to the boom, which was already being raised by the patrol boat stationed there to his port. He'd pass within metres of them on this course and he didn't want to swamp the damned thing. At this stage of the business, he wanted no trouble with the German authorities.

He turned back to the interior of the bridge. 'Helmsman,' he commanded, 'careful as you go!'

'Ay, ay, skipper,' the man replied dutifully, as the boom swung open and the German in charge of the operation waved lazily to them, and then saluted formally in the German style.

Svenson smirked. He obviously knew his Swedes and

their 'generosity'. He'd be another one whose palm would have to be greased with coffee and American cigarettes the next time they ran into Lübeck. Then he forgot the boom ship Commander and the three fishermen to starboard. Instead he raised his glasses and swept the horizon to his front. No sign of aircraft, German or otherwise; and no sign of their patrols. Within the hour he would be outside their territorial waters. Then it would be 'farewell Germany'.

At the helm, the rating seemed to sense the skipper's feelings, for he grinned and freeing one hand made an obscene gesture in the direction of *Tyskeland*. Stern disciplinarian that he was, Svenson grinned, too. He'd had enough of *Tyskeland* for the time being. Then his grin faded and he was businesslike again. 'Good. Now, helmsman, I'm going below for breakfast. Keep your eyes skinned.'

'Ay, ay, sir,' he replied smartly and added under his breath, 'skinned like a peeled tomato, skipper.' For he knew what the skipper's breakfast would consist of – half a bottle of strong *aquavit*, plus a pot of black coffee. Then he concentrated on the expanse of muddy green waves ahead, whipped and combed into a frothy white by the stiff sea breeze, the big blue and yellow Swedish flag cracking cheerfully overhead.

In the *Volta's* wake, what looked like an empty rowing boat bobbed and juddered in the white frothy water, being carried steadily back into the harbour, until finally it disappeared altogether.

CHAPTER 10

'*Patrol boat*,' Svenson said in disgust. 'German patrol boat.' He lowered his glasses to his chest, breathing out the *aquavit* fumes and ordered, 'Both slow – dead slow.' The telegraph clicked and the *Volta*'s speed decreased steadily as out of the thin mist which now hung over the Baltic, the slim grey shape of a German motor torpedo boat started to turn in their direction. The Germans were obviously going to stop him for one of their damned, irritating, time-consuming spot checks. Already their aldis lamp on the bridge was beginning to click off and on urgently.

Five minutes later, with the *Volta* wallowing heavily in the waves, the German craft hove to on their port bow, the boarding party in their leather jackets, rifles slung over their shoulders, already lining up on the deck of the long lean sinister craft.

The German skipper, a tall hawk-faced boy, who looked to Svenson no more than twenty, raised his loud-hailer and cried, 'Afternoon, Cap'n! Permission for boarding party to come aboard, sir?'

Svenson muttered an obscenity beneath his breath. Aloud he said, 'Yes, permission granted, Captain. Send them over.'

Smartly and swiftly, the young German sailors in their outsize caps, with the ribbons blowing straight out in the stiff northern breeze, clambered into the rubber dinghy, which already wallowed in the swell between the two craft. The motor caught life at once and they began to putt-putt towards the Swedish craft, while, as Svenson noted with some alarm, the gunner on the torpedo boat's upper deck swung his quadruple 20mm cannon round and directed them on the big merchantman.

The young German Captain must have seen the sudden look of alarm on Svenson's face for he called, 'Just routine, Cap'n. Besides, it's a Bofors, made in your country.'

Svenson waved his hand in reply, but said nothing. He wondered when all these young silly men would stop playing soldier and let honest, Christian seadogs get on making a modest living without so much damned warlike interference.

A few minutes later, the German seamen, commanded by an older, hard-faced Petty Officer, whose broad chest was covered by 'tin', as the Germans called their decorations, were clambering up the 'Jacob's ladder' on to the deck of the *Volta*. 'Routine search, Captain,' the Petty Officer announced with a perfunctory salute. Svenson could see at once from the look on his ugly face that the German didn't like Swedes. 'Have I your permission to commence?'

Svenson indicated he had and told himself it was no use offering this swine a bribe to get it over with quick. He was a real German 'current-crapper', strictly routine, who went by the book. He'd do his job, even if it took hours of precious time.

The young ratings knew what they were doing. They had obviously been well-trained and well-briefed. They knew all the nooks and crannies and general hidey-holes employed by merchant seamen to conceal their bits and pieces of contraband. They burrowed into the coal bunkers, checked the goods in the holds, even unscrewed the nuts on the coal shutes and slides down the narrow chutes into the space beyond. And all the time the officious tough Petty Officer was behind them, elbowing the crew out of the way, ensuring that his men missed nothing.

After half an hour, he insisted that they had to search Svenson's cabin, which proved decidedly embarrassing when they found the skipper's treasure trove of French pornographic magazines which he kept hidden from the stewards. He told himself, red-faced with anger and shame,

237

that it would be all around the ship within the hour. The steward who had seen the Germans find the dirty books was a real chatter-box; *he* certainly wouldn't keep it to himself.

Thus while the Swedish Captain fumed, the Germans went over his ship metre by metre until finally ratings began to report, '*Nix, Herr Obermaat*, no blind passengers at all', using that strange expression the Germans employed for stowaways.

But still the tough-looking Petty Officer didn't seem satisfied. Standing next to Svenson on the rear task, he pointed to the tarpaulin-covered dinghy tied to the stern, bobbing up and down wildly in the swell. 'What about that?' he demanded.

'It was thoroughly searched by your police before we sailed, Petty Officer,' Svenson snapped, growing ever more irate at the German's dogged persistence.

The German didn't seem to be listening. He said, 'Well, it ought to be searched again, Cap'n. Orders are orders and schnapps is schnapps.'

Svenson shrugged his shoulders. 'Well, if you want to risk a ducking, Petty Officer, it's up to you. I'm not going to have the derrick crew bring it up for you. It's up to you.'

The German gave him a confident smile. 'Don't need a derrick, Cap'n. I'll go over the side myself and shin down to her. I was brought up in the old *Deutschland*. Sailing ship, you know. I've climbed up and down worse bits of tackle than that! ' He showed the skipper his set of perfect teeth. He was obviously quite a show-off, Svenson told himself, and hoped the *Volta* would give a sudden roll and toss the supercilious bastard right into the drink. A cold dousing would take him down a peg or two.

'You . . . and you!' the *Obermaat* commanded the two nearest ratings. 'Grab a hold of that rope and haul it tight. Look lively now –'

'– Aircraft to port!' one of the sailors sang out suddenly.

238

'Tommies?' someone asked fearfully.

The *Obermaat* paused momentarily at the rail and flung a glance in the direction of the two black dots in the grey sky. He sniffed contemptuously. 'Don't go creaming yer skivvies, you lot o' piss pansies. Them's Dorniers!' And with that, as the two ratings pulled the rope attached to the dinghy below tighter, he stepped over the rail and grabbed the rope.

Expertly, the big Petty Officer took hold with his hands, then swung his feet up so that he straddled the rope which now went down at a forty-five degree angle to the dinghy a good twenty-five metres below. Now as the drone of the two flying boats' engines grew louder, he started to lower himself, moving down the swaying rope with practised ease.

On the deck Svenson raised his glasses. He had seen the German flying boats, the Dorniers before. But the two white-painted planes heading straight for the ships wallowing in the trough didn't look like Dorniers to him. Hastily, he focused the binoculars and the first white shape slid into the circle of calibrated glass. He ran the binoculars along the plane's fat rump. There it was – the red, white and blue roundel of the Royal Air Force. The flying boat was a Tommy!

Hurriedly he let the binoculars drop to his chest. He cupped his hands to his mouth, mind racing. If the Tommy had spotted the German motor torpedo boat – and what a sitting duck it was at the moment – he would attack. By now he knew the Tommy fliers. They wouldn't give a damn that he was a neutral, lying alongside the German. They'd attack and the *Volta* would get its share of the bombs. 'Ahoi, Captain,' he yelled urgently. 'English aircraft to port!'

'Great crap on the Christmas tree!' the young MTB skipper cried in alarm. Then he acted. 'Withdraw that boarding party,' he bellowed above the roar of the planes' motors. 'Engine room, start both – on the double now. *Los . . . los!*'

Now things began to happen fast. As the engines of the MTB coughed and spluttered, with thick white smoke billowing out of the exhausts, the boarding party doubled frantically across the deck of the *Volta* for their own craft. Up on the bridge, Captain Svenson was also snapping his orders into the speaking tube. All was controlled haste. For it was clear that the two craft had only moments left before the two Sunderlands came roaring into the attack.

Halfway down the rope, the tough *Obermaat* paused, hanging there grimly, wondering what he should do as he recognised the planes for what they were – British. Should he go on? Or should he scuttle back on to the deck of the Swedish tub before it was too late? Already he could hear the first throb of engines from below and the ship's rump beginning to vibrate. It was getting underway. But the *Obermaat* was typical of the breed, the backbone of the *Kriegsmarine:* one of those stubborn Petty Officers, who once they had got an idea in their heads to do something would never let up until they had done it. He cursed and started towards the dinghy again. Even as he did so, he knew he was being unreasonable and the skipper would be cursing him for holding up the MTB. But he had always been like that; always would be.

Startlingly the Sunderland came dropping out of the sky, followed a few metres to its rear by the second big flying boat. There was a burst of smoke. Bright blue lights flashed. Suddenly a stream of white glowing tracer was hissing straight towards the bows of the *Volta*.

'Goddamned British!' the skipper cursed and shook his fist at the white blur of the pilot's face. To his port, the engines of the MTB burst into life. The German, at least, was sheering off. '*Full ahead!*' he cried into the tube. The *Volta* started to move forward in the same instant that the MTB's multiple flak cannon burst into frenetic activity. A solid white wall of shells erupted into the sky.

240

As the Sunderland swept over the two vessels with a tremendous, ear-splitting roar, the MTB lurched. Abruptly its nose rose into the air at an angle. Almost instantly twin bursts of white angry water rose at its bows. The young skipper was going to make a run for it before the second flying boat came roaring in.

Desperately Svenson sought to save himself, the German forgotten now. The second Sunderland was coming in low, roaring flatly over the sea. Did they carry torpedoes, he asked himself. He didn't know. But he wasn't chancing his vessel being in the path of a tin fish intended for the German. '*Hard to port!*' he yelled at the helmsman.

The sailor reacted immediately. Svenson grabbed for support as the *Volta* heaved violently and the evil black eggs came pouring from the flying boat's fat blue belly.

The *Volta* heeled and reeled back and forth, as the bombs exploded in the water only metres away. Huge spouts of boiling white water shot up on both sides of the Swedish ship as she was straddled by bombs. The helmsman screamed with fear as a great torrent of seawater swamped the boat momentarily. But the freighter ploughed on through the crazy maelstrom, shell-splinters the size of a man's fist hissing everywhere, slicing through the rigging as if it were string, ripping the length of the superstructure, leaving the deck a mess of gleaming twisted silver scars.

Blinded by a roaring torrent of falling spray, his mouth and lungs full of acrid cordite fumes, the Petty Officer clinging to the rope midway between the deck and the tarpaulin-covered dinghy below, clung on to the rope with all his strength. He was not afraid, although he seemed to be all alone in the world; he sensed the skipper had shoved off with the MTB. He didn't blame him. He would have done the same. Now as the Sunderland, its bombs gone, roared back into the sky, he shook his head and told himself that 'If it's the last shitting thing I ever do, I'm coming to have a look inside that shitting dinghy!'

Doggedly, as the sea below subsided, he shook his head

clear. Then he drew a deep breath and began his progress downwards once again. But not for long. The burst of machine gun fire from the Sunderland's rear turret, drowned by the roar of the twin engines as the pilot took her up, caught him in the back with a blow like that of a sledgehammer. His shoulders disappeared in a sudden welter of bright scarlet through which gleamed the specks of broken bone fragments like polished ivory. He could hold on no longer. The scream of absolute, unreasoning fear followed him down, as he plummeted to his death on the bow of the wooden dinghy to lie there like a bag of abandoned red rags . . .

Ten minutes later the angry tumult was over, with the two Sunderlands racing after the MTB, which zig-zagged wildly, its flak barking all around, as it attempted to escape destruction from the air. Now the snarl of engines and the chatter of the angry machine guns was replaced by the steady throb of the *Volta*'s pistons, as she steered her course for Sweden once more. Slowly, very slowly, the tarpaulin moved. A furtive hand crept out, tapped its way along the blood-soaked canvas until the fingers rested on the body slumped over the bow. A groan. Someone heaved. Slowly the inert shattered body slipped over the side. The hand disappeared. A moment later the corpse of the dead Petty Office slipped beneath the waves. The *SS Volta* ploughed steadily northwards.

Envoi

The keel of the little dinghy grated as it rammed the shingle of that desolate shore. Behind them out to sea the *SS Volta* plodded on, unaware that she had lost her three stowaways, her blue and white flag waving cheerfully in the stiff breeze, as if in parting salute.

With a grin, despite the coldness of the dawn, Ami came to the position of attention and put his frozen hand to his cap to return it. 'Thank you for the lift, Swedes,' he said.

Polack grined too, as he heaved the dinghy further up the shingle. Karl, for his part, remained sombre as he looked out to sea. They had come a long way, he thought, and they had finally made it – after five interminable years of trying. Once they had been the 'Goulash Cannon heroes'*, lauded by *Reichsmarschall* Goering himself: 'Any army where the cooks win medals for bravery, *mein Führer*, is unbeatable,' the fat crook had chortled that day in France back in what seemed another age now. Since then many good comrades had died. Now Germany was virtually beaten, but before that happened, more honest young men like themselves would die, too.

Karl thought of 'Howling Mad' Mueller and the terrible manner of his death, the fat homosexual soldier-priest, *Pan Comendant* and the 'brother-in-law', the fat Gestapo man, the dead Petty Officer killed so dramatically moments before he was about to discover them hidden in the boat . . . Had they all been creatures of chance? Had their lives, intermingled so strangely with their own, been simply a matter of idle fate? Or had there been some purpose to it all? What did it all mean in the end? The young man's handsome face creased in a perplexed frown.

*See *Rebel One – Cannon Fodder* for further details.

But there was no answer to that overwhelming question: one that all young men who have been through the dread dangers of war must ask themselves some time or other, if they are the least bit sensitive. There never has been an answer — and there never will be. Somehow at that moment, standing on the desolate coast of Sweden in this first few moments of his freedom, his mind filled with the past, Karl realised that truth. Life was fate and the only certainty in it was – *death!*

He shook his head, as if trying to wake up from a heavy sleep. Next to him, Polack touched his arm gently and said softly, as if he knew instinctively what was going on in his old comrade's mind, 'Karl, up there on the bluffs, look! There are some cottages.'

'Food!' Ami said eagerly.

Karl turned. The cliff was lined by a group of wooden houses, all spick and span with bright new paint, so that they looked like grown-up dolls' houses.

'What do you think, Karl?' Polack asked. 'Do you think they're safe? ' His voice was still and concerned.

Karl's stomach rumbled loudly. '*Safe?*' he roared with sudden energy – and hunger. 'How in three devils' name do I know, you big horned-ox? But there's one way to find out, isn't there?' Grinning hugely, he thrust his arms through those of his comrades. 'Let's go and see, eh?'

'But what then, Karl?' Polack persisted, refusing to move.

'Why worry about that now,' Karl chortled, exhorting all his strength to make Polack move up the beach. 'You know what I always say – let's take it step . . .'

'By STEP!' the other two roared in unison.

Next moment they were on their way up the beach to the cottages, linked arm in arm, laughing and giggling happily like three young schoolboys released from school at last.